Woman from Spillertown

❧◎❧◎❧◎❧◎❧◎❧

A Memoir of
Agnes Burns Wieck

❧◎❧◎❧◎❧◎❧◎❧

David Thoreau Wieck

With a Foreword by Thomas Dublin

Southern Illinois University Press   Carbondale and Edwardsville

Copyright © 1992 by the Board of Trustees,
  Southern Illinois University
All rights reserved
Printed in the United States of America
Designed by *Patricia St. John*
Production supervised by *Natalia Nadraga*
95 94 93 92   4 3 2 1

Library of Congress Cataloging-in-Publication Data

Wieck, David Thoreau, 1921–
    Woman from Spillertown : a memoir of Agnes Burns Wieck / David
  Thoreau Wieck : with a foreword by Thomas Dublin.
          p.   cm.
    Includes index.
    ISBN 0-8093-1619-6
    1. Wieck, Agnes Burns, 1892–1966.   2. Trade-unions—United States—
  Officials and employees—Biography.   3. Labor leaders—United
  States—Biography.   4. Trade-unions—Coal miners—Illinois—History.
  5. Women's rights—Illinois—History.   I. Title.
  HD6509.W54W54   1992
  331.88′092—dc20
  [B]   90-24460
                                                                         CIP

Excerpt from *The Thirties* by Edmund Wilson. Copyright © 1980 by
Helen Miranda Wilson. Reprinted by permission of Farrar, Straus and
Giroux, Inc. Excerpts from "Illinois Household" from *The American
Earthquake* by Edmund Wilson. Copyright © 1958 by Edmund
Wilson. Reprinted by permission of Farrar, Straus and Giroux, Inc.
Excerpts from Ralph Chaplin's "When the Leaves Come Out" and
from the song "Solidarity Forever" reprinted with the permission of
the Washington State Historical Society. Excerpts from the letters of
Mary Van Kleeck are reproduced by permission of J. Dyck Fledderus,
executor of the Estate of Mary Van Kleeck.

Frontispiece: Agnes Burns Wieck.

The paper used in this publication meets the minimum requirements of
American National Standard for Information Sciences—Permanence
of Paper for Printed Library Materials, ANSI Z39.48-1984. ♾

To all trailblazers, everywhere,
in the cause of social justice

Contents

Foreword

Thomas Dublin

Coal mining in the United States in this century has known a tumultuous history. Beginning with the Anthracite Strike of 1902, through "Bloody Harlan" of the depression decade, to the drawn-out Pittston strike in 1989, the experience of this industry has commanded public notice. Its history speaks to the growing role of the state in industrial relations and to the necessity of state intervention in such areas as occupational health and safety. The history of the United Mine Workers of America reflects a pattern common throughout the labor movement of struggle, growth, and ultimate decline in the face of social and technological change. Finally, the precipitous decline of coal mining in recent decades has been shared by numerous other industries as manufacturing in the United States has steadily given way to a service economy.

Typically, historians have examined these developments by focusing on particular events or individuals of national significance. The stories of the Molly Maguires, of the 1902 Anthracite Strike, and of the Ludlow Massacre in 1914, for instance, play prominent roles in our understanding of the coal industry. Similarly, such national labor figures as John L. Lewis and Mother Jones rightfully command our attention.

On rare occasions, surviving sources permit us to explore beneath the major public events and public figures and expand our vision. A case study of a single community based on particularly rich documentation—as in the case of St. Clair in the Pennsylvania anthracite region—or the study of a single individual—as in the case of Richard L. Davis of the United Mine Workers of America—may often speak to considerably broader themes.[1]

Woman from Spillertown offers just such a perspective. It is in part a memoir—based heavily on the diaries, letters, and writings of Agnes Burns Wieck. It is also a biography, as the author, Wieck's son David Thoreau Wieck, draws on a range of sources including diaries kept by himself. Finally, the book is in part autobiography as the author integrates an account of his own coming of age and wartime draft resistance with the story of his activist mother. The result is a compelling narrative that explores in detail the life of one labor activist while placing that life within a broader social and familial context.

Too frequently, public figures display little interest in revealing their personal lives. Mary Harris Jones—Mother Jones to contemporaries and historians alike—was a towering figure in labor protest in the United States between the 1890s and the 1920s. David Thoreau Wieck points out the influence of her example on his activist mother. Still, *The Autobiography of Mother Jones* reveals little about the influences that operated within Jones's life.[2] She covers the first forty-one years of her life in a scant three pages. Her marriage in 1861 and her husband's death of yellow fever in Memphis six years later occupy a paragraph and a half. Her autobiography, though dramatic, is not very revealing about Mary Harris Jones, a person who chose activism and protest as a way of life.

In contrast, *Woman from Spillertown* offers a much richer view of the creation of a labor activist. We enter into the childhood of Agnes Burns as her family moves from mining camp to mining camp. Daughter of a miner, she learned firsthand of insecurity, frequent migration, and the value of union solidarity. After the death of her mother when she was ten, Agnes Burns raised her younger brothers. She was not a miner, but coal mining was in her blood. Family was central to her life, and through her family she learned the values of the labor movement as much as if she had served an apprenticeship as a miner's helper underground.

As the story unfolds and traces her years as a teacher, her marriage to Edward Wieck, her writing for the *Illinois Miner*, and her renewed coalfield activism in the 1930s, we learn much about labor and reform movements in the nation more generally. She met Eugene Debs, charismatic leader of the Socialist Party, an event that evidently made a deep impression on her. Her emergence as a labor organizer came through a training program held in Chicago under the sponsorship of the Women's Trade Union League. In the 1920s she wrote for the *Illinois Miner,* which brought her into close contact with the socialist editor and humorist, Oscar Ameringer. Finally, in the 1930s she repeatedly crossed swords with John L. Lewis who successfully smashed the insurgent union, the Progressive Miners of America, which she worked mightily to promote. Through her story, then, we learn much about broader developments in the twentieth-century American labor movement.[3]

Agnes Burns Wieck made an unusual contribution to organized labor in the coalfields. She also made an articulate case for the importance of women in the movement even if they were not wage earners. As she said in a speech before a district convention of the United Mine Workers of America: "The labor movement has a place for every honest man and woman earning an honest living. And don't you think those women in the homes are earning an honest living? I do" (p. 44). She understood that wives of miners were just as much working people as their husbands. Hers was an insight that academic labor historians have only come to embrace in recent years, but which she learned in the course of growing up in the coal mining communities of southern Illinois.

Wieck proceeded to apply this understanding in her writing and her organizing over the next two decades. In the *Illinois Miner* she addressed a female audience offering education and consciousness raising. In the 1930s she served as president of the Women's Auxiliary of the Progressive Miners of America, criss-crossing the state of Illinois, making speeches, rallying women strike supporters, and generally acting as a "coalfield hell raiser." The fifth chapter of the memoir offers a revealing grass-roots view of labor insurgency in the coalfields of southern Illinois in the depression decade and the role of one courageous woman organizer who sought to articulate the grievances of miners in the region. It also makes clear the central role of miners' wives in the labor struggle, an element rarely emphasized in the institutional or biographical treatments of labor struggles in the depression decade.

With the defeat of the Progressive Miners of America, the memoir shifts focus and we learn much about the less public side of this activist family. The final chapters of the memoir round out the picture of the Wieck family and offer insights into the lives of the husband and son of Agnes Burns Wieck. Once again, the story touches themes relevant to broader developments in the nation's history. Edward Wieck, blacklisted for his union activity and unable to work in the mines, found employment under Mary Van Kleek at the Russell Sage Foundation and conducted a number of germinal studies of the coal industry. The son of Edward and Agnes, David Thoreau Wieck came of age in the late thirties, graduated from college just before Pearl Harbor, and became a self-conscious opponent of the draft during World War II. The memoir traces the family dimensions of Wieck's refusal to be drafted and his noncooperation with authorities during his lengthy prison term. The focus in the final chapters shifts away from Agnes Burns Wieck, but the result offers a fascinating view of the reproduction of radicalism within a family across generations.

All in all, *Woman from Spillertown* has much to offer readers in the 1990s. It recreates the world of working-class radicalism of an earlier period and demonstrates the transformation of that radicalism over time. It permits us to understand the making of two generations of American radicals and to reflect on the meaning of radicalism in the United States in the twentieth century. It is a story that has much to offer us as we prepare to make our way into an uncertain future.

Prologue

In central Illinois, in the town of Mt. Olive, there is a Union Miners' Cemetery. Inaugurated as a burial-ground for the union dead in the "Virden Riot" of 1898, it also is the site of the grave of Mother Jones, whose body, by her instructions, was brought from the East for burial alongside her "boys" in December 1930. On the reverse of a black-bordered funeral notice, my mother wrote: "Your Daddy and I pronounced it the biggest and most striking labor gathering we ever saw. We hoped it would be treasured in your memory and an inspiration." I was nine and I remember the occasion but faintly; I must admit that my recollection of Mother Jones in her casket is confused with my vision of another woman who died near that time, a great-aunt, who like Mother Jones had lived to an astonishing age.

Now, in the fall of 1985, for the first time in many years, I was returning to my home state. The occasion: a scholarly conference on Illinois coal miners' history. The date: October 12, anniversary of that gun-battle by which the union miners defeated the Chicago & Virden Coal Company's attempt to bring a trainload of strike-breakers to its mine. The location: Jacksonville, thirty miles west of Springfield, in farming country; a pleasant county-seat town, dating from the 1820s, that once served as a station on the Underground Railroad. The site: Illinois College, modest-sized, itself almost as old as the town, whose first graduate served as governor of Illinois during the Civil War and whose most famous, William Jennings Bryan, aspired repeatedly to the presidency of the Republic.[1] Among the sponsors: the Illinois State Historical Society, the Illinois Labor History Society, and District 12 (Illinois) of the United Mine Workers of America.

We drove, my companion and I, the 1,025 miles from Troy, New York—ever since the federal government broke the Air Traffic Controllers' Union, we don't fly. As I explained to a friend at the conference, there is for me an invisible picket line around the airports. I know too well the past and present of labor unions to have illusions about them—as institutions, they are not very different from the other institutions of our society. But there are certain principles I abide by, and one of them is solidarity. I remember vividly, January 1933, in Springfield, when my mother, a miner's daughter and miner's wife, led ten thousand women assembled before the state capitol in singing "Solidarity Forever"; they had come to protest the reign of terror in the Illinois coalfields. How many times, that day, did I hear that chorus!

Our route from the East had taken us through the old coalfields of northern Illinois. My family had lived downstate and I did not know this region. The mines are gone but I caught sight of names of towns, Carbon Hill, Coal City, Braidwood, Braceville, all of them off the course of the undeviating highway, that I had often heard mentioned when I was young. Braidwood! Birthplace of John Mitchell, president of the United Mine Workers union during the great strike in the Pennsylvania anthracite in 1902. I looked also for signs of Cherry; but no, Cherry was to the northwest many miles. A dozen years before I was born—I am getting the figure now from a book on prevention of mine disasters written by my father—259 miners perished there in an underground fire, "the Cherry fire."[2] And Braidwood! just off the road we were traveling—hadn't there been a tragedy at Braidwood also? Yes, Andrew Roy's old history of the miners tells the story. Back in 1883, sixty-nine miners were drowned in the flood when the waters of a lake broke through a hundred feet of earth to the workings below.[3] Only once in my life have I been down in a mine—but fire, flood, explosion, men killed or backs broken by roof falls, men killed or legs lost in haulage accidents, how often in my hearing did talk among my father and his friends turn to those topics. Angry talk, bitter talk. Underground mining was dangerous, but the greed of mine owners multiplied the risks.

As we neared Springfield there came to mind an old coal camp, named Tallula, a few miles from Petersburg. (We were in Lincoln country now.) My grandfather, my mother's father, had worked in the mine at Tallula. My grandmother died there, more than four score years ago.

At the conference next day, those presenting papers were scholars of labor history digging into a now-distant past, even well into the last century. In the audience were a number of miners and other working people, among them a man who had particular reason to remember Agnes Burns Wieck. On the day of that Springfield march, he told me, he had at my mother's request accompanied the delegation of women who went to the governor's office to present their grievances and demands. An organizer of the jobless, he was assigned to make the case for unemployment insurance legislation and for increased "relief." His idealism undiminished, Paul Rasmussen continues from his Florida home to be active in the cause of democratic unionism.

My memoir was the last event on the program. I was introduced by Ralph Stone, professor of history at Sangamon State University, with whom I had been in touch for some years and who had been of crucial assistance. He told about our finding each other; already interested in my mother's life, he had happened upon an article of mine in an anthology of writings on anarchism. When I lived in Illinois, that would have scared the daylights out of most everybody. Times have changed somewhat.

First, I needed to clear up a small confusion. Ralph had pronounced "Wieck" as I do, with a long "e", but people in the audience who knew of Agnes had heard it "Wick" as often as not, and very naturally, with a final "s," "Mrs. Wicks." I was going to stick to the Illinois pronunciation.

To begin, I gave a rapid sketch: "Imagine a smallish woman, not much over five feet. Stocky, short-legged. A bit round-shouldered. Black hair, brown eyes, freckles. An open face, pleasant features. Liked to think of herself as Irish. Quick to smile. Laughed easily." Then I began a telegraphic chronology: "Born 1892, died 1966. Born in Sandoval, Illinois, January 4th, 1892, daughter of Florence Burns, born Florence Wilhelm, and of Patrick Henry Burns." I named the six Illinois counties, including Sangamon, where the family lived in Agnes's first ten years; told of Tallula and of the family's journey, after Florence's death, down into "Egypt," to the village of Spillertown in southern Illinois, and of her five years as a school teacher and why she had quit at twenty-two in order to become involved in the labor movement; spoke of her encounter with Eugene Debs; mentioned briefly her work with the Women's Trade Union League and her years in Chicago and Philadelphia and Boston; told of her return to Illinois to marry a coal miner, and of her journalistic and educational work for the Illinois miners during the twenties. Then I reached the center of the story, the climax of her Illinois years, toward which I was hastening: "November 1932, elected president, for a one-year term, of the newly organized Women's Auxiliary of the Progressive Miners of America. During which time, news headlines were announcing 'another Mother Jones.'"

The Illinois Labor History Society has a nice ceremony of recognition of persons significant in Illinois labor history. As the last event of a banquet-evening, two persons were inducted into the society's "hall of honor." The first was Daniel McLaughlin, a Scottish miner active in the union in the old country who came to America in the 1870s and became one of the leaders of the unions that preceded the United Mine Workers of America; the second, Agnes Burns Wieck. There was a rightness about this conjunction, for Pat Burns was one of those old-time miners who spoke up for the union, answered every strike call, experienced the blacklist.

The plaque for Agnes characterizes her this way: "Eloquent, tireless, courageous and inspired, educator and rebel organizer of her people in Labor's Cause, the 'Mother Jones' of Illinois." Mother Jones led marches of women; Mother Jones knew all the dramatic gestures; Mother Jones confronted the troops and the gunmen; Mother Jones was frequently at odds with union officials. Parallels enough; besides which, for Agnes in her youth, Mother Jones had been an idol. But comparisons with persons like the larger-than-life Mother Jones have metaphoric value only. Life-size exactly is what I have striven for in my portrayal of Agnes Burns Wieck.

Do You Know What "Radical" Means?

At the International convention of the United Mine Workers of America in January 1934, all resolutions not to John L. Lewis's liking were disposed of swiftly. Among the more unwelcome was a proposal to form a women's auxiliary of the miners' union. The vote done with, the president had a few words to say.

"You will remember," he told the delegates, "that men who are members of the United Mine Workers will continue to do the fighting for the organization. The Chair wants to express his gratification on the action of the convention, because if there is anything that has caused us great concern in some of our industrial conflicts, it has been the tendency of certain men to shove their women out on the picket line while they remained at home and did the cooking."[1]

Lewis was speaking obliquely, as he often did, just how obliquely will soon be evident. But the delegates could hear the scorn, the heavy sarcasm. They could tell that he was issuing a warning, and they knew just which "industrial conflict" he had in mind.

Certainly, Lewis had reason enough to become enraged at the very thought of auxiliaries. The reason: ten thousand women— wives, sisters, and daughters of Illinois miners—organized in an auxiliary of a rebel union, women who hated "King John" and who had caused him great concern indeed. ("Why doesn't somebody take a shot at Lewis? That would settle it"—I paraphrase letters I have read.) A career begun in Illinois more than two decades earlier had seemed about to end there; for Lewis, it was a nightmare just now dissipating. As he spoke to the convention, one of the ten thousand, one particular woman from that nightmare, may well have been in his mind's eye.

Significant rebellions are most often sparked by outrageous betrayal. The rebellion in Illinois in the summer of 1932, in the face of the worst economic depression in the nation's history, was no exception. Illinois was the last union stronghold in the soft-coal industry. Under Lewis's leadership the organization of which he had taken command in 1917, when it was nearing its peak strength, had suffered defeat upon defeat.[2] The Illinois coal operators were insisting upon another large wage cut. The union officials recommended acceptance, and twice the miners voted the contract down. The results of the second referendum were never made public (unofficial but reliable press calculations showed a clear negative); the officers announced that the return-sheets had been stolen, a tale no one believed. An "emergency" no one had authority to declare was declared, and the miners were ordered back to work under the new contract.

For months, since the old contract expired, there had not been a payday, and for a long time before that work had been slow. But the right to determine the wages they worked for was a precious right. A paycut was inevitable in these hard times but the officials could surely have struck a better bargain. Worst of all was the insult of being asked to swallow a story that even a fool would laugh at.

Faced by widespread refusal to obey, determined to break the strike, Lewis deployed all his resources. In Franklin County, Illinois's major coal producer, in the southern part of the state, the United Mine Workers' union, the "law," and the companies joined forces: picket lines were broken and two miners were killed, one of them, a strike leader, assassinated. Fear and confusion of loyalties had their effect.

Among embattled miners, long marches were an old tradition. In such fashion, "General" Alexander Bradley, a veteran of Coxey's Army, had helped spread the strike of 1897 that established the union in Illinois. Now in the late summer of 1932 processions of cars and trucks packed with strikers from the northern and central fields streamed together in a single caravan that stretched over twenty-five miles of highway, to bring support to the "shot back to work" Franklin County miners. The marchers, their number estimated at twenty thousand or more, meant to camp in an adjacent county and march on foot into Franklin County and picket the mines. Detoured by state police and county authorities into a well-prepared ambush, the unarmed caravan was smashed by a small army of sheriff's deputies. There were no dead this time — clubs did most of the work — but many would die before this war was over.

Smashed at Mulkeytown was not only a caravan but thirty-five years of loyalty to the United Mine Workers of America. Eight days later, the Progressive Miners of America was formed. At the constitutional convention that convened on October 3, ninety-five local unions with a membership of thirty thousand were represented — an overwhelming majority of the miners in the northern and central regions.[3] There was good reason to expect the miners of Franklin and neighboring counties to rejoin the rebellion, and there was hope that the new union might spread to the states from which the old union had been driven and become in fact as well as name a new national organization of miners.

Among the founders an idealistic and radical spirit prevailed. In its early days the old union had been democratic and anti-centralist to a degree that very few present-day unions exhibit; over the years those traditions had eroded, gradually and then more rapidly. John Lewis, opportunistic, shrewd, ruthless, quick to exploit the vulnerabilities of colleagues and enemies, had been able in a short time to achieve a personal dictatorship. The Illinois district (District 12), while preserving the forms of democracy, had rotted; it had become more and more obvious that the bitter conflicts between the district officials and Lewis were in essence a rivalry for power and control of union treasuries. John Walker, president of District 12, and his colleagues were now collaborating fully with their long-time enemy, for the good reason that they shared a dangerous common enemy, the rank and file in rebellion. Of Lewises and Walkers the Progressive Miners wanted no more.

The constitution of the new union was designed by the radicals on the committee that wrote it to guarantee — so far as constitutions can guarantee anything — rank-and-file control. Progressive officials were to receive miners' wages with minimal fixed expenses, were prohibited from self-succession, and were denied opportunity to surround themselves with a palace-guard of appointees. Among the union's stated objectives was the following: "To unite women and to educate them on the struggles of the workers, politically and industrially, and to organize them into Women's Auxiliaries."

On the last point the constitution gave endorsement to a movement well underway. The first Illinois auxiliary had been organized at West Frankfort, coal capital of Franklin County, early that summer;[4] the idea had spread northward rapidly. When John Walker showed up in Johnston City, a mining town just south of Franklin County, to advocate acceptance of the hated contract, he was "stoned by infuriated women." When Lewis spoke at Benton, county seat of Franklin, he had found it necessary to "pack the hall with gunmen to protect himself, not from the miners he had betrayed, but from their wives."[5] On the picket line where Dominic Laurenti was killed, women were among the wounded. Many hundreds, perhaps more, were in the march that ended at Mulkeytown. By early November, when 157 delegates, dressed in the white uniforms with white headbands that had become standard, arrived from thirty-eight "ladies' auxiliaries" to form a statewide organization, the auxiliaries had long ceased to be service-units limited to soup-kitchen work.[6]

A crucial moment in the auxiliaries' rapid evolution came in October, three weeks before the founding convention. The Peabody Coal Company—largest in the state and locked into Samuel Insull's public utility empire—had reopened two of its strikebound mines in the Taylorville field in central Illinois. The "old union" was recruiting strikebreakers; the state militia stood guard at the mines and patrolled the town streets. On October 12, forty miles away, Progressive Miners and their families had assembled for the annual memorial at the graves of General Bradley, Mother Jones, and the "Virden Martyrs." In her report as auxiliary president, a year later, Agnes Burns Wieck referred to that day: "Word reached Mt. Olive that in Taylorville the memorial march had been attacked, the strikers jailed and their women driven off the streets with bayonets. We who were there well recall how the news made our blood boil. We told our men to go home and mind the children, we were going to the aid of our sisters of the Auxiliary. In the moonlight of that October night, a long caravan of determined women moved northward into Christian County." On the picket line next day, "choked with tear gas, jabbed by bayonets, the women hurled their defiance at the military power." A striker was shot to death by a soldier.[7]

At the auxiliary convention Agnes Burns Wieck of Belleville, a solidly Progressive district, emerged as leader. In her address on the opening day she rallied the delegates to a militant program, to more than a fight for an honest union. Unemployment was beyond reckoning, starving was no figure of speech, "the system" was bankrupt. An observer quoted her:

> We, sisters, have got one fact to face—there is no peace for labor! We must fight on and on because capitalism makes us fight.
>
> This movement is going to educate you and some morning you are going to wake up and wonder if it is really you. You are going to be radical. Do you know what radical means? I looked it up in the dictionary. Rad means root—radical means getting at the root of things. And that's what we're going to do—get at the root of our troubles.[8]

Agnes was elected president—one year, no self-succession, no salary, no expenses reimbursed. ("I just didn't want the fine idealism spoiled by paid workers.")[9] She was a natural choice; she knew these women and could articulate their feelings. She had more education but she spoke a language they all understood, with no "talking down to." An experienced and powerful speaker, Agnes knew how to inspire an audience with her emotion. "Intense," "charged with nervous energy": such was the impression, magnified perhaps by her short stature and conveyed by her words, gestures, and expression. She also understood those women who wanted the auxiliaries to be "ladies'" auxiliaries and had the right kind of patience to bring them around.

Nor was her name unknown to the women who came to that convention. During the middle and late twenties she had been a writer on the staff of the weekly *Illinois Miner*, which went into every miner's home. During those years, too, she had frequently been invited to speak at miners' celebrations and memorials. But Agnes had not gone to the convention with any thought of running for office. Hard battles were ahead and she had doubts about her physical endurance; her health was worse than "not good," and she needed rest badly. But Mt. Olive, Taylorville, and the convention at Gillespie revealed in many of these women a spirit she had longed for. If she could help, she had to help; she would have to rely on what she had in abundance, "grit," "determination," "stubbornness," favorite words of hers, and also "guts."

There were personal reasons as well. She shared their anger and feelings of desperation. Her husband, Ed Wieck, a miner with more than twenty years' experience and still a union member, hadn't had a job in the mine for five years or any job for two. A Progressive Miners' victory wouldn't put him back to work but a militant union, especially if it should become part of a new and militant labor movement, would fight for the unemployed. She worried about her boy's future. She still had people down in Johnston City, where she had once lived and taught school; some of the rocks aimed at John Walker were, I am morally certain, thrown by her sister, Amelia.

It was not only for husband, child, and kinfolk, however, that she was ready to fight. For a long time she had had a dream of an "army of women." Now, in spontaneous answer to brutal realities, such an "army" had come to be.

Babies, Strikes, Shutdowns, Blacklists

As I turn back to write about Agnes's childhood and youth I am aided by certain reminiscences that she recorded in a diary ten years before the time of the Progressive Miners and the Women's Auxiliary. The entry I shall quote first is for January 4, 1923. Agnes, two years married, has a year-old baby. "Today is my birthday. Thirty-one years ago, I was born in a little mining town of central Illinois, not in a hospital as was my own baby, but in a company house. I have heard my father and sisters tell of the bitter cold weather and the hard times of that winter."[1] There was more drama on the day of her birth than Agnes has told of here. According to notes she made later, a "girl" who was hired to "help out" had upset the kitchen stove "and a boiler full of wash on top of it." "All hands had to turn to, fighting fire and flood."[2]

The diary continues:

I was the fifth baby in a family already unable to live decently. Just two years earlier the United Mine Workers had been established [i.e., founded] and like the miners' families was going through some trying times. For the sake of this new national union the men in the forefront of the fight risked everything—their women in the background suffered and proudly bore the penalty of unionism. Before I was many months old my father sought work in a new place—from pillar to post—and I carry no memory of my birthplace. A few years ago when my father was job-hunting through the state he went again to the old mine where he had worked when I was born. A queer thought struck him—it might be well to go back and try it over again. He had liked the little town and wanted to try his luck there once more. But he found that work was pretty dull [i.e., slack] and he did not tarry long. He went down into

11

Rheinhart Row and looked again at the little house where I was born and though he never confided it to me, my sister told me that he had brought back home a piece of the weather-boarding off the little old weather-beaten house and tucked it away in his trunk among some things he kept in memory of my mother.[3]

Two days later, on January 6, came a different anniversary:

Twenty-one years ago today my mother died. The dreaded and terrible disease of consumption had rapidly undermined her health. She made a courageous fight against it but died within a few years. As I look back upon her life I ask myself, how did she bear her cross? She had never known anything but hard work and hard living and then that horrible hideous death! At fourteen a wife. Nine times a mother. Dead at thirty-nine.

I was ten. The night she died we younger children were asleep. As I awoke the next morning I heard neighbors' voices in the kitchen. I hurried in to ask if she was worse. They would not speak. I ran into her room. The bed was gone, so was my mother. Her body, draped in sheets, lay stretched out before me. That was the end.

The funeral—I shall never forget it. We were so terribly poor. My father was burdened with debts. He was working like a mule and making next to nothing. It was winter weather and we had nothing to wear to the funeral. Mrs. Kerby, who owned the mine, brought us suitable clothing. The one woman coal operator I have known of—the one coal operator who ever showed us human kindness.

I have often wondered about my mother's girlhood about which I know too little. When my father came into her life—himself a mere youth—I am sure that she began to dream as every woman dreams. Never enough to live on, always another baby coming, debts, sickness—the wonder is not that she died so soon but that she lived to bear so much.[4]

The marriage of Patrick Burns and Florence Wilhelm, as Agnes heard it told and related it to me, had indeed the character of romance. Florence was living with her family somewhere in the "backwoods" of western Kentucky when Pat, three or four years older, passed that way in the course of his youthful wanderings. Son of a baggage-master in Louisville, he had run away from home at an early age—there was something about a stepmother and a poker that Agnes could not interpret for me. He had worked on the building of the Eads Bridge across the Mississippi, had done farm labor, and then had gone into the mines. In Florence's eyes he must have been a romantic figure, for Pat could embroider a good Irish tale. A real romantic elopement it was. Florence's father, James Wilhelm, a liquor-fond butcher known locally as "Wild Bill'helm," was ready to kill both her and her sister Arty, who was abetting the young lovers. Florence's stepmother hid the girls from "Wild Bill'helm's" wrath and Pat and Florence, accompanied by Arty, succeeded in reaching the Ohio River ferry and were married in Illinois by a priest of Pat's Catholic religion.

Florence's life after marriage, and her death, as told so far, would be an unexceptional tale of the poor. But that life and death had a larger meaning for Agnes.

> The years when my mother bore her children were the years when the miners' union was struggling for its existence in this country. Babies and strikes and shutdowns and blacklists—from one mine to another, moving, always moving—like bands of gypsies went groups of coal miners' families through the coal fields in those years. Before the union was firmly established my mother had stood by while my father took one reduction after another—already living on too little she was forced to feed her family on less. Where the union was most active, work was always the poorest—work for less, steadier work, was the operators' ruse. If the blacklist drove my father to seek a new job under a new name, my mother managed somehow to save us from starvation while the job-hunt was on. The union demanded no sacrifice too great for her.[5]

The birthplaces of the seven Burns children who survived infancy tell something of the story of migration. Mag, the eldest: Equality, in southern Illinois, a dozen miles west of the Ohio River. Jim: Evansville, Indiana. Amelia: Kinmundy, south-central Illinois. Dan: Providence, western Kentucky. Agnes: Sandoval, about twenty miles from where Amelia was born. Gilbert and Gordon, the youngest: Fairmount, eastern Illinois, near the Indiana border. After the other moves for which I can account are included, the number more than doubles and an average of once a year for those decades becomes more than plausible.

> [Florence] saw the United Mine Workers of America come into existence—she cherished this union as something sacred. She saw it grope and grapple for its endurance. She suffered through hard-fought strikes that ended in failure. Victories here, defeats there, and then the big

strike, the strike of '97. The miners had nothing, naturally the union had no treasury. Delegates to the national convention called to consider the strike rode in box cars. Everyone knew there could be no financial relief and nobody had anything to start on. We might as well starve striking as to starve working, was the attitude everywhere. The response to the strike call was indeed remarkable. Men grimly set their faces toward the future. Women steeled their hearts. Children went hungry. Children died. Hunger, sickness, death, but silent and unshaken stood the strikers and their families. For six hard months they struck.[6]

By that strike the miners won a victory without precedent in American labor history: a wage agreement for the whole of the Central Competitive Field, from Illinois to western Pennsylvania, and the eight-hour day.

My very earliest memory goes back to a day of this strike. My mother and women like her went out among the farmers to ask for food. Each morning saw them, baskets on their arms, making their daily rounds. One morning my mother took me with her. I carried back a doll, I remember. My mother carried back a basket of food that I'm sure she never forgot.

Behind the men who won that great strike stood an army of women. They had taken no union vows but within their own souls they had pledged their lives to the Union. They went to no meetings but in each little home counsel was always taken as to the next move. They formulated no policies but they gave full-hearted support to action. Unfaltering, unwavering they stood, like a wall that nothing could batter down.[7]

And that must have been an especially difficult time for Florence. According to Agnes's record of births and deaths, her mother was probably three-and-a-half months pregnant, assuming delivery at full term, when the strike began.

Agnes, who had a weakness for absolutes and superlatives, idealized the solidarity of the women as she tried to bring to life something about which she had too little specific information. But there is no reason to doubt the substance of it. For those who lived through it, the strike of '97 had a character of the sacred—the difference between slavery and freedom, and something more.

Brightly Colored Pictures

Further back than the image of Florence's death was a childhood-remembered of a different tone. These memories were of Fairmount, to which the family had returned after the big strike. The diary continues:

> I was too young to realize the hardships of those years [of the strike]. Memories of my childhood — in the days when I had a mother — are to me like brightly colored pictures of a story-book. I was not quite six when I first went to school. Union recognition was then a reality throughout the Illinois coal fields. We were living in a little prairie town. The mine had been sunk a mile away but we didn't go to live in the Patch — all those company shacks were red — we had a pretty white cottage in town — the only miner's family on Main Street. Jim had left school for the mines. Mag hired out. My mother kept boarders. The union could not bring us a good living overnight but it had brought light and hope and a large measure of freedom. The blacklist gone, my father had at least the security of a job. We lived in the little white house a long time — that was the first and only house we ever thought of as home. To me it is the brightest spot in my life.[8]

> I love to remember my mother in the setting of that little white house on Main Street. The big maples along the brick walk, the white picket fence, the fruit trees, the grape arbor, the old smokehouse covered with gourd vines, the moss, the chicken yard — how different from the miserable company shacks she had known before that first big union victory.[9]

Agnes saw her mother — or more exactly, came to see her in retrospect — as a woman of very strong character, stronger than the father she loved but whose failings she knew. Florence's forebears — her mother was a McHenry, or MacHenry — were, Agnes surmised, among the Scotch-Irish and German pioneers, courageous people in her imagining, who had moved across Kentucky a generation or two earlier, to end up not much better off. My impression is that they were striving toward lower middle-class or slightly higher status. Florence, certainly, never let herself be demoralized by poverty. "Ma was a great manager," Agnes wrote, citing as authorities her older sisters. "She knew how to manage Pa and he was not an easy man to manage."[10] She knew how to manage Pa's drinking, I take it, and casualness with money.

But Florence's managerial talents, which Agnes "inherited," were not confined to "managing Pa." Making that house into a comfortable home was not easily accomplished. In the next passage, which concludes Agnes's reminiscences of Florence, the phrases "work out" and "wash out" refer to exchange of labor, the latter by washing clothes, for things; "remlets" are remnants. Belle Cullom and her husband, Lee, had accompanied the Burnses during a number of their "gypsy" migrations.

> How comfortable my mother made that little home! Fixing, always fixing, I have often heard my father say of her. I remember how she used to work Saturday afternoons at old lady Hall's hotel—she would work out a piece of discarded furniture—sometimes she brought home old clothes. Many a night she sat for hours at the sewing machine making over old clothes for her children. She was a great hand at creating new things out of old.
>
> I shall never forget how she once made over an old sofa—it was just at that time that the old-fashioned sofa was giving way to the new-style backless lounge. Belle Cullom . . . had an old sofa that she had "washed out" years before—it was worn through to the springs and Belle declared she could do nothing with it. My mother bargained with her for it and got it for a quarter. After dark one evening Dan and I were sent with a wheelbarrow to bring it across town. My mother ripped off the back for the upholstery job she was so good at. On one of her bargain trips to the county seat she brought back among a variety of "remlets" some carpet covering, fringe and brass tacks. How proud she was when that new lounge was sitting in the front room. I was so pleased with her achievement that I considered it worth boasting about and one day I gave the secret away in front of company—the look in my mother's eyes was a lesson I never forgot.
>
> When "Crazy Miss East" locked herself in and set fire to her house, Dan came running home from school with the news that the furniture saved was being sold. My mother hurried to the sale and for a very few dollars bought an oak bedroom set—the talk of our house for years. My mother's taste for nice things, her natural talents, her unceasing labor worked wonders with the little we had.[11]

Discipline was strict. Mother and father were "Ma'am" and "Sir." "In our home," Agnes later wrote, "there used to be an unwritten law that no child should be spoken to twice. . . . We never took a chance on finding out what would happen if we didn't move the first time." Poor they were, but the kids should be brought up "decent." Sinners got their just dues—except for Agnes, who never spoke of being punished. As youngest daughter, tiny and no healthier "than the law allowed,"[12] she enjoyed a certain favoritism but it is not my impression that Agnes gave her mother much trouble. Exaggerated, but perhaps not by much, is the story that Florence beat Amelia, still a little girl, "to a frazzle" when it became known that Melie had destroyed a neighborlady's pansy bed. For the boys, a woodshed whuppin'. Another story tells of Jim's receiving a frightful stroppin' for stealing from a store in which Pat was a partner.

One other significant glimpse of young Agnes, perhaps at Fairmount:

> This morning another Christmas present—from Amelia. A picture— not much in size or cost but full of sentiment. A little old-fashioned girl, in bonnet and curls, sitting beside a tree. She sits quietly, her doll rests on her arm, but her thoughts seem far away. On the back of the picture Amelia has written: "Sis, when I seen this picture I thot of Mrs. Minnus, Mrs. Corncobb, Mrs. Shucks and Mrs. Rainwater all at once and I said to Mag that is for Ag. It looks just as you use to look when you played. This isn't much of a Xmas present but I have a dandy ordered."[13]

Agnes continues: "I am sure I never looked like this little girl—I know I didn't have curls. But something about the picture brought back memories of a little sister who liked to steal away and play alone, who would sit for hours beneath an old tree, her only company a doll and the characters of her imagination."[14] With two baby boys on her hands, and probably already unwell, Florence may not have had much time for Agnes.

Of Agnes and Amelia, five years her elder, there is a faded but lovely studio photograph. Despite Florence's efforts, Agnes's hair is straight. "Amelia," Agnes wrote on the back, "was gifted with good looks and beautiful hair," as is visible. "She married before the year was out, age 15." By the time I knew Amelia, those looks were gone. Too many pregnancies, too much hardship. But what spirit! Agnes and Amelia always remained close.

Down into Egypt

Only slowly did the union's victory bring stability to the Illinois coalfields. In our family a postcard was called a "John Hogg" in memory of Agnes's uncle by marriage, forever on a freight train in search of better and steadier and safer work, or just plain work, who in this manner courteously kept his family informed of his luck.

But it puzzled me that the Burns family had left Fairmount for the town where my grandmother died. Then I found a note of Agnes's: her father just had to get away "from that rock roof."[15] This helped me decipher a letter in which her older sister Mag tried to answer Agnes's questions about the early days, one of which seems to have concerned mine accidents. Mag didn't remember anyone being killed at a town about which Agnes was inquiring, "but my God at Fairmount was where they got it."[16]

Instead of a Fairmount, Agnes was going to live her growing-up years in Spillertown, a farm-village become coal camp, in Williamson County, in the very heart of Little Egypt, as that southernmost part of Illinois is popularly called. On the map, Egypt would be an inverted pyramid with its southern tip at the town of Cairo, where the Ohio and the Mississippi rivers join; a line running east from St. Louis, through Sandoval, Agnes's birthplace, approximates its northern boundary. Culturally, Egypt was continuous with Kentucky and southern Indiana and inter-migration was common. Spillertown was just a few miles from Florence's birthplace, a log house near the courthouse square of Marion, the seat of Williamson County.

Infertile yellow-clay foothills in the main, Egypt was no land of plenty for poor-whites who tried to farm it or for the rapidly growing number of miners in the booming Williamson County coalfield. Many of the miners were "hunkies" or "dagoes", but that brought no slightest alteration in the dominant culture, which regarded these immigrants as "furriners" and their religion as no such thing. For the Peabody Coal Company, which operated Slope Mine No. 1 at Spillertown, and whose coal rights in the region Agnes estimated at a million acres, it was a land of plenty. For miners there was plenty of work and, a relief for Pat, "a coal seam where a man can stand up like a man,"[17] unlike the pitching coal seams only a few feet thick, where miners often had to work on hands and knees, that were common up north.

Agnes had lost both her Fairmount and her mother, and Spillertown horrified her; their new home was a company house on Easter Row, painted red. (If I'm not mistaken, Easter Row was so called because of its sequence of Easter-egg colors.) Although the "Bloody Vendetta," the family feuds of the rural culture of the seventies, belonged to a past now covered with layers of coal dust, violence was a constant presence. Pat was in his forties now, and more than a little weary. His oldest son had taken his own road and the older daughters were married, but there were four youngsters to look out for. Toward the end of her life, Agnes wrote some notes for a story that would begin in 1912, when, after ten years, the family moved from Spillertown to a town nearby. She recounted what her father had said to her then—as she remembered it fifty years later. Its like has appeared in many novels and films but I wouldn't doubt its substance; the circumstances are the most ordinary of proletarian life. How many times did I hear the expression "out of the frying pan into the fire" and its cousin "from pillar to post."

"I told you when we come down here in 1902, after your mother died, you would have to learn to like it here—sure, it's not like your mother wanted but I'm through jumping out of the frying pan into the fire. I promised your mother when she was dying I would keep you kids together and do the best I could. I sure can't leave you kids anything after I die but I can leave you an education, if you want to take it."[18] About education, Agnes needed no persuasion. "Learn to like it" she never did, even though, long after she left it, never to live there again, Egypt was still "home."

It wasn't very long after the move to Spillertown that Agnes, the youngest and only unmarried daughter, became by her choice the woman of the Burns family. Apparently, Pat had decided not to interpret "keeping the family together" absolutely literally, and Agnes rebelled. Some years later, speaking to a miners' convention, she told it this way: "Many good people there wanted to take care of me and educate me. My father, not wanting me to be raised without a mother in a coal dump let me go several times, but I always came back home. And the last time I said to Dad, 'I am going to stay; I will learn to cook and we'll stick together through thick and thin.' That evening he taught me how to fry potatoes."[19] Agnes could not have been much past twelve. She was keeping house for Dan, by now digging coal, and for the younger brothers, ages five and seven when the family "descended into Egypt."

When Florence died, Agnes was old enough to understand death yet still very much within the web of mother-father-child emotions. This "duty" she now insisted on fulfilling was not only an expression of "belonging" and a sense of "Burns" identity but a way of resolving emotion about her mother's death. If she had been jealous of her younger brothers, who usurped her place in her mother's attentions, she was now, from duty, their mother. If she felt guilt about her mother's death, she was atoning by taking her mother's responsibilities so far as she could, upon herself. If she wanted to be sure she would not lose her father to another woman, she was herself the woman of his house in consequence of an act of loyalty. There was an additional factor: those "good people" who wanted to take care of her would have been of another class, and Agnes may already have been developing a certain class consciousness. Whether any of these interpretations are true or not, it is beyond doubt that Agnes's early experience as surrogate mother and housewife had a significant bearing on the course of her life.

Now it was Agnes's job to fix breakfast and pack the lunch buckets. "I recall that the five o'clock whistle at the mine was always followed with a sharp calling of my name, and like an automaton, I would bound out of bed and wake up afterward. To this day if I am awakened out of my sleep, I exclaim 'Sir?' I am ready for the next command."[20] The "Sir?" habit stayed with her until the end of her life.

Agnes cooked and scrubbed and did what else she had strength for; unless money ran short, they could hire a woman to do the washing (pit clothes were heavy). She was not very big, not very strong; "will power" was her most important resource. She felt it was up to her to "keep the standard of living high in our home, although it was very low in the camp." A "low" standard meant surrender to bedbug and cockroach and fly, floors that were bare, newspapers tacked on bare walls, an outhouse that stank, garbage and tin cans in the yard, corncobs instead of catalogues for toilet paper. (I bring to mind a house I saw, when young, in a coal camp a few miles from Spillertown.) Agnes, in her diary, wrote of her mother: "I have often tried to think of what she might have done with the red house in Easter Row."[21] My grandmother would have been sorely tried, though not as never before. Agnes attempted flowers, but that hard clay, plenteously sprinkled with cinders and coal dust, had its mind set on weeds.[22]

Young Agnes did her best. Her chief responsibility was to keep the boys in school. "I longed to see my brothers, whom it was my duty and privilege to mother, become doctors and lawyers."[23] To kill two birds with one stone, of an evening the boys would take turns with her in reading to their father the adventures of Nick Carter and

Deadwood Dick and Jesse James, that nemesis of banks, as counter-attractions to the saloon.[24] Pat liked those stories he couldn't read and surely liked his kids to show off their learning. But he didn't always stay home, only more often—a pretty good bargain.

Family

The word "tribal" pretty well describes the Burns family. Both of Agnes's married sisters lived within walkable distance from Easter Row; Pat even exercised, initially, a semi-patriarchal authority in Amelia's household, which he believed (not at all to her liking) to need his management. Over the years there were the usual bicker-ings and jealousies and hurt feelings, but Agnes was not part of that, either as "aggressor" or "victim." Those negatives, however, can be seen as functions of a powerful sense of connectedness, and therefore of expectation, that eventual geographical dispersion did not affect. It should come as no surprise that women married into this hypercritical family at their peril.

My grandfather, of course, I knew only as an old man. A jovial gram'pa, a very heavy-set five-eight—none of the children were tall—with twinkly blue eyes and an impressive tobacco-stained, handle-bar mustache. He ran a little store, along with his son Dan; behind the store was a poolroom and a small speakeasy (these were Prohibition times). He was free with credit and with candy for children, and full of grandfatherly tricks; he had, my mother said, "the Irish sentimentality and gambling spirit." She, by no means ungenerous herself, thought he let himself be taken advantage of. He most always had something on the side, if only a card game, to supplement, maybe to lose, what he made in the mine. His son Gordon, who would be an authority, had great respect for "the old gent's" poker-playing. He was a damned good coal miner, said my father; when miners got together they would soon start "digging coal" and you could tell pretty quickly.

Although socialism had a strong following among Illinois min-ers, to the point that being known as a Socialist or claiming to have voted for Gene Debs was helpful to those ambitious in union politics, my grandfather was not in the least radical. "In the days of free silver Bryan's picture held an honored place in our home—I can remember my parents going over to 'Old Squire Mulvaney's,' in whose home was one of the few talking machines of the town, to hear the famous 'cross of gold and crown of thorns' speech" (this was in Fairmount during the 1900 presidential campaign). For the poor, "free coinage of silver" was more than a monetary policy that might allow them to climb out of debt; gold was as ever the emblem of the wealth that kept them down. "Just as Jewish children have always been taught that the Messiah is yet to come, so were we children taught that William Jennings Bryan was yet to be president."[25]

But 1902, when the family reached Spillertown, was the year of the great Anthracite Strike and now John Mitchell's picture replaced Bryan's. "Politics ceased to cause excitement in our home."[26] But the Burnses faithfully voted the Democratic ticket. Illinois Socialists and the radical labor people who founded the Industrial Workers of the World at Chicago in 1905 saw Mitchell as another of the "labor lieutenants of capitalism." In Williamson, such talk would have received a bad welcome; a very bad welcome from Pat Burns, who believed that the mine owners had a right to their profits. Of course, the kids were sent out in the wintertime to steal coal off the railroad cars at the mine-siding, to fuel the stove that cooked the food and boiled the clothes and warmed the house. Agnes and the younger boys toted it home. "Carrying a sack of coal on your back in the dead of winter will make an indelible impression on the mind of anyone,"[27] Agnes said later. Pat, who didn't have Agnes's Puritan conscience, didn't worry about whether his family had a right to make ends meet by stealing coal.

The children were baptized Catholic, and Florence was buried in a Catholic cemetery, but religious denomination does not seem to have been important. The children went to Protestant churches and Sunday schools if that was what was available. The identity that mattered to Pat—equal to "union man"—was "Irish." A grandson, Dan's boy, Patrick James, remembers Pat's instructing him, as a small child, to answer "I would be ashamed of myself" if asked what he would be if he weren't an Irishman. "He would sit me upon the bar and have one of his Irish friends ask me the question, and everyone would have a big laugh at my response."[28] And Pat was of the "fighting" Irish; the Burnses seem to have acquired, in Williamson County where that took some doing, a certain reputation.

As for the Burns children, all the boys went into the mines and all the girls married miners. Amelia Ann, married to Lee Cobb, will reappear frequently in Agnes's story; no more need be said of her for now. First-born Margaret Jermima ("Mag"), married to Neal Tolbert, would be the mother of five daughters and a son, and a mother to grand-children. I knew Mag only slightly but what I saw conformed to my mother's characterization: goodhearted, incredibly kind, terribly downtrodden. A dozen years older than Agnes, she hadn't had any schooling worth speaking of in the procession of coal camps through which the family moved in the late eighties and early nineties. Agnes so often prefaced "Mag" with "poor." Still, Mag made it to eighty-two, the longest lived in the family. Agnes loved her sisters—and couldn't stand it that they'd always be as poor as Job's turkey and resigned to it.

The only one to separate himself from the family was James Myrl, the oldest son, who never married and of whom I know nothing but the year and manner of his death: shot dead in his early thirties, in a coal mine at Pocahontas, Illinois. Some said the problem was a woman, and some leaned to cards, at which Jim made most of his living and was just too skillful. Jim, my mother said, thought that only "damned fools" would break their backs digging coal. The older of the boys whom Agnes raised, Thomas Gilbert, the child Florence was carrying during the strike of '97, became an object of family expectations and seemed headed for an honorable career in the labor movement. But he died at thirty-three, leaving a wife and three small children—a victim of incompetent doctors, my family was sure. In Johnston City schools and businesses closed for the funeral. Honorable his career would have been, for Gil took Agnes for a model. Gordon Patrick, "Red," the youngest boy, went to Detroit in the early thirties to get away from the mines; pumped gas (and cursed Sun Oil), cursed Budd Wheel and Briggs Body, drew customers to any bar he tended, worked in a book, ran a small poker game, knew when to call and when to fold. Belly-laughing, beer-drinking, possessed of Pat's generosity and more, Red was loved by all his nephews and nieces. Married once, he was a ladies' man and a sporty dresser. In his youth quite a semi-pro ball-player, Gordon all his life loved to play and lived to play; will never change, Amelia said about him over and over.

Unlike Gil, who was drafted but wasn't sent overseas, Daniel Victor did see action. A few years Agnes's elder, dark like his mother, he was a miser with words in a family of talkers. In his youth, Agnes said, he was "a hard worker, too much so, wanted to save and plan." Dan was gassed in France in World War 1 and was no longer able to work in the mines. Reclusive, bitter about the war, bitter about his life, Dan "batched" with his father, then eventually married and had a son. He remained down in Egypt, a stone's throw from where Mag and her family lived, across the state highway from a worked-out coal mine, long after everybody else in the family was dead or gone. Agnes felt terrible about Dan. Out of school and into the mines at age eleven, he was a whiz at math and liked to work problems in his son's college texts. "Mickey," or "Mick," as Dan liked to call young Pat, was so far as I know the only grandchild of Pat and Florence, besides myself, to go to college. Dan always told his son, "If there's an *A* given in that class, you'd better get it."[29] He didn't want his boy to get stuck like himself. But he was a loving and gentle father.

A Social Conscience

Agnes's first break with convention, of which I have knowledge, she assigned to age twelve, two years after the family moved to Spillertown. She reminded me of it many years later when I was involved in a strike against Jim Crow. "Do you recall the story of your maternal grandfather reprimanding your mother who came home and told of sitting in the same seat with a Negro passenger on the train? 'Your mother would turn over in her grave,' he told me. 'They never do such things in Kentucky where she grew up.' I'm sure that was the first colored person I had ever seen in that region. When my father asked me why I had done such a thing, I said, because all the other passengers deliberately passed by that vacant seat and I couldn't bear to see anyone humiliated."[30]

Pat was right about Agnes's mother. Mag recalled the time, when the family was living in the central Illinois town of Assumption, that the woman who taught the Baptist Sunday school asked Florence if Mag could attend; she would have the company of two girls who lived across the street from the Burnses. "Do you mean them niggers? No, my God no, not my kids go with niggers."[31] But Pat was no different. In my time Agnes's brothers and sisters found it hard to remember not to use "nigger" in her presence. Although Illinois north of Egypt was not culturally southern and had pro-

vided many of the soldiers of the Union army, racism was the rule
througout the state. The policy of union-fighting coal companies to
recruit blacks from the South as strikebreakers engendered an
additional labor union racism, for not too many whites cared about
why black men would be willing to take their jobs.[32]

Agnes cannot have been unaware of the "rules" of the culture. If
her feeling for the humiliation of another is concordant with the
best of Christianity, it was certainly not Christianity as interpreted
in Williamson County. "I have often speculated on how I escaped
such prejudice, rife on both sides of my family, with all my
ancestors from the South. Maybe the experience I had in Danville's
colored slums, looking for the wash-woman that bitter cold day."[33]
(This must have been in Fairmount days, Agnes pre-school.) As I
recall her telling it, she was supposed to meet her mother, or wait
for her mother, got lost, was taken in, shivering and scared, by a
black family, folks much poorer than her own, was treated kindly,
hospitably; and was by their help reunited with her mother.

"I couldn't bear to see anyone humiliated": all the time I knew
her, she literally experienced the other person's suffering or humiliation, experienced it in her body; she seemed to have no callous, no
boundary that defined an individualistic separateness. If empathy
is our original nature, our true social nature, from which we are
taught to retreat, perhaps there are experiences that reinforce that
nature. There may be a clue to Agnes's feelings. I am conjecturing
and there is no way I can validate the connection that I imagine but
each time I return to the thought, my intuition says yes to it. The
first experience fixed in Agnes's memory dates from "the big
strike," age five and a half, surprisingly late and isolated. Earlier,
both Agnes and her mother had "the fever." (Scarlet fever. Typhoid, which missed Agnes but did not miss Dan, was "typhoid.")
Accompanied by high temperatures in its onset, the disease commonly stretched out over a number of weeks. Mag told Agnes of two
details: "You pulled all your hair out and tore up a watch chain";
Belle Cullom "come down and scraped all the dead hide off of Ma's
feet when she got better."[34] Whether this illness accounts in some
measure for Agnes's chronically sub-par health I can't be sure—in
its more virulent forms it could do damage to heart and lungs. (That
this illness probably left Florence vulnerable to tuberculosis is very
probable.) What I see is an experience of pain, of delirium, of the

gradual peeling of outer layers of hideously discolored skin as the disease subsided—together with awareness of what her mother was undergoing—that may help explain Agnes's inability to bear others' pain, that quick empathy.

More or less contemporaneously with the incident on the train, the meaning of "the union" became dramatically real for Agnes. Ever since 1897 the union miners had been forced to put up with a non-union operation at Carterville, to the west of Spillertown, but its end was foreseeable; it was an anomaly rather than a serious danger.[35] The new mine at Zeigler, to the north just across the Franklin County line, the first shaft to be sunk in that coal-rich county, could not be ignored. The project of the Leiter family, Chicago millionaires, the mine at Zeigler incorporated advanced coal-mining technology; it had the capacity to outproduce by far any mine in the state. More important, more ominous, the town of Zeigler, built beside the mine, foreshadowed the new-style company towns that appeared in great numbers a decade later in West Virginia. It had broad streets and a park, housing far above coal-camp standard, a brick schoolhouse, and a hospital—no "coal dump" this, but the equivalent of the company town of Pullman in the Chicago area and the U.S. Steel town of Gary, Indiana. It was a clear challenge to the union.

As soon as the mine began hoisting coal, the miners demanded union recognition and union scale—not part of Joseph Leiter's plans. The miners struck, and they and their families were immediately evicted from the company houses. The mine compound was turned into a fortress within the Leiters' twelve-square-mile property; barbed wire was strung and heavy machine-guns were mounted in stout two-story blockhouses.

In an article for the *Illinois Miner* some twenty years later, Agnes wrote about her memories of the Leiter mine. "If they could not rely upon native labor, they could import scabs from other fields."[36] From fields as far away as Hungary, in fact. "They could house them in barracks. They could build stockades around their property. They could station gunmen at strategic points. And all this they did. And when their work was finished and they called it good, they placed upon the tipple of the big mine an enormous, revolving searchlight to expose the 'invading army' and to broadcast their deadly warning."[37] That mine-tipple was considerably taller than a ten-story building. "Our daddies could protest against injustice in the mine and the Union would protect their rights. Over in the Leiter mine the miners had no rights. . . . We heard our daddies call them slaves. We, too, lived in company houses, but far worse were those awful barracks. In the quiet of the night in the union camps some child would shout 'There it is!' And across the sky would flash the ominous light."[38] The more ominous because the light was indeed searching—searching out or feigning to have located armed intruders, of whom in the first year of operation there were many, along with frequent exchanges of heavy gunfire.

> At such times our daddies would speak in earnest tones that brought disturbing thoughts to us children. To us that warning in the night suggested some fierce monster who had the power to sweep down upon a little mining community and compel the people there to do its bidding. But there was the Union! The Union would save us from the fate of Leiter's miners.
>
> And then, as memory recalls it now, there came a terrible disaster in the Leiter mine, and in the work of rescue, so we heard, the ladies of the Leiter family hurried down from Chicago to lend aid to the heroic nurses.[39]

That explosion on January 10, 1909, five years after the mine opened, followed by a second explosion a month later, persuaded the Leiters to abandon their venture. The new technology and high-speed production multiplied the risks of mining a coal seam where methane gas was present in large quantity (a "gassy" mine). All told—there had been an even worse disaster in the mine's first year—eighty miners died in underground explosions, the result in each case of gross violations of the safety standards that the union had obliged the state to accept.[40]

It was probably in the year after Leiter's mine began operations, when Agnes was thirteen, that a book entitled *A History of the Coal Miners of the United States from the Development of the Mines to the Close of the Anthracite Strike of 1902 including a Brief Sketch of Early British Miners* found its way into the Burns home. The author was the Hon. Andrew Roy, former miner and the first mine-inspector in the state of Ohio. On the copy I have, in addition to the name P. H. Burns there appears "Agnes Burns, Spillertown, Ill., 1905." A much later flyleaf note of Agnes's tells an anecdote about apple-

butter-smeared schoolbooks and says "this book saw much of that
when the Burns kids were growing up." Very sympathetic to the
cause of unionism, Roy told about the early miners' unions, the
strikes, the mine disasters—Agnes treasured that book. It is likely
that she took particular note of a quotation from a speech by John
Mitchell following the settlement of the Anthracite Strike: "The
victory of the great strike belongs to the men who struck; but
behind them were a great force, whose names never got into the
papers. They are the brave women and children who endured the
suffering without perceptible murmur—they deserve the credit. I
desire to pay a tribute to the men, women and children of the
anthracite coal mines."[41]

Quality Hill

The experiential, not merely geographical, distance between Spillertown and Chicago was vast; Agnes's horizon had a radius of
perhaps a dozen miles. Except as the force behind the Zeigler mine,
those Chicago capitalists had for her no concrete reality, no more
than did the owners of the Peabody Coal Company for which her
father worked. But even Spillertown had its "Quality Hill"—or so
Mag named it—that overlooked the company houses. One belonged
to Pete Henderson, the mine superintendent, but the house that
stayed vivid in Agnes's memory was not his. Many years later she
used her visit to that house as the lead-in to an article about Jane
Addams's "big house," Hull House.

> In the smallest community there is at least one big house that stands out
> in sharp contrast to the little houses of the working people. I remember
> the "big house" on the hill in the mining village where I grew up, and
> how like a king's palace it seemed to us who were condemned to live in
> the ugly little houses provided for the miners. And I remember how
> curious I always was to look within the "big house." I heard about the
> carpets that seemed to lift one up and down, so soft and velvety they
> were. In fancy I closed my eyes and tried to imagine the sensation. Then
> it so happened that I was once "summoned" to the "big house" to receive
> a gift from the Lady Bountiful. I was very nervous when I found myself
> treading the velvety carpets, but my eyes took in the rich hangings, the
> brilliant chandeliers, the big beautiful pictures and costly ornaments.
> How I hated to go back to that ugly little red house down in the Row.
> Often afterwards I imagined myself possessed of some magic power with

which at one stroke I wiped out the dingy little houses and created in their places beautiful homes for everybody. And on the hill stood the biggest home of all, with its doors open wide to all the people.[42]

Further on in the article Agnes referred to this house of the people as a "dream of my childhood."[43] (She rarely bothered with dates — her memory was not organized around them.) Envy was just not in her nature.

The Downstairs Room

Agnes loved school; she looked back on her first years at Fairmount as a wonderful experience. Colfax and Tallula weren't like that but in Spillertown she found a mentor, Arlo Bratten, teacher of the "upstairs room" and principal, whom she admired. For him she was a star pupil, a girl who loved to read and was eager to learn. Ambitious for her, the family helped every way they could; she, like Gilbert later, was the focus of family hopes. She recalled an occasion, hardly singular, of Amelia's walking her three small children a mile from her house to do Agnes's washing because it was "too much for my strength and I didn't want to miss school," and no money in the house that week to hire help.[44]

In 1908, at age sixteen and with eleven years of school behind her, Agnes passed the examination for a teacher's certificate. Professor Bratten thought it would be to her advantage when she was of age to apply for a job. A year later she was given the first, second, and third grades in Spillertown's "downstairs room." Southern Illinois Normal University, at Carbondale, was handy, fifteen or twenty miles as the crow flies — and she managed in the four succeeding summers to take courses there.[45] ("Managed": Her first month's pay was $32.50. To begin saving up for Carbondale she had, during the summer, persuaded mothers to send her kids who needed help, a dollar per pupil for six weeks.) That she was (to her knowledge) the first miner's daughter to attend the university in Carbondale or to teach in Williamson County, and that the school board had chosen her over the daughter of a rich farmer, niece of the editor of the Marion paper, were points of pride. Pat had refused to help; "I don't believe in influence and I ain't got none," Agnes quoted him. "You got it on your own" was the motto by which he lived. It did help that Pete Henderson was on the board; he was a decent man, Pat felt, who was shielded from coal company pressures by the union's strength and therefore able, as the mine superintendent, to be himself.[46]

Loving, protective, strict, forgiving, patient, conscientious, hard-working, imaginative, Agnes could have been a good teacher, especially for the younger pupils. But the kids were there, most of them, because the law required it; for many it didn't matter whether, at fourteen when boys could go into the mine and girls could (or would have to) think about getting married, they were in fourth grade or the eighth; either way, the future was the same. "Think of teaching children hygiene when you know they don't have milk to drink!" Agnes said about it later. "Teaching little boys the beauty of art when you know they must go to work in the coal mines."[47] She stuck it out for five years, the last two at nearby Johnston City, to which the family moved.

After ten years in that "coal dump" she was now in a town at last; a mining town, but a town. But Agnes's problems did not change much. In the "downstairs room" at Spillertown she had more than fifty youngsters, a count I take from a photograph of her first class, while a picture from her last year at Johnston City's East Side School, also primary grades, shows over sixty. (There is also a photograph of the East Side School's staff—a dozen teachers and the principal strung out as if on a picket line in front of the brick schoolhouse, the ladies all in ground-sweeping skirts. Only a fourteenth person off at one end, the janitor, seems to have anything to smile about.) Perhaps realizing that the change wouldn't be for the better, Agnes had applied at Marion. As customary, she visited the school-board members. Pat had advised against her trying. "Sure made a fool of yourself, going to that banker, didn't you? Professor Bratten might be smart in books but he don't know the ways of the world. Marion's a county seat and rotten like all of them, and the school teachers' jobs go to daughters of business men, not a coal miner's daughter."[48] Pat was right, of course.

"A Wee Bit of News"

Of Agnes Burns at this point in her life I have in my mind a picture of which I feel confident. She is constantly in motion, even while at rest, the kind of person for whom rocking-chairs are made. "Nervous." Physically she is not at all strong, not good with her hands, and not well coordinated (although she has mastered stenography and typing). She depends on her stick-to-it-iveness. She is timid, afflicted by many fears, among them fears of snakes and thunderstorms. She is hypersensitive to pain, but she is not paralyzed by fears and pain—she grits her teeth and endures. She is a talker, can "talk a blue streak." (In her family's eyes, "smart as a whip," "sharp as a tack.") Not a bit shy. She still talks the upstate midwestern of her first school years, but she is "bilingual," can talk Williamson County's Kentucky dialect and make use of its nice turns of phrase. She is well educated by the norms of her county and has tried hard to educate herself. She allows herself no envy or jealousy. She does not envy the rich; she is angry at the poverty of the poor. She has pride in family. She has grown up in a culture of severe Protestantism, where the hard-shell and free-will Baptists debate whether it's predestined or whether you brought it on yourself, a narrowly moral Protestantism that condemns the pleasures which the Devil is thought to have his hand in. She loathes all hypocrisy, counterpart of narrow morality. Although, after trying all the churches, Agnes has finally stopped going—God, I suppose, has a lot to answer for—she has not shaken off the moral code beyond becoming tolerant of the minor sins. (But she hates alcohol and the wife-beating and the rest that the churches don't worry much about.) More important to Agnes is social and economic reform. She cannot be selfish, a very conscientious conscience forbids it; steadily she is developing a spirit of social reform that she sees as one day redeeming her county, her people, a reform centered, of course, in the labor movement. Hardest of all for her, she has no community, no pals, with whom to share her thoughts.

While still teaching, Agnes tried to get involved in the Johnston City labor movement. She described her experience twenty years later in a letter to the president of a chapter of the Progressive Miners' auxiliary, herself a school teacher:

Twenty years ago I began my activities in the labor movement, organizing the miners' wives down in Williamson County, but the old United Mine Workers didn't encourage such a movement as our Auxiliary. . . . While I was still teaching, I was helping the miners and many a time I would be the only woman at their committee meetings for Labor Day affairs, and such things, and no doubt some of the people in Johnston City thought I was doing "queer" things for a young lady. Now and then someone referred to me as "another Mother Jones," making a joke of it.[49]

At one of those Labor Day affairs she made her first public speech. "Twenty years ago the miners' wives couldn't vote and as for the labor meetings, well, some of them went now and then, but most of the time they were too busy with their kitchens and their 'kids' to bother. I did make them come out of their kitchens and join in the Labor Day parades . . . and got them organized in Union Label Leagues."[50] She also tried to stir up interest in building a labor temple to satisfy her wish for a house of the people. It was a live idea in those days of worker self-education; a building erected by working people for common use as meeting-place and as a cultural, educational, and recreational center.

Mother Jones in West Virginia, Mother Jones in Colorado, in the midst of battles for union recognition—fine and dandy. But what business would this would-be Mother Jones have in a fully organized field? Well, it would be all right if she got the women to go talk to merchants about carrying union-made goods and to remind other wives to buy goods with the union label. Agnes also wanted to organize the school teachers, whose pay scale and pupil load she knew very well, but it is hard to imagine her getting anywhere in those towns; the problem would have been with the teachers, first of all. Later she found out that the union label didn't always mean what she thought it did, either. Agnes didn't really know much about the world beyond Williamson County. She needed to get out into that world; there was hardly anything that the county could still teach her and nothing to which she could apply her energies.

Agnes was twenty-two when she quit teaching. The family could get along without her; Gordon, the youngest, was fifteen. She was beginning to think of herself as possibly having talent as a writer, telling the story of the life of working people. Not to be doubted, either, is the lure of the cities and the glamor of the railroad train with its Pullman passenger cars rolling through small towns of an evening on its way to some destination; here, the six-thirty on the C. & E. I., whose through passengers would wake up in Chicago, several hundred miles to the north.[51]

There was in the spring of 1914 an event that served as catalyst, perhaps even imperative, in Agnes's decision to quit teaching and seek a new career. The event, the massacre at Ludlow, was as profoundly significant for many of her generation as the hanging of the Chicago anarchists had been for an earlier one.

By its magnitude and solidarity, the strike of 1897 had taken the coal companies and the other states of the Central Field by surprise. Public sympathy for the miners was strong, and the economy was on the verge of recovery, and the companies could comfortably afford to accept the union. Competition from the "outlying fields" was not yet significant. But the coalfields south of the Ohio and west of the Mississippi remained almost totally non-union and were becoming increasingly important economically. In the mountains of West Virginia and Colorado, class warfare was no figure of speech. Scores of union men, and scores of company-hired gunmen, died in a year and a half of warfare on Paint Creek and Cabin Creek in West Virginia before the miners won union recognition in 1913.[52] (But it would be another twenty years before the state was completely and firmly unionized.) Mine owners determined upon preserving absolute feudal rights would listen to no other arguments. In Illinois the business classes of small towns like Johnston City were not hostile to the union; higher wages were good for business. In the company-store towns of West Virginia and Colorado, miners paid in "scrip" could buy only at the company store.

Agnes hated violence, bloodshed, and pain, but the miners were her people. She remembered the searchlight and the machine guns at Zeigler and the tent city in which the evicted strikers had lived. If the poem "When the Leaves Come Out," written during the West Virginia fighting by Ralph Chaplin, the I.W.W. poet, was known to Agnes by then, she would have understood it, this verse for example: "I will not watch the floating clouds that hover, / Above the birds that warble on the wing; / I want to use this gun from under cover— / O Buddy, how I'm longing for the spring!" Against a ruthless corporate feudalism, working people had the same right to fight back as did the rebels of 1775, a comparison that I heard many times.

In Las Animas County, Colorado, coal miners were striking for union recognition and the rights it would bring, and the eight-hour day; their families, evicted from company houses and under siege,

lived in tent colonies all through a hard winter. On the other side
was the wealth of the Rockefellers, the family a symbol of monopoly
and plutocracy, who owned Colorado Fuel and Iron and had the
state of Colorado at their command. State militiamen, under orders
to destroy the tent colonies, deliberately set fire to the tents at
Ludlow. Among the many dead that day were eleven young children
and two women in a dugout beneath one of the tents. From the
Rockefellers came no admissions and no concessions. In the foreground of a postcard photograph of the strike graveyard, that
Agnes kept, I can make out on the markers the names of four
members of the Valdez family, three of them women or girls;
immediately behind them are three Petrucci children: "Died, April
20, 1914."

At the Women's Auxiliary convention in 1932, Agnes referred to
Ludlow: "I was a good teacher. I didn't know any better. I taught
my pupils the pledge of allegiance to the flag of the United
States. . . . And then one morning I read in the paper of the battle
at Ludlow where women and children were shot by soldiers and
burned to death. Liberty and justice for all! Think of it. I vowed I
would never again teach the children to say the pledge of allegiance
to the flag."[53]

About what she could do, Agnes had no clear idea: some kind of
work with the labor movement. Mother Jones in Colorado, Mother
Jones spreading the story of Ludlow across the country, carrying a
bag of bullets said to have been taken from bodies at Ludlow and
concluding her speech by scattering the bullets across the plat-
form—she was a kind of idol for Agnes. But not a model, for that
old lady, in her mid-eighties at the time, had a style all her own,
inimitable.

Opportunity came that spring in a form that yielded one of those
anecdotes Agnes loved to tell: "a wee bit of news found by merest
accident that Saturday afternoon," "the key that unlocked to me a
big new world, the world of women in industry seeking to develop a
new democracy." A couple of years later she told it this way:

> It was on a Saturday and in those days when I was keeping house for my
> dad and my brothers and teaching school, Saturday was one of my
> busiest days. I was putting down a carpet and was putting some papers
> beneath it. It was with great reluctance that I used some old copies of the

[United Miner Workers'] Journal and I scanned each one before letting it go.

I saw a headline, "School for Women Organizers." Up I sprang from the floor and in that article I read an extract from a speech by Mrs. Raymond Robins. She told of the need of women trained for service in the industrial field.[54]

The National Women's Trade Union League of America, of which Mrs. Robins was president, was starting up a training program in Chicago, "School for Active Workers in the Labor Movement," the first residential workers' education program in the United States. Four months of study were followed by eight months of supervised fieldwork; students would be able to take certain courses at the University of Chicago. The school was intended as leadership-training for trade-union women; Agnes's background did not fit that standard. She referred to having "bombarded the League while trying to get acquainted." Time would pass, more than a year, but in the end she got a scholarship. Along the way, John Mitchell gave valuable assistance.[55]

Her attachment and loyalties were too strong for her not to have seen the road as somehow winding back to Williamson County. She would always remain proud of her origins.

It's Awfully Hard for a Woman to Sit Still

While waiting to be "called" to Chicago, Agnes was not idle. Unlike Williamson County, its eastern neighbor Saline County was very considerably influenced by socialist ideas. With the support of the miners' union, a labor paper, an afternoon daily, the *Harrisburg Chronicle*, had begun publication there. Agnes described her position as that of "associate editor."[1]

Without doubt, the most important day in Agnes's short career with the *Chronicle* was the day Eugene Victor Debs came to Harrisburg to give a speech. She told about it years later in an article in the *Illinois Miner*.[2] The Debs she described, and who moved her so deeply, was the Debs so many people knew and loved. She met a "Christ-like leader of men" to whom children were drawn as if by magic and who nonplussed the local Harrisburg politicians and courthouse hangers-on, waiting outside for a look at this man who had polled 900,000 votes, by shaking their hands and addressing each as "comrade."[3]

One of Debs's gifts was his ability to convince people that they were already socialists but hadn't yet seen how they could be. Agnes was never one to take much interest in theory; she wanted something she could believe in and could explain, in their language, to coal miners and other workingmen and to women. Listening to him, Agnes heard a socialism that matched her own intuition about what is and what ought to be and showed her a way to connect those intuitions to an understanding of capitalist society and an imagination of a commonwealth of labor.

No sooner had Agnes introduced herself, post-lecture, as a reporter for the local labor paper, than she and Debs got into conversation about James Whitcomb Riley, the "Hoosier poet," a friend of Gene's whose verse Agnes was fond of. Debs recited poems of Riley's, and finally, at her request, his poem of tribute to Debs. Agnes thought then to mention a woman, too ill to come to the meeting, who was greatly disappointed at having to miss his speech. Debs, with time on his hands, was eager to visit her.

"I explained that the woman had no home, that I had found her and her husband in an empty house near the railroad tracks just the day before and had written a story of the case for the miners' paper." They went, to discover that the woman was no longer at the house. A coal miner, her husband told them, had come for her; Agnes's story had had quick results. "His woman sent him to bring my woman to their house so she could care for her. He said they had an extra bed that wasn't doin' nobody no good. The churches took up a collection for us this mornin' an' when we git that, it'll help out a right smart."[4]

I quote now the remainder of Agnes's article, except for its last paragraph, which was written with the perspective of ten years' distance. It begins with Agnes's saying to the husband, "You know she said she'd love to see Debs. Well, here's Debs, come to see her."

The man's dull face brightened. Debs reached out his hand and such a greeting as he gave that poor piece of humanity. Debs continued to hold his hand as he spoke words of encouragement. The man's whole being seemed to change. I felt aware of some peculiar presence in the room, so marvelous was the effect of the intense personality of that Christ-like leader of men.

When we left the house Debs was in a quiet thoughtfulness. His face showed pain. Then he began, as if talking to himself. "What that man might have been, who knows? Oh, these tragedies of life! Poverty! Misery! When the earth yields so much beauty! Here, take this. Give it to the woman," and he reached out a handful of silver. "And this," and he was reaching into his purse for bills. "She needs so much, food, clothes, medicine. You know what she should have. Get it for her. Do this for me, won't you?" I protested, assuring him that she would be taken care of. It was not easy to restrain him. I had heard stories of his giving his last penny in such cases and I remained firm in my protest. But he insisted that he give something. "Such things are the greatest sorrow of my life," he said to me. "Seeing such suffering and need and being so helpless to do anything about it." There was a long silence before we talked of other things.[5]

For Agnes, Gene Debs expressed the tragedy and the hope of proletarian life. She wanted poetry and she heard poetry—Debs's kind. She believed that she had encountered the truth and this truth filled a void with which her inability to accept the hereafter religions had left her, filled it by articulating a vision of an ideal labor movement.

Agnes's reminiscences of Debs's Harrisburg visit appeared in the summer of 1925, a year before his death, in the course of a story about an appearance by Debs in St. Louis. In appreciation, he dispatched to Oscar Ameringer, editor of the *Miner,* the following note:

> Will you please say to dear Agnes Burns Wieck when you have the chance that I have read her beautiful personal story in the current issue of the *Miner* and that it touched every responsive chord within me. The very moment I saw the first part of her present name I recognized in her the bright-eyed, alert, zestful young girl reporter I met at Harrisburg years ago. I did not know her married name but I could never forget Agnes Burns for I saw in her at a glance a bright, ambitious, service-seeking girl and I knew she would find her place and make it respond to her high purposes and her laudable ambitions.[6]

A Sermon for the Miners

In June 1915, while working for the *Chronicle,* Agnes was elected by the Illinois State Committee of the Women's Trade Union League as a delegate to the league's national convention in New York City.[7]

Because the league changed over the years, it is hard to give it a simple characterization.[8] Constant was its concern for the welfare of women in industry, especially for those most brutally exploited, those tens of thousands of women, a large proportion new immigrant, employed in the sweatshops of the garment industry and the textile mills. (When Agnes came in touch with the league, the death of 146 women in the Triangle fire, in a New York City shirt-waist factory, was a vivid, recent memory.) The league's mission at its founding in 1903 was to assist the unions of the American Federation of Labor in organizing women workers, especially in industries where women constituted the greater part of the work force. The offer, which could hardly be rejected outright, did not inspire enthusiastic cooperation on the part of the federation's leaders;

when Agnes made contact with the league, it had just about worn out such small welcome as the A. F. L. hierarchy had accorded it. Historically the federation was an association of craft unions, the major exception being the miners' union, which included all mine workers regardless of specialty. With good reason did radicals refer to the members of the craft unions as a self-interested aristocracy of labor.

Unlike its older British counterpart, the league was at no time a general organization of women workers. In the main, its members were either women who had risen through the ranks in their unions or women from the better-off classes indignant about the exploitation and degradation of working women. Many of the latter had their spiritual ancestry in the settlement-house movement; Jane Addams of Hull House was among the league's founders. Margaret Dreier Robins, national president for fifteen years and throughout Agnes's active association with the league, was well-to-do by birth and by marriage—and by no means an honorary president. At the center of activity, organizing and educational, were working-class women, union members, many of them moving along in careers of service and leadership, many of them single women wedded to their work. (With conspicuous exceptions, such as Robins and her sister Mary Dreier, women from the middle and upper classes who associated themselves with the league were defined as "allies," from whom a different kind of help was expected.) The ninety or so women at the New York convention probably included most of the active workers in the league. Relative to the mass of women workers, these women were an elite; there is, however, no question about their commitment, their emotional closeness to the women they were trying to help, or their hope that their assistance would enable those women to learn to help themselves.

During her presidency, Robins was extremely influential in the tone and policies of the league. Politically she fit into the tradition of Liberal-Progressive Republicanism; her liberalism appears to have been thoroughgoing, rectilinear. "Liberal" also meant that when war came in 1917 she pitched in to help make the world safe for democracy; but the imperialist treaty of Versailles outraged her and, like her husband, Raymond Robins, who went on a mission to Russia in 1917, she became an active supporter of recognition of the Soviet regime. Her speeches read well. A strong and resolute woman, she must have made an instant impression on Agnes. Their wealth notwithstanding, the Robinses lived, in Hull House tradition, in a poor neighborhood. In Margaret Dreier's apparently very cooperative marriage with Raymond Robins, Agnes may well have seen the possibility, for herself, of a true marriage.

This was certainly not a radical organization. The aim was "betterment." Were these women feminist? Even now, the word is applied to women and men of extremely varied beliefs and attitudes. If "feminist" is taken simply as signifying belief in the equality of the sexes, then the word would apply to all or nearly all of the league's active workers—but there are many ways of interpreting "equality." Most accurate, perhaps, would be to say that the league was one expression of feminist spirit, in the sense of affirming, by action, women's competence, women's solidarity, women's concern for women, women's equal worth to men, women's leadership abilities. For some years the league was a zealous community of women who felt a bond of love among them and who supported actively the campaign for women's suffrage but for whom the welfare of women workers was the primary concern.

At the New York City convention, Agnes made her presence known by introducing her special concern, the situation of women, both housewives and wage earners, in the towns and smaller cities. She felt encouraged in her hopes of organizing those women. The convention voted to award her a scholarship at the league's school.

From the convention, together with the other Illinois delegates, Agnes traveled to Washington, D.C., to bring the convention's Peace Resolution to President Wilson. The resolution called for an embargo on the exportation of war supplies and the prohibition of manufacture of arms and munitions for private profit. (The Lusitania had been sunk a month before.) As a member of the delegation, Agnes met some "important people": William Jennings Bryan, who had just quit as secretary of state out of disagreement with Wilson's foreign policy, but who thought the league's resolution went much too far; W. B. Wilson, known to the miners as "Billy" Wilson, a long-time U.M.W. official, then secretary of labor; and Woodrow Wilson. (She also did the White House tour and a boat trip to Mount Vernon.) In her autobiography Agnes Nestor, head of the league's Chicago branch, recalled their being "ushered into the presence of our great President Wilson, who greeted each one of us and received our resolution in a formal and gracious manner. It was the crowning glory of our visit to Washington. A day long to be remembered."[9] About this interview I have found nothing that Agnes Burns wrote, but I know that whatever her feelings at the time she did not look back upon that day fondly.

Later in the year, Agnes joined five other women in the league's training program. This was the league's second "class." (Begun in 1914, suspended for a year in 1915 and in 1918, it continued until 1926. Because all students were on scholarship, financing was a serious problem. All told, the school had forty-four graduates.) Magnetic pole for the talent of a great region, Chicago was a city of character. Soon Agnes was forming friendships, something she did easily, with fellow students and with the women of the league's Chicago branch; applying her habits of diligent study to the school's classes; finding, conveniently near the league offices, a marvelous social-science research library, the John Crerar; going to the opera; getting acquainted with Vachel Lindsay, Clarence Darrow, Jane Addams; hearing Scott Nearing lecture; familiarizing herself with the local labor movement and coming to know its leaders, among them the militant president of the Chicago Federation of Labor and good friend of the league, John Fitzpatrick; encountering socialists, Wobblies, anarchists, "every shade, every ism." Carl Sandberg, she recalled, interviewed her and wrote about for the *Chicago Day Book* the Illinois miner's daughter who had quit teaching school to train as a labor organizer. Agnes, looking back a half-century later: a great time to live.[10]

Near the end of March 1916, her academic studies completed, Agnes received an assignment that must have pleased her mightily. In the proceedings of the District 12 (Illinois) convention of the United Mine Workers of America, held in Springfield, there appears an address by Miss Agnes Burns, representative of the National Women's Trade Union League.[11] She was there to seek support for the league's work and to enlist help in getting its *Life and Labor* into the hands of miners' wives: a Mrs. Argo was present to sell the magazine and take subscriptions. Agnes was on a rest and rehabilitation leave—her studies in Chicago had been delayed, or interrupted, by hospitalization for an appendectomy and she still needed to build up her health—but this was an audience that Agnes had many reasons for wanting to address.

Agnes's was an oration in coal miners' tradition. It takes up fifteen pages of the published proceedings; with allowance for her rapid delivery, a good hour and a half of the convention. Although a far from polished orator—this was her first big opportunity and her nervousness was audible—she communicated emotion. Her schooling and teaching had been a useful discipline (elocution was a school subject) and her style told of a lively teacher. She did not mind cliches and neither did her audience. Coal miners liked stamina, a strong voice, and a fighting spirit in their orators, and they did not mind being challenged. They would listen earnestly if there was something to listen to, but they also liked oratory for its own sake, as an art form, one might say. As Oscar Ameringer once remarked, they didn't want to be just settling down in their seats when a Gettysburg Address was already finished.[12]

Even though not all parts could have pleased everyone, the delegates voted to have the speech printed up as a pamphlet and published in the *United Mine Workers Journal*. They had to admire this coal-miner's daughter who (her phrase) had "not yet lived a quarter of a century" and wanted it known that although she had gone forth from the coal camp she was an Egyptian still and proud of it.

Agnes established her presence immediately. She had not forgotten her experiences with the United Mine Workers in Johnston City; no more shunting around.

> Mr. President and Friends: I have waited a long time; it is awfully hard for a woman to sit still and not be able to open her mouth. You have had your say and now I want mine. I don't want the President or anyone else to call time on me. In Chicago I was told the condition of my health was such that I might break down if I came. I said it would break my heart if I did not come. I came down here yesterday and was frozen out. I came here yesterday afternoon thinking I would have a chance to speak. I told President Farrington to have business go on and I would speak later; and then that man Frick kept on reading resolution after resolution and I didn't get a chance. Now, that man Frick is terribly interested in me— he's an undertaker—so I am not going to die.[13]

The stenographer nowhere records "laughter," but it is more than likely that Agnes had found in the chairman of the Resolutions Committee a target of which her audience approved.

Now that she could have her say, there were so many things she must tell them! She wanted them to know what this union had meant to her family and what it meant to her. She wanted them to remember Mother Jones's role in the miners' struggles, a place that few of these men would deny. "Some day that story will be given to the world; and her story will be our story."[14] She wanted to assure them that she had not been fooled by the clever arguments of Chicago professors who favored "scientific management," the Taylor System, profit sharing, anything to keep the unions out.[15] She wanted to tell them about the league and its school. She wanted them to know how good she felt about the brave fight for union that the Chicago public-school teachers were making. She wanted to put a word in on behalf of the teachers of southern Illinois ("If there are any teachers lower paid than they are, God pity them"), and another good word on behalf of John Fitzpatrick, who had been under attack by trade-union conservatives. She wanted to instruct them, those who needed it, in what they ought to believe about the profit system, and for that made use of her coal-stealing story: "I have often wondered since why my dear old dad did not see then, and why so many of you dear old dads do not see now, that all of the coal of the earth belongs to all of the people of all of the earth and not to a few coal barons who happen to control the machinery of its production."[16]

But there were two topics of preeminent importance to her. First, the women of the coalfields. She approached that question by speaking of the working women who have joined the labor movement.

> Woman now feels she is a conscious and important part [of the] great scheme of the world's affairs. . . . The awakening comes to the working girl through her sense of the need for change. . . . In many a factory and workshop there are girls who, with the development and training necessary, would soon become leaders among their fellows. . . . Men have developed naturally into these things, but women have not, because it is only such a short time since women were considered so inferior that if they had an interest outside of their homes they were surely "out of a woman's place."[17]

So far, she had explained the importance of the league's work with women in industry. But she was ready before long to talk to these men about their wives.

"Now I am coming to my 'sermon,' and it is no suffrage 'sermon.' I have been called a suffragette many times by the people in the little towns who know me. I am a believer in woman suffrage, and so are you. Any sensible person is." She was preparing for the argument with which she would sum up her sermon: "The labor movement has a place for every honest man and woman earning an honest living. And don't you think those women in the homes are earning an honest living? I do." Her method of persuasion was emotive; rigorous argument was not her forte, but she built a case.[18]

"We know that the men and women in the unorganized fields are an injury to our cause and that when organized they will become a source of strength, not only to themselves, but to us." ("Us": she wanted it understood that she as much as her audience was a part of the labor movement.) But it was not only the workers in non-union mines and factories who were unorganized. "Men, have you ever thought of the thousands right in your own ranks, right in your own homes, with whom you have been so little concerned?"—those many thousands who "perform a function in our economic life that is not the least difficult nor the least important"?[19]

"I don't believe union men, and especially coal miners, believe an autocracy is good for any division of society, and certainly not for the home."[20] With not many exceptions, of course they did—for the home—and she knew it perfectly well. To get around them, she told a story:

> But I believe you are like the Canadian farmer, you forget. The Canadian farmer, we are told, went to town one day and transacted his business in a most careful manner. On the way home, however, he was firm in the conviction that he had forgotten something, but what it was he could not tell. Three times he went through his pockets in a vain endeavor to discover what he had forgotten. He arrived home in due course of time and was met by his young daughter who exclaimed, "Why, father! where have you left mother?" Now, men, that is the question I want to put to you—where have you left mother? If she is not in a rut it is through no fault of yours; and I repeat that the woman in the home performs a function in our economic life that is not the least important, nor the least difficult.[21]

To support this last claim she offered a lengthy description of a day in the life of a miner's wife, beginning with her getting up early in the morning, "when the corporation whistle blows three times," signaling work-today, to fix breakfast and pack lunch-buckets. "Unless she has a most remarkable, a most extraordinary husband, she makes the fire." Again she jabbed—but she avoided comparison between the housewife's physical labor and the miner's. She wanted recognition for women, not pity, and she was not challenging the division of labor. What she talked of was the woman's responsibilities, her importance as manager of the life and economy of the household, her responsibility for the children, and of the stake she had (too often without understanding it) in the struggle for a better world.[22]

The vision she put forward, then, was of a time when "these women will be fighting with us and standing with us with as strong and firm a spirit of unionism as that of any band of union men on earth. . . . I know these women in the homes. I know them like Agnes Nestor knows the working girls in the large cities. I know their hearts, their hopes, their language."[23] She wanted to see these women organized—and educated—and she wanted organized labor's support, practical as well as moral, for an organizational effort.

Of course there is a problem with Agnes's syllogism whereby "earning an honest living" entitled women to a place in the labor movement. Historically, the labor movement was defined by wage labor and collective bargaining, not by "earning an honest living." But the problem is interesting and worth pursuing.

What she wanted to do, concretely, she described to the convention in just one sentence: "We [the league] have plans under way whereby we will gather into our organization the women working in the trades in the small towns and the women who, though they work in the homes of union men, can hold no union card."[24] The rationale could be worked out this way: directly or indirectly, all these women were victims of exploitation; as such, and as women, they had a natural solidarity of interest, a natural community. Whether employed or not, they were of the working class, they were proletarian women, and therefore they had a community of interest with men who worked for wages, and so there was a class solidarity. This would not be a trade-union concept of "labor movement," but rather a class concept.

What would these women do? Community activities, labor education programs, legislative and political activity, cooperatives, union organizing and agitation in the style of Mother Jones? In the larger towns and small cities, there would be women factory-workers to organize; even in the small towns, there would be teachers, waitresses, stenographers. All these women could assist in strikes and organizing campaigns. But she was thinking chiefly, I feel sure, of the first step, women learning to work together, educating themselves, and thereby becoming ready to engage the problems of their locality. "Autocracy in the home" could not be the first item of business. Had she possessed a deeper understanding of patriarchy than I think she did, and had she acted on it, Agnes would have separated herself immediately from "the masses." Above all, practically speaking, the awakening of the coalfield women would be many times more difficult, if not impossible, if it began by setting the women against the men.

The most serious problem about Agnes's project is that she could not have had much evidence that it corresponded to a need already felt. Agnes was young, Agnes was enthusiastic, Agnes saw a what-ought-to-be. How much opportunity she had to try out her ideas I don't know; the league, always straightened financially, was in no position to undertake such a project without substantial help from the labor movement.

Her other principal topic, another "sermon" really, for her no less important, was reserved for the end of her address. The war in Europe was on her mind. She began by talking about school teachers, with a confession. "There is a new spirit abroad in our schools today and many of the teachers are realizing that much of the history and literature and even the songs have been uncon-sciously developing the spirit of militarism. For many years I taught the so-called patriotic songs to my little ones." The little girls would sing, "Who in the years to come, will play the fife and drum, loudly the bugle blow, bravely to meet the foe; Who in the Nation's need will every war cry heed, who'll be our loyal men, who'll be our soldiers then?" And the little boys would respond, "I! I! I! We'll be the soldiers then." To Agnes's delight—for she had come to realize what she, as a "good teacher," had been doing—she had, on a recent visit back home, heard one of her former pupils singing "There'd be no war today if mothers all would say, I didn't raise my boy to be a soldier." To her further delight it turned out that young Hannah had learned this song in school.[25]

In Chicago she had heard a visiting member of the Women's Trade Union League of England speak about the war. Agnes conveyed Isabelle Sloane's message. The men of England and of Germany, fighting in the trenches, "bodies broken" but "spirit coming to life," wanted to say to their brothers, "We are not fighting you, we have no quarrel with you. We realize you are our brothers, but we are fighting because we were told to fight, because we were led to believe we were fighting for our country and our liberty." Then Agnes: "Will the time ever come when the workers of America will be plunged into a deadly struggle with their brother workers in any country on earth?" She wanted to believe that the war was creating revulsion against war, that a "new spirit" was being born, that "great changes" were going on. She ended her speech with lines from James Russell Lowell, whose opposition to the Mexican War had received new attention since the Spanish-American War and the conquest of the Philippines. The first and last lines: "Where is the true man's fatherland?" "His is a world-wide fatherland."[26]

When war came to this country just a year later, Agnes was not among those who changed their minds: theirs was not the true patriotism, or true love of country.

A Forced Vacation

In early May, a little more than a month after that convention, her health still not satisfactory, Agnes was obliged to take a rest/ vacation that lasted through the summer. One of her correspondents was John Walker, president of the Illinois State Federation of Labor; in the John Hunter Walker Collection at the University of Illinois library, three letters of Agnes's from that summer survive. Although Walker had been expelled from the Socialist Party, rather understandably, for putting his idol John Mitchell in nomination as Democratic candidate for governor, he still professed socialism. He was also prominent in and a leading advocate of the co-op movement, which was making rapid headway in Illinois coal towns. "The more I think over the condition of affairs, the lives of the workers," Agnes wrote to Walker, "the more I look to the cooperative movement for the solution."[27]

At the date of her first letter to Walker (June 9, 1916), Agnes was staying at a farmhouse a mile from Lake Michigan, near Fennville,

Michigan, in the heart of the fruit-belt, a long way from Chicago. "Get lots of exercise and good country food—and sunburn. . . . Wish I had a wheel, could see some of this country. . . . Lots of Fords about, get a spin occasionally." Though she was doing fine and had gained seven pounds, she couldn't "help but think of the value of time." She didn't believe in "vacations for the mind." Teaching was still her true vocation and in that she was frustrated there.[28]

> Was thinking last night of Colorado and there in those mountains I could see health and something more—the opportunity to give opportunities (such as I have had) to those yet denied them. I could see myself teaching those who needed it to read and write or even to learn the English language. Such "missionary work" is needed in Southern Illinois, I know, and I feel sure worse conditions obtain elsewhere. I would rather be doing that down there than nothing here but I thought of Colorado because there health could come. . . . The spirit within me becomes so restless I could almost take what money I have left and hie away where I could use this time and at the same time gain health.[29]

She found herself to be in a "G.O.P. hot bed."

> Also a hot bed of Union antagonism. But it only shows how big our problem is, the ignorance to be overcome, and that the real task is education. If we could have our boys and girls educated (as boys and girls) instead of such organizations as Boy Scouts, etc., the task might show some sign of solution. . . . Our boys and girls need to read more of "Our History" instead of the history as it has been written.[30]

> Am trying to read Charlotte Perkins Gilman's "Human Work." Think she's got the conception of things—so far as I have read. I can't get it from anything else and I'll never be satisfied until I can have a reasonable conception of the relation between the race and progress. Some of my best friends think it's in the Bible—no where else—but I can't see it there. And I can't see their God.[31]

Two months later, on August 4, Agnes wrote: "My vacation has been extended, thanks to the gods of Fate and Finance. The change in plans has proved very beneficial. I love the water and it seems to be doing me a lot of good. I am right on the lake now."[32]

But she thought of those who could not be there, and of those who could.

I long for the time when our people may have vacations. My physical environment is conducive to restfulness and growth but my mental environment is such that forever places the class-conscious person on the defensive. The aspirations and ambitions of the would-be capitalists!

But I came here to rest and I refuse even to defend my class at this time. I have not hesitated to answer direct questions and as one lady put it, they are anxious to get the "anarchist started"—but *she won't start.* These and their kind have cheated our kind out of vacations and most every other good thing and I am determined they shall not cheat me out of this one.[33]

A third and last letter was sent to Walker from Fennville on August 19. Walker, she had read, was going to make another try for the presidency of the United Mine Workers of America. (He would come up only six thousand votes short, and it is very doubtful that he got a fair count.) Anything but unambitious, Walker could imagine himself succeeding Gompers as president of the A.F.L. Apparently, Agnes caught on to this and neither encouraged nor discouraged his pursuit of higher office.

It's the (darn) political maneuvering necessary that clouds the big things. John P. White [the incumbent] has the confidence of a great number of people—possibly not a majority—you may have the situation correctly sized up. I don't know. I wish I knew a lot of things I don't know. I wish I knew Mr. White. His friends tell me they wish I could know him and judge for myself. I really doubt if the average miner knows much more of the situation than I do and I know very little, despite the fact that I am intensely interested and I feel I am entitled to know. As to what I would really like to see happen I am almost ready to say with the Professor, "I have ceased to be interested in individuals or personalities." The interests of society are so much larger and of greater importance than any of us.

When children first become interested in history, they become hero worshippers. Personalities loom larger than the really big things. I really think my first insight into the labor world was much the same way. But I have come a long way just in the last two years.[34]

She was much more interested in trying to persuade the *United Mine Workers Journal* to give her a page devoted to the needs of women and kids. But then she realized that she had not told Walker anything he really wanted to hear.

I see the [league's] *Life and Labor* used your article on the Cooperative Movement. That was good.

Do you really feel that you can do more for that movement as head of the International?

Here I have written nearly four pages and what have I said that is worth that much of your time? As you say, I can't vote anyway nor can I help in any way. But there was something I wanted to say — don't know that I have it clear —

Good luck? — well — Yes.[35]

She held the letter long enough to write a postscript six days later on other topics.[36]

A Letter

By the end of the year Agnes received an assignment with the Philadelphia branch of the league and she would not be back to Illinois, except briefly, for four years.

Before following her to Philadelphia it is useful to read a letter that Agnes wrote to Margaret Robins, dated "October 6, 1916, after the Dinner." It is not an easy letter to interpret but it is significant. On a number of occasions I heard my mother speak of Robins but not in a way that gave me a sense of her importance to her.

Dear Mrs. Robins:

I must say this to you tonight.

Your few words whispered to me so hurriedly, yet so lovingly, seemed to come in answer to my need for inspiration for the message I hope to carry to the miners next Thursday. And it will carry me farther than that. What you said inspired me for a lifelong journey.

The inspiration was in this, "That is why I love you." I could not answer you then. Love to one who has known so little of it and who has had so great a need for it, is like a beautiful vision that bursts upon us unexpected — and love is the most beautiful and most powerful force in all life.

And I hope that this fact — that you have the beauty and the power of this force — may help to add to your message as you give it in the journey across the continent. For while we may differ in a particular case or situation, we who are devoted to this, the greatest cause in the world, always remember that we are journeying toward one great end and that we journey together. And I know it would be impossible for you not to hold our banner high on any occasion or before any people and I am confident that our story will go out to the men and women who gather to hear you along the route of your travel.

You have shown me that you loved me and it was as fine to have it told as lovingly. You showed me first and told me later.

Because of what you have chosen to do for me I can prepare to go back among my own with a message of love and hope. And oh, how much strength is needed for that work. And no, I can never forget them. They are pulling at my heart strings always. They are a part of me and through me your spirit, so big, so fine, so wonderful, shall go to them.

You have helped me in an immediate problem—how to answer a letter from my sister—a letter that carried only despair. I couldn't do it this morning. I can now.

You make me feel that "to me also has been given control over life" and I shall face my task bravely and, I hope, nobly.

God bless you, Mrs. Robins.

> Always your loving and grateful friend,
> Agnes Burns[37]

Except for one detail and for one fact that may help in understanding the letter, I don't know the local context. "The message that I hope to carry . . .": that Thursday would have been October 12 and Agnes had been invited to speak at Mt. Olive, at the memorial, on the anniversary of the Virden Riot. More important, the "journey across the continent" on which Robins was about to embark was a women's campaign tour for Charles Evans Hughes, the Republican candidate for president. Although he conducted an equivocal campaign, Hughes was regarded as the candidate more certain to lead the nation into war. A half dozen years later, a stranger recalled having heard Agnes Burns speak in Chicago on the Sunday before the election; her heart, I know, was with the socialists but like many of the socialists she hoped that "the president who kept us out of war" would continue to do so. (I remember her recalling a number of times the sense of relief she and her friends experienced the morning after the election when the news came that Wilson had carried California.) This may well be the "particular case or situation" about which "we may differ" and that differing is conceivably the "that" of Robins's "That is why I love you."

More important is what the letter tells about Agnes. "Love to one who has known so little of it": surely Agnes had the love and admiration of her father, brothers, and sisters. But she needs the love that is "the most beautiful and most powerful force in all life." I wonder about her mother—and not just about Agnes's loss of her mother. Absent from her celebration of her mother in the diary from which I quoted (chapter 2) is mention of a "loving" mother; Florence appears, rather, as a "stern" mother. If a powerful need to achieve is commonly associated with a feeling of being unloved, I was wrong to be surprised that Agnes felt herself so unloved as this letter says.

I observe also that this letter could have been written, word for word, by many a young missionary. The language—inspiration, hope, spirit, force, beauty, love, vision, journey, greatest cause, one great end—is of that order. Agnes would not have minded being called a crusader and she certainly felt that she had a mission. Elizabeth Anne Payne, in her 1988 study, speaks of Robins's "Great Mother quality" and cites as example Agnes Burns's "to me also has been given."[38]

Finally, taking this letter in conjunction with Agnes's letters from Fennville I become aware of something I have been overlooking, "vacations for the mind." (Walker, by the way, disagreed with Agnes and thought that they were valuable.) Agnes was always a "nervous" person, easily startled, hyper-alert, hypersensitive to physical stimuli, needing to be constantly active. Had she had what was called a "nervous breakdown"? Hints in the Walker correspondence, taken together with the length of her stay at Fennville and her vagueness in conversation with me about that episode, lead me to think it very possible. According to Payne, breakdowns in health and "nervous exhaustion" were not uncommon among women of the league, including Margaret Robins in her youth.[39] About Agnes I have no basis for a definite conclusion.

Philadelphia Stories

The years 1917 to 1920 I think of as Agnes's *Wanderjahre,* partly because she was all over the map on a trail of which I lose the track, but also because she was completing her education through encounters with many different worlds: that of immigrant Jewish garment workers, of Irish telephone operators, of union leaders both men and women and at all levels, of feminists and women's suffrage militants, of upper-class philanthropic women, of literary folk, a list that is surely incomplete.

Around the beginning of 1917, Agnes began work as organizer for the Philadelphia branch of the league. From her time in that city two experiences stood out in her memory, stories that she liked to tell. About the first she wrote a brief report in the league's *Life and Labor* and, nine years later, a long two-part article for the *Illinois Miner.*[40]

Early in 1917, two thousand shirt makers came out on strike; wages and hours and collective bargaining were the principal issues. The union called upon the league for help—two-thirds of the strikers were women, mostly young—and Agnes devoted all her time and energies to the strike, which lasted two months. It was a tough strike: "striker after striker was thrown into jail, the police forbidding picketing."[41]

One day well into the strike Agnes was on duty at a peaceful picket line at a factory gate when, at quitting time, a patrol wagon arrived and police descended in force and grabbed the pickets— Agnes, eight "girls," and a man who was probably an organizer for the union—and dragged them into the wagon. The charge: inciting to riot. Agnes's immediate task was to cope with the fears of these young immigrant women who had no idea what to expect. In the police precinct, until well into the night, the women sang strike songs at Agnes's encouragement—to the amusement of some of the other prisoners and to the annoyance, expressed in "vigorous profanity," of drunks trying to sleep it off. (One of the strike songs, to the tune of "Tipperary": "We are striking for right and justice, We are striking to win! / The bosses are out to bust us, But we never shall give in! / If the bosses can make their own shirts, Let them do it—we don't care! / We shall never, never, never go back, 'Til we get what's fair!"[42]) In the morning they were brought before a police magistrate who of course accepted the testimony of a policeman who, Agnes was sure, had not been on the scene. The only "riotous" behavior had been on the part of the police who, by collaring the pickets, had attracted a crowd; the scabs had already been let out another gate to avoid the pickets. But the policeman swore solemnly that his men were saving a deaf-and-dumb job-seeking woman from attack. The sentence, for disorderly conduct: fine or jail, the latter thirty days in Philadelphia's grim Moyamensing Prison.

Agnes assured the women that they would be bailed out and that the conviction would not stand, so they chose to make a test case of it. Posting of bond by one of the philanthropic women associated with the league was frustrated by the magistrate. Later in the day the women were packed into a Black Maria for transportation to Moyamensing; a vehicle well-named, its interior lightless and airless and, needless to say, terrifying.

In prison, Agnes worked to keep up her comrades' morale and seized every opportunity to do educational work. While they were still together in a reception room she got them singing again and taking turns at making brief strike-speeches. She tried to persuade the Jewish women to eat the bean mulligan, "to keep up your strength."[43] They experienced the usual prison routine and were stripped, searched, deloused of imaginary lice, issued prison clothing, assigned two-by-two to cells.

Locked in, Agnes like all new prisoners wondered about escape and sub rosa communication. She recited for her companion—I am not sure it cheered her—verses from the "Reading Gaol." "And never a human voice comes near to speak a gentle word: And the eye that watches through the door is pitiless and hard: And by all forgot, we rot and rot, with soul and body scarred." And also lines from a poem that Agnes had recited publicly as a child, "The Independence Bell," which celebrated that "quaint old Quaker town" and which provided opportunity for Agnes to explain the difference between political and industrial liberty and the meaninglessness of citizenship "unless we have self-government in the factories and mills and mines." She remembered her companion, asleep, "her long dark hair waving across her shoulders, her beautiful face recalled the Madonna picture I had hung in my school room a few years before."[44]

(While she was writing her story for the *Miner,* Agnes's four-year-old son must have overheard talk about jails. "As I write my own little boy is playing with his blocks. I hear him saying 'This is the way they ought to build jails, big and strong like this.'"[45])

They were all bailed out the next day, to learn that the day after their arrest "a throng of college girls" mobilized by the league had showed up on the picket line. The judge in the Court of Common Pleas, finding that the defendants had done nothing unlawful and were being denied the right to peacefully persuade, dismissed the charges. And the strike, Agnes wrote, ended in victory. She must have thought it so but victories in those struggles to organize women factory workers were, she soon learned, few and often short-lived. In her Organization Report to the Philadelphia league that fall, she noted that the Shirt Makers Union had not won a closed shop and that the form of "union recognition" that the companies had conceded was a very weak one. In short, the union was "going down."[46]

When she left Philadelphia, Agnes carried with her one undying hatred—for John Wanamaker, well-known philanthropist, owner of the biggest department store in Philadelphia. She had put great effort into helping organize the women upholstery workers of the city. The women, all "Americans," mostly of English and Irish descent, were badly exploited. Top wages for skilled work, often on assignments outside the shop, with responsibility for decisions, were around ten dollars a week, far below the New York City scale. Their work carried them "from palaces to battleships," the latter a battleship for the Argentine Republic.[47] In September 1917 a joint strike of men and women upholstery workers was called. The men in the trade, already unionized, were giving the women full support; "they consider the women their fellow workers."[48] The women, some two hundred, were asking for union recognition; for both men and women, wages were at issue.

Agnes had a knack. In her Organization Report to the Philadelphia league, she wrote:

> In [the women's] ranks was one who attracted little attention in the early meetings but who had latent within her the qualities of leadership. This was Agnes Brown who has since become president of the [women's local] union and who has proved the backbone of the strike. Miss Brown said to me one day during the strike, when I was asking her what she thought about the venture on that first meeting night, "It was all entirely new to me. But after you addressed the meeting, explaining this thing the men had been talking about, and telling us all about the labor movement, I said to Mayme McGinnis, next to me, 'Mayme, something inside of me has cracked tonight.'"[49]

The smaller shops agreed to terms quickly; Wanamaker's led the resistance. In one of their strike songs the women christened the very Christian John Wanamaker "Holy John." The store hired inexperienced workers to replace the striking women, and to shield the scabs from picketing and persuasion the upholstery shop was moved into the enormous store. As I recall Agnes's story, the women's strike, still underway when she wrote her report, was defeated but not before she had a chance to get into the midst of the action. A young member of the league, a hosiery worker, was sent into the store to "scab"; several days later, Agnes and one of the league's organizers-in-training were able, with the "scab" as guide, to make their way to the eleventh-floor upholstery shop.

> On guard at the shop door were detectives and managers who had encountered us on the old picket line, but we hurried into the work room like faithful employees, right at the heels of the "scab." In the work room we delivered our message and of course its conclusion was an exciting one for we were pitched out of the room, but not until our purpose was achieved. Five men threw the two of us out and proceeded with us to the head office. . . . The trip to the office afforded a fine opportunity to inform other employees of the trouble. They would not arrest us for they will not permit any publicity on the strike.[50]

And then on a Saturday, when the store was thronged, came a "picturesque" action which Agnes helped plan but which was executed by "the men." First they distributed leaflets to the balcony customers. Then,

> When they were out of the store there came down from the balconies above a regular snow storm of little white circulars. The sight was beautiful to behold, with the little white messages floating through the air, playing about like snowflakes before they fell to the counters and floor below. People gazed with open eyes and open mouths and cries of "Liberty Bonds! Liberty Bonds!" were heard. Then as they reached and secured the little papers they could be heard reading aloud the message sent from above: HAVE YOU HEARD THIS TUNE ON THE WANA-MAKER ORGAN—Women Upholstery workers in Wanamaker's forced to strike for a living wage![51]

The Wanamaker organ was as familiar to Philadelphians as the Liberty Bell.

One other Philadelphia memory was of the Gabin sisters, Clara a dressmaker, Yetta a waistmaker, both of them active in their union, both members of the league. Agnes commemorated their friendship ten years later in an article prompted by a card from Yetta telling of her graduation as a nurse from a New York City hospital; a

commemoration intended also, it is plain, to educate Illinois mining people whose notions about Jewish people had been her own
when she was growing up, namely, that they were merchants and
peddlers, an alien race, who always got the better of you somehow.[52]
If she had carried such notions to Chicago, as she may have, she
must have heard all about the Hart, Schaffner, and Marx strike and
the Amalgamated Clothing Workers of America, its leadership and
a large part of its membership Jewish, in the building of which, in
defiance of the A.F.L., the league and Mrs. Robins individually had
a significant role. What seems to have impressed Agnes about the
Gabin sisters was their knowledge of literature, music, and politics,
the cultural wealth they possessed. They put her to shame by their
familiarity with European writers and advanced thinkers and their
acquaintance with Thoreau and Whitman. They took her to hear
Stokowski's orchestra, fed her Jewish food, and lectured her on the
conservatism of the American labor movement. If she was going to
catch up, Agnes had a lot of work to do.

Visits and Verses

Meanwhile, Agnes kept the railroad lines busy—traveling to conventions, going home for visits. One of her trips to Illinois turned
out to have a significance that she could not possibly appreciate at
the time.

On the first of May, 1917, in the mining town of Staunton, some
fifty miles south of Springfield, a "mortgage-burning" ceremony
was held at the splendid Labor Temple erected by the miners' local
union. May Day, that international "labor day," would not have
been an accidental choice. This was a town where the socialist
Appeal to Reason was home-peddled by newsboys and the "Rote
Fahne" was still the beer-drinking song in saloons patronized by
miners of German origin. One of the invited speakers was William
Green of Ohio, secretary-treasurer of the United Mine Workers of
America, who succeeded Samuel Gompers as president of the
A.F.L. eight years later. The other was Miss Agnes Burns.

Long after, on the back of a photograph of the building, Agnes
noted of the occasion "Ed in crowd, probably a critical onlooker."
An appraising one, no doubt, but Ed Wieck was already "stuck on"
Agnes, the effect of an earlier chance encounter in the union's

Springfield offices, a meeting that Agnes never succeeded in recalling; probably, she had been "introduced around." Staunton was
Ed's home town and it is likely that he had a hand in the invitation.
Rather shy with women, at the age of thirty-two a confirmed
bachelor, he did not seize the opportunity to speak to Agnes; for
her, he did not yet exist. Some months passed before anything
developed between Agnes and Ed.

In the summer of that year Agnes took a vacation from Philadelphia. There might be more than a bit of nostalgia in some verses,
"Vacation Vaporings," written while she enjoyed herself at the
shore, north of Boston. (Friends of the league took care of its active
workers.) The verses came into the hands of Victor Olander, editor
of the Illinois State Federation of Labor's *Weekly News Letter.*

> Agnes Burns, Formerly of Johnston City, Ill., Recently of Chicago and
> Philadelphia, But Sojourning August 25, 1917, at 25 Puritan Road,
> Swampscott, Mass. . . . Nearly all active trade unionists in Illinois
> know Agnes Burns—a good, live, hustling trade union girl. . . . All
> who are mentioned in her lines will feel honored—but others will be
> troubled by the suspicion that she forgot all about us while vacation-
> ing."[53]

It would be nice if Ed read Agnes's poem and was stirred to
initiate correspondence; for all I know, it might be true.

Certain glosses on Agnes's verses will be useful in carrying this
story forward.

Vacation Vaporings

Down in Springfield, Illinois,
The State Capital's location,
There lives a crowd of radicals
With reform as their vocation.

It often happens that some nut
Comes drifting into town,
Then at the luncheon table
They all must gather round.

His is an ism not yet heard,
And oh, 'twould give them joy
To have it made into a law
First in Illinois!

> When he has finished his harangue,
> They have a sort of forum.
> For they must always hear themselves
> Regardless of decorum!

First described is Duncan McDonald, socialist, one-time president and for the past six years secretary-treasurer of the Illinois miners. For the latter position, John L. Lewis, arch-conservative politically, had contested him twice; had carried out, with assistance of family and friends, a campaign unprecedented in Illinois miners' politics for its scurrility; and had twice been defeated badly.

> Duncan McDonald, called upon
> Much against his will,
> Assails conditions that obtain
> In workshop, mine and mill.
>
> "The working class throughout all times
> Has suffered persecution.
> Down with the capitalists' misrule!
> and up with revolution!"

Lewis's attack on McDonald at the Illinois miners' (District 12) convention in 1912, following their first contest, offers a wonderful example of Lewis's florid style. "Beyond peradventure of doubt," said Lewis, McDonald is "one who grafts. Those are hard words, but there are absolute facts, and it is up to me now to prove my assertions or else I am a defamer of character and he is an honest man. . . . I have crossed the Rubicon, I have burned the bridge, it is up to me now to show whether I speak truth or not." After detailing a series of harrowing allegations, Lewis continued: "And I say to you now that if the men at home had known of such actions you would first have heard a muttering and then a murmur, louder, louder, and that murmur would have swelled into a mighty rumble, and by the time it had reached the zenith it would certainly have destroyed this idol who was guilty of such acts!" Pointing dramatically at McDonald: "There is your idol! Behold his feet of clay!" There is more that I must deny myself the pleasure of quoting, ending with the reprise, again with dramatic gesture, "There is your idol! Behold again his feet of clay!" The gestures I know of from my father, present as a delegate. For each of Lewis's charges, McDonald had documentary disproof; in the next election, despite endorsement by Frank Farrington, also a conservative Republican, who won the district presidency, Lewis finished a distant third.[54]

Next in Agnes's poems appears John Walker. Despite her misgiving about his ambition, Agnes sees him as "human, tolerant" and "out of the party but still quite Socialistic":

> He has the great solution
> Which happiness will bring
> To every human being,
> And every living thing.
>
> It's coming, coming like the tide
> Which steals upon the shore;
> It now has its beginning
> In the Co-operative Store.
>
> "If we are to make progress,
> You must be forced to see,
> It is the co-operative movement,
> For all humanity."

Ed Wieck knew a rather different John Walker. Early that summer of 1917, Ed initiated a "Dear Sir and Brother" exchange with Walker—lengthy letters in which each expounded his stand on the war. For Ed, as for the anti-war wing of the Socialist Party, the war was a rivalry between the capitalists and owning classes of the great powers; soldiers on the battlefield and workers at home, the lower classes, were making the sacrifices and the Morgans were harvesting the profits; but the labor movement, and John Walker, were collaborating with the capitalists. In his replies, Walker made it clear that he saw no merit at all ("Christian Science," he called it) in an extract from Tolstoy that Ed sent him, about which Ed wrote that "it in many ways states my opinion" on military service and conscientious refusal. For Walker there was just one enemy, the Kaiser. And he did not fail to insinuate that Ed's opposition to the war could be explained by his German ancestry. Small wonder, then, that Walker was now telling whoever would listen that from the cabin in the woods to which he had retired that summer, to remain apart from the world at war, Ed was in secret radio communication with Wilhelm II in Berlin.[55]

After Walker comes Agnes Nestor, Agnes Burns's friend from Chicago who organized the women glove-workers of that city. She has her own priority:

> Agnes Nestor, who has come
> Down the State to lobby,
> With facts and figures in her bag,
> Starts out upon her hobby.

> "The eight-hour day is what we need
> For future generations:
> And for this cause I bid you plead
> And cease all protestations."

George E. Lee, adherent of Henry George's system, whose wife was active in the Women's Trade Union League, is allowed to point out that everyone else is wrong, that the Single Tax (on land) is the only solution.

I suspect it is the last luncheon-table speaker, Harriet Reid, who troubles Agnes most. From 1907 to 1912 Reid had served as John Mitchell's private secretary. On the first issue of the league's *Life and Labor*, in 1911, her name appeared as business manager. For the last few years she had been working in Springfield for state mining agencies. The next year Reid became McDonald's private secretary and two years later the first woman arbitrator on the Illinois Industrial Commission, which appointment came only after a bitter struggle: right qualifications, wrong sex. (She wrote to Ed that John Walker worked against her.) After sixteen years she was ousted for political reasons. Reid was a friend of Agnes's and of Ed's, and his copy of *Walden* bears Harriet's inscription: "To Edw Wieck—Staunton's future H.D.T.!!" She was quite definitely an "independent woman," acquainted it seems with everyone who was anyone in arts and letters or the labor movement in Illinois, and possessed of a reservoir of gossip about each and every, a fact that did not stay either of my parents' respect for her.[56]

In Agnes's poem Harriet is allowed no more than a protest against the others' views:

> "What foolishness!" quoth Harriet Reid,
> "Why do you still extol
> All these reforms so petty
> And ignore Birth Control?"

Whether Agnes had yet come to see birth control as a crucial issue, I
don't know. But there is a better quote from Harriet or paraphrase
in Agnes's diary, five years later: "What salvation can the labor
movement bring women, when they find themselves in a whirlpool
of poverty and degradation, continually pulling others in?" And
by then, if not before, Agnes would wonder: "I have about come to
the conclusion that Harriet Reid was right when she used to tell me
that this problem [birth control] supersedes all others in importance."[57]

A Romance Falters

At summer's end Agnes was back in Philadelphia, and some time
late in 1917 she and Ed begin to exchange letters. In a photograph
dated 1915, I see a very youthful, very intense woman of twenty-
three. There is a photograph of Ed, also dated 1915, when he was
thirty-one. Ed is all dressed up (probably attending a miners'
convention) in a three-piece suit, derby, white shirt and collar and
small bow-tie, and a gold chain leading to the gold watch in a vest-
fob. He is much fleshier than I remember him; his face gives
nothing away.

Of this initial correspondence just two letters exist, both Ed's.
The first is dated March 7, 1918, Chicago. A month previously he
had barely escaped a vigilante mob in his hometown. Ed's letter is
an autobiography, full of names, dates, places, schooling, jobs,
travels, political and union activities—a response, it is clear, to
Agnes's desire to know more about this man whom she had not yet
met.

A very private man, Ed answered reluctantly. At the end of his
letter, expressing that hesitancy, he revealed much about himself.

> Now I have spent an hour and a half writing down a lot of stuff about
> myself and you don't know anything yet. You know you can't find out
> anything about anybody by asking them. They won't tell it. It is natural.
> Even at that I have told you more than I have ever told anyone. And I told
> it to you to satisfy your curiosity, no one else's. Not that I care in
> particular but I have broken a rule of mine in telling you all this.
>
> Agnes I am going to brave your wrath and preach a bit right now
> before I close. Since I announced beforehand that it is preaching I might
> get by with it. And I am absolutely sincere about it. With all your 26

years (you see I remember too) and the experience they have given you *I* must tell you that there are no supermen or women. We think that sometimes, at first glance, but on closer examination and aquaintance [*sic*] we find they are all the same flesh, tempted by the same foibles and weaknesses as all other men and women. I am saying this in answer to the statement you make as to your conception of me as a "real" man. How many times has your opinion of persons changed for the worse after you became better aquainted with them. Think it over.[58]

A month later—there must have been an intervening exchange—Ed terminated the correspondence abruptly in a letter from Los Angeles. Why, is not fully clear. "Apparently letters from me are no longer welcome."[59] Agnes might have shown resentment at his "preaching" or perhaps she was annoyed at his disparagement, in the March 7 letter, of women of the Prohibition Party at a political convention he attended in Chicago, one of whom "delivered a tirade against rum and tobacco," "tobacco worse than drink, cause of all ills."[60] (Agnes, hater of saloons, was a convinced Prohibition-ist.) Perhaps he was fearful of becoming trapped, of losing the freedom to which this bachelor was much accustomed, and had found a pretext to break off. Harriet Reid, who expressed to Agnes her wonder, after Ed and Agnes married, whether Ed's roaming days were really over, might have favored the latter interpreta-tion.[61]

To judge by another letter of Ed's, Agnes took the Los Angeles letter as a slap in the face. But it was true that Ed had gone to the West Coast with the intention of staying clear of the military draft, should it be extended to include men of his age, and also of being unavailable if the net of prosecution of radicals should reach out for him. The month of the vigilante action in Staunton, the federal government had rounded up the entire general executive board of the I.W.W. Stories like John Walker's could do him no good, in the midst of what is called, rather generously, the "hysteria" of war-time. He did not know where his journey would take him ("I will be a blanket-stiff instead of a tourist"[62]). But perhaps his explanation in a letter of apology later on should be taken seriously, that he had enemies who "would not hesitate to harm me, or try to, through others they might know were dear to me." In the paranoid climate of the nation at war it should not be surprising that a person in Ed's shoes should have irrational fears; but then, by the same token, his fears may not have been entirely irrational. Almost two years went by before Agnes and Ed resumed communication.

Boston and Return

I don't know how long Agnes stayed in Philadelphia. After September 1917 the first firm date and place I have is Armistice Day, 1918, Chicago. She was working then in the employment service of the U.S. Department of Labor; while on that job she had a battle with a Marshall Field's manager over her refusal to refer job-seekers at the low wages the department store was paying.[63]

In January 1919, the Telephone Operators' Union, growing rapidly all across the country, received formal recognition as a department of the A.F.L.'s International Brotherhood of Electrical Workers. Its headquarters in Boston, its president Julia O'Connor, was a fellow student of Agnes's in Chicago and a very good friend. Agnes became office secretary. Her job entitled her to membership in the Stenographers' Union, the only union I know of that she ever had an opportunity to join; it also allowed her to preserve connection with the Women's Trade Union League through membership on the executive board of its Boston branch. She seems to have tried to organize stenographers in Chicago during her "training" days, but it was a hard trade to organize.

The Telephone Operators' was an exciting union to be associated with. It was "the only labor organization of an international character officered by and composed wholly of women," Agnes wrote for the league's *Life and Labor,* after the union's New Orleans convention in the fall of the year. "Its executive officers came direct from the 'tools.' The delegates were all girls in the[ir] twenties. . . . From Boston and New York came girls well schooled by seven years' experience in trade unionism, girls who have established the best system of collective bargaining in effect in any industry. The New England Telephone Company and the Providence Telephone Company, both of the American Bell, are solidly organized, as was demonstrated in the six-day tie-up of New England's telephone service last April." A "splendid victory."[64]

I sense, here and there, enthusiastic exaggeration, but those New England operators had stood up to the U.S. postmaster-general and to Massachusetts' governor Calvin Coolidge, who threatened to seize the lines and break the strike. Most of the women were Irish; of course, Agnes had a special Irish pride in their courage.

In my mind—and it must be from Agnes that I got that feeling— the Philadelphia she lived in was darkened for her by a God-awful black cloud, the war. Except for the long-awaited revolution in Russia, the destruction of tsarist autocracy and the proclamation of socialism, there had been very little in which people like her could rejoice. Her naive optimism was gone for good, but if she could not share in the public celebration of military victory—she would think only of all the dead—it was possible to believe in a new beginning.

The year 1919 was indeed eventful. With ratification of the Eighteenth Amendment Prohibition was the supreme law of the land, a great victory for women, so it seemed. Alcohol, the saloon as its symbol, had drawn much of the blame for husbands' brutality and irresponsibility. Alcohol exculpated the men who were portrayed as victims of their peculiar weakness. A great deal of feminist energy was invested to achieve a sorry victory. Her own enthusiastic support for that cause Agnes was to regret early and bitterly for many reasons, but, especially because—paradoxically—the demise of the saloon opened the world of drinking and drunkenness to women, especially young women. She never quite got over the feeling that a drunken woman was a sorrier sight than a drunken man. For Agnes, Prohibition was going to be a lesson in the enforcement of morals.[65]

The woman's suffrage amendment was also moving along to passage, though Agnes came to see it as a rather hollow victory. Agnes liked to recall a big suffrage parade in New York City in which she marched and to tell of seeing John Dewey carrying a placard inscribed with the slogan "Men Can Vote; Why Can't We?" The right had to be fought for but she knew that if voting women, like their husbands, chose between the Tweedle-dee and Tweedle-dum of the Republican and Democratic parties, as in fact they mostly did, the world would be little different.

It was a notable time in labor history also; locally there was not only the telephone strike. For Agnes, an enthusiast of the "legitimate theater"—which the movies never replaced in her heart—a high moment was a strike of actors and actresses in New York and Boston that led, as she remembered it, to the founding of Actors' Equity. Ethel Barrymore on a picket line! With the labor people of

Boston, she shared the tremendous excitement of the police strike of September 1919, a brief and glorious time. ("Took a hand in it," she once told a reporter.[66]) Governor Coolidge feared, as union people hoped, that policemen, if allowed to join a bona fide union, might be inclined to sympathize with their union brothers and sisters in times of strike. He fired them all, broke the strike, and earned the reward of election to the vice-presidency a year later. The months of October and November 1919, were also very emotional for Agnes; a half million striking coal miners stood firm in confrontation with the federal government and won a pretty good settlement. But the great steel strike of that fall was crushed violently. During the summer the deportation of foreign-born radicals had begun. On New Year's Day in 1920, there were deportation raids all across the country; in Boston hundreds were led through the streets in chains.

I find it hard to develop a satisfactory image of Agnes in Boston. She had, I know, brought with her many kinds of enthusiasm: the very idea of Boston, the Boston of Lexington and Concord, of New World culture and learning, of the anti-slavery movement, of the agitations for woman's rights, was thrilling. She went to concerts and museums; the tea-rooms knew her; she came to know a lot of people of all social classes and styles of life. (I remember her speaking of having been at Rose Kennedy's home.) Mary Donovan, active in the Socialist and labor movements, later on secretary of the Sacco-Vanzetti Defense Committee, had an apartment in Cambridge near Harvard Square. Agnes and a young woman they called "Wizzie," who specialized in bringing Harvard students home for dinner, roomed with Mary. Fun memories. Did Agnes have a love-life? Never a hint.

In her own eyes she was a writer-to-be. "The pen is mightier than the sword," she liked to say. Agnes could not have seen herself as *just* a professional writer: she would have to write as a voice of the working people. As models or inspiration she may have had Zola, Dickens, Sinclair, and Dreiser. (Sinclair may seem out of place but *The Jungle*, through which he exposed the Chicago stockyards, was on its own terms masterly.) Agnes had a thousand true stories in her head. She wanted to write a novel—*that* was how to reach people. Earlier, an astute warning from a league friend had probably dissuaded her from attempting a biography of Mother Jones. First, her friend's advice: "I tell you what, you get Miss Henry [Alice Henry, editor of *Life and Labor*] to help you with it. One of you should balance the other. Miss Henry is a dabster for references and raking up information, she fears neither the post nor the telegraph offices and knows how to make a thing academically convincing and you would supply the fire and vim." A sound judgment of both parties. But then—"I should love to hear the snub you get from the old dame as two mere females of the species when you approach her for she is quintessentially androcentric."[67] A sound judgment, too, of Mother Jones.

The Burns family did break into print, pseudonymously, with Agnes's help. In December 1919, under the heading "Letters from a Miner's Wife," *The New Republic* gave three pages to a group of "Dear Sis" letters written during the national coal strike just ended; the first four from "Julia," in Amelia's inimitable style, and two short ones from "Tom," whom I am unable to identify.[68] It delighted Agnes that a "literary lady of Boston" refused, third-party assurances notwithstanding, to admit the authenticity of Amelia's letters. "The literary touch is insufficiently concealed."[69] That literary touch was Amelia's natural eloquence, something "the lady" was unwilling to credit in a miner's wife. Amelia wrote on the sixth day of the strike: "Of course, we're not fixed for a strike, never would be for that matter, they never give us enough work to lay anything ahead, but they can freeze before they can starve us and operators [mine owners] can't dig their coal or beg it and we can beg unless they run an injunction against it."[70] On the ground that the Armistice hadn't ended the war, a federal judge, at the government's request, did "run an injunction" against strike relief though not against begging, and threatened to jail the union officials. John Lewis, then acting president, pressured the union's policy committee to call off the strike, saying "We cannot fight our government," but the miners in the stronger union fields ignored the order and stayed out another month. Lewis's friends claimed that the order was not meant to be obeyed, a view that "Tom" reflects; there is much reason to doubt it, as "Julia" did. Wrote "Julia": "This is the miners' strike, not Lewis' strike, but the Government and the public don't seem to know that."[71]

Indeed it was the miners' strike, for it is questionable that Lewis would have moved to abrogate the wartime wage agreement, although it was far out of line with the post-war "high cost of living," were it not for the pressure brought by the "1919 Wildcat" strike that originated in the Belleville subdistrict and was spread to other parts of the state by bands of "Crusaders."[72]

Around January 1920, the month after publication of the letters, Agnes and Ed, at her initiative, resumed correspondence. Ed was in Illinois again, living in a small town near Belleville and working in the mine. A temporary assignment from the Telephone Operators' Union had brought Agnes back to Illinois.[73] I believe his statement in one of his letters that he had never stopped thinking about her, but I also believe that he had put himself in a corner by his letter from Los Angeles—an embarrassment that could have kept him cornered indefinitely. But they did not meet until the fall of the year. Ed's letters in the months preceding and following marriage are truly love letters, not lacking the madness of love. In one he charts their elaborate "trails" on the scroll of life, in their infinitely small region of a vast, indifferently watching, yet somehow amused cosmos; trails that drew closer, moved apart, wandered, and finally converged so happily. Ed was a loner, had long been such, who felt more at home with books, with nature, perhaps even with chance acquaintances on the road than with most people he met. He liked to see Agnes as a wanderer like himself; in his letters she is "Gypsy" or "Little Gypsy," a reference both to her "Egyptian" origins and to his difficulty in keeping up with her journeys.

Agnes and Ed weren't youngsters anymore. When they married on January 21, 1921, Agnes was just past twenty-nine and Ed seven years older. At the Chicago courthouse that day he gave her a copy of a book by one of his favorite philosophers, *Leaves of Grass*, from which he had quoted copiously in his letters. He had carried Walt in his knapsack on his journeys around the country.

My Soul Aflame with Indignation

When Ed's father, Henry J. Wieck, was a small boy the entire Wieck family, peasants from the vicinity of Kiel, then under Danish rule, transplanted itself to the farmland of Macoupin County in central Illinois. At eighteen Henry enlisted in the Union Army, First Missouri Cavalry, and served three years. After the Civil War he worked as a bridge carpenter on construction of the Union Pacific Railroad; helped rebuild Chicago after the fire; worked on river steamboat construction; then married Clara Bretschneider, some dozen years his junior, and settled down in Staunton, from which base he built houses, churches, and business-places in the coal towns of the region.

Though Henry had only six months of school, he commanded a large English vocabulary, had no accent, and (Ed said) was a "great reader." Other veterans liked to swap war stories; not Henry, who refused to join the Grand Army of the Republic. (But he retained his loyalty to the North and voted the Republican ticket faithfully.) He did tell Ed about Pea Ridge, Arkansas, the one major battle in which he took part. He and another soldier were sitting side by side on a rail fence waiting for the order to go into battle, when a cannonball, whose sound he did not forget, split the distance between them. (An uncle of Henry's, on the other hand, was credited with shooting a Confederate general off his horse.) Perhaps to discourage any thoughts of war's glories, Henry also told Ed about the involuntary bowel movements of green soldiers under fire; not much else.

Clara, who died in her middle forties, had come over as a young woman from Grimma, a small city of Slavic origin in Saxony; from a photograph I find it easy to imagine a part-Slavic ancestry. To her was due whatever warmth there was in that family. "Mother was just a mother," Ed wrote to Agnes. "A great lover of flowers, house and yard always full of them."[1] She too liked to read. John, the older son, called "Fod," was born when Henry was around forty; Edward was born three years later, and then Elvin. Henry's life was cut short by an apoplexy that coincided with a "rebellion," cause unknown to me, by the younger son. (When I began to learn about "Prussians," I had already, from stories about my grandfather, an image on hand.) The funeral was Masonic; nobody in the family belonged to a church, though Clara had regularly attended one of the churches the sound of whose bells my father translated as "a nickel'll do," as opposed to the sonorous "bring-g-g-g a quarter-r-r-r along-g-g-g" variety.

At thirteen, after a year of high school—he had probably exhausted what the school had to offer, including a little Latin—Ed went to work but not at his father's trade, which was also a "rebellion." While clerking in the post office, after several years as a barber, he read the incoming Socialist papers, become convinced, and joined the party. He gave himself a severe regimen of continuing self-education, not uncommon then among radical workingmen. He turned down a chance to read law with the lawyer-postmaster, whom he had impressed, and went to work in the mines; they didn't work every day and before long he found the one that shut down first in the slack season. Like many radical workingmen he did not want to rise above his class; he wanted to rise with it. Nothing commanded his respect more than skilled and useful work, conscientiously executed—here was beauty—but he also thought there was more to life than work. He roamed the country, boxcar or cushions, as circumstances dictated or permitted, and saw just about every northern state west of New England. He worked in a mine office and in a logging camp and in shipyards and dug for chrome ore; shoveled coal in the engine-room of a coastal boat and picked fruit along the Great Lakes, and did a two-year stint in the Illinois miners' offices as assistant to Duncan Mac-Donald, chiefly as a favor to Mac. He went no closer to a factory than a warehouse in Chicago, where he didn't stay long; he always went back to Staunton and to the mines, where you worked with a "buddy" and seldom saw a boss. He examined his needs carefully.

How many pairs of shoes can you wear at the same time? (He mentioned with respect a man on a beach north of San Francisco who had done the very Thoreauvian thing of reducing his housing needs to the coffin-shaped wooden box he slept in.) He was a very self-disciplined person and an effective pit-committeeman: "He who loses his temper loses his cases." He did, to be sure, have an O. Henry streak. Once in southern Illinois he hooked up with a grifter; their specialty was the cleaning of already-clean cisterns after demonstrating the need for it by stirring up the bottom. Their victims were people of the business class. Ed didn't mind "skinning the bourgeoisie"; he despised people who lived off the labor of others. In his way he was a playful person, less serious than Agnes, but most people mistook him; his eyes were a bit mischievous.

Over the years Staunton's Socialists had literally been "building the new society within the shell of the old." A Labor Lyceum erected by German-speaking Socialists hosted amateur theatricals, provided meeting-rooms and a bar, and offered adult-education classes in its library. Polish and Bohemian Socialists built their own hall along similar lines. The miners' local union #755—Staunton was a mining town in a farm region—acquired a store building, bought staples in carload lots, and built a warehouse near the railroad to store surplus stock and to handle the sale of coal. And it built the Labor Temple, dedicated in 1914, which housed offices, a reading room, a theater and other meeting halls, including one for lodge meetings. The store and coal yard cut sharply into local businesses and the Labor Temple's movies destroyed the competition; before the war, Ed said, the Socialist Party had been "on the verge of taking over political power."[2] In all these activities Ed and his brother Fod were prominent; their younger brother, the Labor Temple's first janitor, became projectionist and (after the war) manager of the theater.

On February 12, 1918 a mob led by the police chief set out to purge Ed's hometown of its "unpatriotic" citizens. Staunton's Socialists were mainly of German descent and mostly anti-war. Such people were of course called "pro-German"; no doubt some were but Ed was an internationalist on socialist principle and the Germans he honored were those who did not support their government and refused to vote war-credits.

A miner in a nearby town had been arrested under the Espionage Act for allegedly anti-war and anarchistic activities. On the night of the twelfth, Local 755 met at the Labor Temple and re-affirmed its decision to give Severine Oberdan financial assistance in his legal defense. As the meeting broke up, the vigilantes moved in. Oberdan and his lawyer were beaten, tarred and feathered, driven out of town. "Progressive leaders of the miners were beaten up or cowed by indignities or humiliation"; many were arrested.[3]

Not knowing the cause of the ruckus that developed when the meeting was adjourning, Ed had gone to the hotel where he boarded. Warned that he was being sought, he decided to get out of town. As he left by a side door he heard someone mounting the front steps. "Standing in the shadow at the side of the house, I saw a dozen men enter, the leader with a rope."[4] In writing about these events, Ed could not resist comment on the moral worth of such individuals: "I recognized the leader as one who had been at various times a saloon keeper, tinhorn gambler, and petty foreman in the mine. His last job in the mine had been lost because so many brass fittings had disappeared, to turn up later at a local junk dealer's establishment."[5] Ed hustled out of town, down the Inter-Urban tracks. "As I left the town behind me I could hear the sound of confused shouting which had become louder and was now punctuated by an occasional pistol shot. The glare of the lights over the town as contrasted with the surrounding darkness gave the impression of a large bowl, partly lifted and under which had crept some malign influence to harass and injure a peaceful population. Again I was beset by doubts as to whether my course in leaving town was right."[6] (I connect this last remark with a German Mauser rifle that was in our home. I know that Ed had it in Staunton. He must have carried that rifle, slung over his shoulder, as he left town.)

Down the tracks Ed ran into his brother Fod, also wanted. Not finding Fod at home, the mob broke in and carried off all the money they could find, along with the deed to the house. A young member of the Socialist Party was forced to carry a heavy flagpole twelve blocks from his home to the town park; "struck, beaten, pelted, and even spit on" en route, "knocked, buffeted and kicked into unconsciousness" on arrival. Lacking, Ed thought, was only the crown of thorns.[7]

In the West, while working in the shipyards, Ed picked up an I.W.W. red-card. He admired the Wobblies for their industrial union program and militant organizing. But in the debates within the Socialist Party he had stood neither with the "possibilists" nor the "impossibilists." He was scornful of "sewer socialism," the municipal-ownership program of the right wing. But he was by nature, as if by inheritance, a builder. In Staunton they had built and they had contributed importantly to the building of the United Mine Workers' union, which had brought a better life and a measure of freedom. By forcing the owners to accept uniform labor contracts, the union had partially stabilized the chaos of capitalist competition in the production of the coal the world needed. Agnes had been listening to arguments that the U.M.W. was too conservative and should be supplanted by a more militant union; Ed agreed with the diagnosis but not with the solution. True, the rank and file, Agnes's dad for example, was losing confidence in the union's leadership. But a new organization would be composed of "the same general timber as the old"; too many belonged to the union "only as a matter of course" (once hired, you had to join).[8] Ed did not idealize the working class.

In temperament Agnes and Ed were quite different. Her strong quality was her fire, emotion, quick responsiveness. Ed on the other hand spoke in measured terms, and only to say thoughtfully what he thought was worth saying. Much the more systematically reflective, he framed questions in historical terms ("the long term"); he studied and analyzed a concrete situation as though it were a union contract full of ambiguous clauses that needed resolving. A sharp critic (he always thought my best efforts to be not entirely unworthy first drafts), he could help Agnes. Whether his criticism would sometimes be intimidating, whether their views on certain things would come to convergence to her detriment, I hesitate to assert, though I suspect it.

A Gemütlich Town

It hadn't been clear where Agnes and Ed were going to live. She was in Springfield in a responsible job with the Tuberculosis Association, which she could not just walk away from. In Belleville, Ed was living with brother Fod and his wife and getting more impatient by the hour ("married, no wife"). Why shouldn't her fellow workers call her "Mrs. Wieck"?[9] They both regarded the marriage license as

a legal formality — understood, it seems, a little differently by each.
Of course a "Mr. Wieck" and a "Miss Burns" couldn't live together
respectably in a town like Belleville; but what did the town have
that Agnes wanted? St. Louis, that was a city.

Oscar Ameringer, a socialist, a veteran labor editor with a first-
rate head for business and a superb knack for extracting money
from fat liberal wallets, had a scheme for setting up a chain of daily
labor papers across the country. One of those was to be the *St. Louis
Daily Herald*, a project with which Agnes became involved, but it
didn't pan out. Ed had a job in a mine near Belleville, and he and
Agnes had between them hardly any money and no clear prospects
for any kind of work in St. Louis. The upshot, Agnes quit her job
and she and Ed set up housekeeping in a small flat a block and a half
from Fod and Mayme's.

Belleville's courthouse square sits just about fourteen miles
southeast of the river crossings at St. Louis.[10] To reach it from St.
Louis you had to pass through East St. Louis, host to slaughter-
houses and railyards and heavy industry; an ugly city, site of one of
the worst of the end-of-war "race riots." Leaving East St. Louis
behind, and having ascended the high bluffs above the Great
American Bottoms, you soon arrived at the beginning of Belleville's
eight-mile long main street, a pretty good length for a town of
maybe twenty thousand souls. Within pleasant walking-distance
from the square you would have found many handsome examples of
nineteenth-century non-Victorian architecture. By geographical
definition Belleville lay just within the northern boundary of Little
Egypt and the very first settlers had come from the South. Culturally, however, there was no kinship. To the east of town spread the
"Looking Glass Prairie," a rich farming region, wheat predominantly, christened it was said by Charles Dickens on his 1842
American tour; by our time, progress had torn down, in favor of a
movie theater, the Mansion House at which he stopped. Eight miles
to the east, not yet of more than marginal significance in the life and
economy of Belleville, was Scott Field.

Belleville had proud traditions dating from the first influx of Germans in the early 1830s, among them university graduates and professors known as "die Lateiner," liberals driven to emigration by the
reaction that followed the aborted revolutions of 1830. The characteristic rhythms of local speech remained the German sing-song that

prevailed across the river in South St. Louis. An astute reader of the editorial page of the *Belleville News-Democrat* would have recognized in its owner-editor, Fred J. Kern, an admirer of H. L. Mencken. The line of descent of Belleville's public library was continuous from the Deutsches Bibliotheksgesellschaft of 1836. In the same tradition, Belleville residents took keen interest in public education.

The 1911 edition of the *Britannica,* near enough to date in all respects but one, speaks of mines, stove and range factories, flour mills, rolling mills, distilleries, breweries, shoe factories, copper refining works, nail and tack factories, glassworks, and agricultural implement factories.[11] Coal, conveniently near the surface, had been discovered in 1825 and St. Clair County, serving St. Louis, had until the end of the century remained Illinois's major producer. Mines and foundries were now the major employers. The distilleries, and eight breweries of splendid reputation, had been sealed shut by Prohibition, which decentralized brewing—every home, so it seemed, was a brewery. A local justice of the peace ruled that a debt for home brew was collectable in Belleville, the Eighteenth Amendment and the Volstead Act notwithstanding.

The short-lived American Miners' Association, the first national union of miners, was founded in (then) West Belleville during the Civil War. During the strike of 1897 Belleville miners were slow to join the movement—"General" Bradley had to lead his "army" down there to persuade them—but they were solid union men ever since. Miners of the Belleville subdistrict were in the vanguard of the statewide "1919 Wildcat" and were still inclined to troublemaking when coal companies got out of line or union officials didn't do their job. There were no coal camps; the miners lived in town or in nearby villages or in the country and many owned their own homes.

If the reader gains the impression that this was a "bürgher" town whose business people constituted a very well-to-do and very self-satisfied dominant class, then I have conveyed the right impression; local industries were nearly all owned by long-established families.

Belleville was in most ways tolerant. (Black faces of course were rare; Belleville wasn't *that* tolerant, although I did know a few black kids in school. Outside the city limits, nearby, was a small black community.) The Ku Klux Klan, which appeared in Williamson County in 1923 and had ambitions of spreading further, made only a brief, quickly reconsidered attempt to gain entry to Belleville—no cooperation or sympathy from the law, and laughter and ridicule from the pages of the *News-Democrat*. There were good reasons. Belleville had a sizable Catholic population with the bishop of the diocese in residence, and religious tolerance was in the town's tradition. Equally important, enforcement of the Prohibition laws was at the top of the Klan's agenda. Bad enough that the town's major industry had been wiped out.

It took a fair while — Belleville was a rather placid town — but Agnes grew to like it.

Two Families

Oscar Ameringer never ran short of ideas. If he couldn't have his chain of papers, maybe he could get the Illinois miners' union (District 12) to publish an official organ under his editorship and administration; there would surely be a place for Agnes. In late April or early May 1921, Agnes was in southern Illinois with Oscar and his companion and associate, later his wife, Freda Hogan. Agnes was using her connections and knowledge of Egypt to get pledges from the miners' locals. Frank Farrington, president of the Illinois miners, liked the idea of an official organ for his district — the *United Mine Workers' Journal*, Lewis's organ, was a dreary affair, and strictly self-serving. Ameringer could tolerate Farrington's conservatism, a match for Lewis's; in exchange for the paper's unquestioning endorsement of Farrington's policies in the political struggles within the union, Ameringer would have (otherwise) a free hand.

Agnes and Ed both wanted a child or two, but had no plans yet. Fearful of childbirth — with reason, given her chronic not-good health, chronic over-extension of herself, and (more recently) palpitations and shortness of breath — Agnes had been reassured by a physician. Ed prescribed a regimen of exercises. But of course it happened; a 100 to 1 shot, said Ed. That baby, whose sex he took for granted, was now calling the tune. And the baby arrived on schedule, December 13, 1921. (The *Illinois Miner* would soon begin publication but although Agnes's typewriter was not idle, the baby was nearly three before she began writing for that paper.)

Agnes had sought out St. Louis's top gynecologist/obstetrician, the head of a maternity hospital, and bore a healthy baby. She followed the most advanced scientific routines of the day: the baby was circumcised, fed on schedule, and weaned early. Snapshots of babe and mother (her hair "bobbed") show the glow of motherhood, I think it is called. But there was something she never told me, that I learned only recently: the birthing was "indescribable agony," a "terrible ordeal"; she thought the problem was "the bones not giving." The experience "haunted her"; "the fear of another pregnancy" had "about wrecked her nervous system."[12]

Ed, who introduced Agnes to Thoreau, wanted to name the boy after the Concord philosopher; Agnes liked "David." (They probably didn't know that Thoreau, christened David Henry, chose to be Henry.) On my first birthday, Agnes wrote in her diary: "We have been asked if we expect to give the world another David Thoreau. We have no plans for our boy. What natural gifts may be his, we have no way of telling. The choosing the name of Thoreau was doubtless the expression of a hope within us that we might bring up a boy to honor such a name. If David has his father's love of nature, his philosophical turn, his high ideals, he will have a strong claim upon the name of Thoreau."[13] At Christmas in 1922 I received a present from Elizabeth Christman, of the Glove Workers, a friend of Agnes's from the Chicago League, a present I wasn't ready to appreciate: a 1915 (London) edition, from a Simple Life series, of Thoreau's "Life Without Principle." A visitor remarked to Agnes that were she to have a child she "would let it run wild, natural and uncurbed—which is about what we do with young David, a practice not evolved from theory but from compulsion,"[14] the compulsion being crowded quarters and an active child. Perhaps—but these rebels weren't much disposed to discipline. Mayme, who took care of the baby on occasion, was of the no-nonsense persuasion. A breath-holding baby could scare the daylights out of Agnes; Mayme's medicine was a fast splash of water. But by the time I was on my feet, I had the run of her house too.

When I was six months old, a tiny baby weighing less than three pounds was born in Belleville to Laura Yereb, also the wife of a coal miner. Soon after the birth of Helen Marie, Agnes visited the Yereb home. As *St. Louis Post-Dispatch* reporter Robertus Love told it later on in a feature story for its Sunday Magazine, "She looked upon the mite of humanity and made mental comparison with David Thoreau at home. Then within her radical soul was wrought a mighty indignation. Mrs. Wieck knew John Yereb and his story. She went home and wrote the story."[15]

The opening paragraph of Agnes's "A Deportation and Its Aftermath" (published in *The New Republic* in 1922) reads as follows:

> Two years ago [March 31, 1920] Palmer's Red Hunters invaded Belleville, an Illinois mining town across the river from St. Louis, and retiring to that city, took with them two coal miners. After much questioning both men were released without bond and sent home with the admonition to attend closely to their own affairs. Time passed and Belleville forgot the incident. Last April, two years afterwards, one of the men was ordered to St. Louis where he was informed that his case had been decided at Washington and that he was to be taken to Ellis Island immediately for deportation. He was not permitted to return to his home to bid his wife goodbye. Mr. Daughterty's agents started him for Ellis Island on the noon train. Within a few days John Yereb was on the high seas and on his way to Austria, his birthplace. Back in Belleville was his wife who would within two months give birth to a baby.[16]

Agnes's article focused on the human meaning of this deportation: the family broken up, the mother unable to make ends meet. Mrs. Yereb: "I don't know what I would of done after they took John away if it hadn't of been for the good union men here in Belleville, God bless them."[17] But on Agnes's second visit fifteen cents was all that was left. A neighborhood doctor, he and his wife "good Christian people," active in charities, refused to help: "the government knows what it's doing." But Agnes did not fail to include the crucial legal point:

> This man's crime against the government was membership in the I.W.W. when as a single man he had been a migratory worker. The other man taken with him in the Red Raid proved himself an American citizen and has not been bothered since. Yereb was under the impression that he was a citizen and had voted in a presidential election. When a lad of fourteen he had come to this country with his step-father who became naturalized and this, Yereb thought, gave him citizenship.[18]

By the time Agnes's article appeared, John Yereb, who was not going to abandon his family, was no longer in Austria. He had gone to Hamburg; from there he worked his way on a freighter to Vera Cruz and from there to Tampico and finally to Portland, Maine, where he presented a passport, in his own name, which he had procured from the U.S. Consul at Hamburg. He was of course arrested. But Agnes's article had roused up the *New Republic*'s liberal readers, the recently born American Civil Liberties Union was providing help, and the *Post-Dispatch* was beginning to ask the right questions. (A rabbi in Oakland, California sent Agnes five dollars for Mrs. Yereb and then another contribution, saying "I shall eat less on the train," and he wrote to the government official who would be handling the case.[19]) The government admitted no error but after due consideration it decided to withdraw the order of deportation: Yes, he was a citizen. After nearly seven months' absence from home, John Yereb rejoined his family in Belleville.

It was during Yereb's stay in jail that Robertus Love interviewed Agnes and Mrs. Yereb. Lest the word "raid" as a description of Yereb's first arrest be taken figuratively, here is what Laura Yereb told Love: "I returned home one day to find my husband on the sidewalk in front of our home, handcuffed. Inside I found men ransacking our rooms. They had opened John's trunk and found his old card in the I.W.W." These items appear to have been the entirety of the evidence against Yereb. "They had taken up the rug from the floor and searched through the old newspapers which I had laid under the rug to protect it. They had ripped open the mattress to our bed. They had upset everything in the house." Their first child was born dead two months after the raid.[20]

Love reported also his impressions of the Wiecks, of this "young woman of culture" and her coal miner husband who "used to be known as the 'H.D. Thoreau of Staunton.' . . . Incidentally, if anybody imagines that a coal miner's family is just that and nothing else, a visit to the Wiecks of Belleville should go a long way toward disproving that notion. Both Mr. and Mrs. Wieck can 'talk' literature and philosophy, and even the modernly popular science of psychology, with a knowledge and insight calculated to put to shame the cultural pretensions of many persons who live in fine houses and drive the latest models of high-priced cars."[21]

Union Politics, Union Troubles

The fortunes of the miners' union were very much on the minds of the Wiecks and their friends. During and immediately after the war, the United Mine Workers had made great headway but the coal companies of the southern Appalachian region had not reconciled themselves to unionization. Southern West Virginia, where new major fields were being exploited, was crucial to the future of the union.

In August 1921, perhaps 15,000 union miners, many of them war veterans, took part in the "Armed March" from the Kanawha Valley over Blair Mountain into Logan County in the southernmost part of the state. The immediate cause, or provocation, was the assassination by thugs in the employ of the Baldwin-Felts agency, of two union men, one of them Sid Hatfield, chief of police of Matewan and already a folk hero to union miners, on the steps of the courthouse where they were to be tried, a second time, for murder in the shootout in Matewan a year earlier. The deeper motive was the barbaric industrial feudalism against which union men, their cause quite literally freedom, had been waging a losing guerrilla war. The miners' army, proceeding with military discipline, routed the company gunmen in pitched battles before federal troops forced the miners' retreat and abandonment of their plan "to bring West Virginia into the United States." Indictments for murder and treason were numerous.[22]

At the same time the union, nationally, was in the turmoil of a furious internal power struggle. The tendency of organizations, large or small, however democratic in their founding, is to evolve — perhaps "devolve" is the better word for it — in the direction of concentration of power at the top. In the miners' union John Mitchell's charisma had been his power and when that faded he chose not to run again, leaving its democratic structure essentially intact. But his successors worked systematically at changing the rules of the game in order to centralize power in the union's International headquarters at Indianapolis; long strides in that direction had already been taken when, in early 1917, John L. Lewis, in semi-exile as an A.F.L. organizer in the Pittsburg region, made his way into a modest position in the headquarters bureaucracy. When President John P. White resigned to become labor advisor in the wartime Fuel Administration, his successor, Frank Hayes of Illinois, appointed Lewis to the vacated vice-presidency. A likeable fellow, a bit of a poet and a bit of a socialist, poor Hayes, a drinking man, seems to have lost the battle to John Barleycorn. Lewis, who had never gained an elective position above the local

level, was very soon de facto president of a union whose membership was rising toward half a million.[23]

After a year, Hayes took a leave of absence for his health, a leave
from which he was never to return—which did not prevent his re-
election, and Lewis' as vice-president, by a membership that was
kept in the dark. With the prestige of the 1919 national strike
behind him, Lewis won the formal presidency a year later.

A flash of John Lewis in his late thirties, in his time of ascent. A
letter from Agnes to me, 1945:

> I am using, or trying to use, my fountain pen of many years ago, a gift
> from the president of the International Brotherhood of Electrical Work-
> ers in World War I, when we were in Montreal at an A.F. of L.
> convention. That was when I pointed out John Lewis to Julia O'Connor
> who made the remark, "Why he looks like a second-story worker."
> Lewis was standing slumped up against a pillar in the hotel lobby, hat
> pulled down to one side and scowling. The other U.M.W.A. delegates
> were anti-Lewis and he was unnoticed and as yet unsung.[24]

Lewis's power threatened union politicians with bases of power
of their own, among them Frank Farrington, president of Illinois's
ninety thousand miners. Allied with Farrington was Alex Howat,
president of the small Kansas district; or, rather, each was trying to
use the other, for their philosophies of unionism were diametrically
opposite. Because of Howat's defiance of Kansas's strike-outlawing
Industrial Court Law, for which he did sixteen months in jail, and
his long harassment of recalcitrant Kansas coal operators and his
flouting of union presidents who tried to bring him to heel, Howat
was (also) the hero of the union's left wing.

Ed Wieck and his brother John knew Lewis and had no illusions
about him, but they also knew Farrington's dictatorial ways and
could not forgive his employment of strong-arm tactics and expulsion of members in putting down the 1919 Wildcat strike (at that
time, Ed was still in the West). In Howat's judgment and character
they had no trust whatsoever. By now, also, the Communists were
emerging as a small but significant force, different from the old
Socialists in that their first loyalty was to their party. The Wieck
brothers were by nature conservative, though not at all in the sense
that Farrington and Lewis were. The building of a national union of
coal miners had taken decades and the struggle for power was

putting the union in jeopardy. About these matters, Agnes would have trusted Ed's judgment.

Ed was a delegate to the International convention in the fall of 1921, the last that could be called "free." I quote from a letter to Agnes from Indianapolis:

> This afternoon when the uproar was at its height I met [William] Petry of the W.Va. delegation, and district vice-president, in the corridor and he showed me a telegram stating that two deputy sheriffs had been to Charleston after him with three indictments for first degree murder in connection with the recent fighting. I asked him what he was going to do. He answered that W.Va. was his home and that he was going back after the convention. I could not help remark to him that were I in his place I would take a look at that mob in the hall and then study a long time before I would decide to die for them. He cursed them and repeated he was going back to W.Va.[25]

At this convention Lewis succeeded in changing convention rules to the permanent disadvantage of any opposition. He had done so, by bare majorities, with the support of blocs of West Virginia votes—votes of loyalty to the president who controlled the treasury on which they depended for financial support and whose organizers had their ears. The result was a terrible animosity between "Illinois" and "West Virginia." During the national strike of the following year, Farrington threatened to break solidarity by signing a separate contract for Illinois; Lewis broke solidarity with sixty thousand miners in non-union fields of central and western Pennsylvania, a strike in which Communist organizers had played a very positive role; and each sought to blame the other for the trouble that came to Illinois that summer of 1922.[26]

Tragedy in Egypt

For many years, strikes in Illinois had been strictly contests of will between miners who lost work and coal operators who lost profits, both groups acting collectively. The national coal strike beginning April 1, 1922, should have been no different. For reasons never made clear, the Illinois district officers granted permission to a strip-mine owner. William Lester of Cleveland, Ohio, to operate his steam shovels to uncover coal but not to move it. By shipping that coal into a fuel-starved market, he could make a very neat profit; no one thought he would take that risk. Lester's mine was located in Williamson County.

Once the overburden of earth was removed Lester fired the union miners and brought in a new steam-shovel crew (members of a strike-breaking "union") and armed guards in equal numbers. Lester's workers never left the compound—afterwards, some told of having been recruited under false pretenses and of being held virtual prisoners. Aggressively and provocatively, Lester's superintendent and guards kept the surrounding area clear of inquirers but the miners in neighboring towns learned that a coal train had gone out. Lester knew that the union miners would not sit by. If he was making rational calculations, he was calculating that when his mine was attacked the National Guard would be sent to protect his operation. Nobody wanted any of this—not the union miners of course, not Williamson County's law or its business class, and not the coal companies on whom Lester was stealing a march.

On the ninth day of Lester's strikebreaking operation, hundreds of miners equipped with rifles and dynamite besieged the compound. Firing commenced; three men on the union side were killed, none in Lester's party. The militia was not called. Lester's guards were vastly outnumbered; as more miners joined the siege, it became obvious that his operation was doomed. From Chicago, under pressure, he agreed to close the mine, he had waited too long. On the morning of the tenth day, June 22, guards and strikebreakers and the superintendent came out in surrender; the union men, their number augmented by new arrivals (there were women too in that crowd), began to march the prisoners toward Herrin, five miles away. If anyone was in charge no one would admit it; the miners' subdistrict officials studiously sheltered themselves from responsibility. A mile toward Herrin, the superintendent, C. K. McDowell was killed. Further along the procession stopped and the prisoners were lined up in front of a barbed-wire fence and told to make a run for it; they were hunted through the woods like rabbits. The wounded were tracked down; those who died speedily were fortunate. On the outskirts of Herrin a small group was dragged to a cemetery for execution, to the cheers of children from the neighborhood. Most, some with help from union men, did make it to safety, but nineteen of Lester's men besides McDowell never made it. With the Herrin Massacre, Williamson County regained title to the epithet "Bloody Williamson." Lester did not make out badly after all: to avoid costly lawsuits, the Illinois union bought his mine at a handsome price.[27]

Whether any of Agnes's relatives were involved—the mine was just a few miles from Johnston City—I don't think she wanted to know. None were indicted. Years later her brother Dan told his son of having picked up a gun and gone to the mine, and arriving after it was all over. But those scabs "got what was coming to them." Many held it to be God's view that it was no sin to kill a scab.

After two juries found no one to convict, the prosecution gave up. Angus Kerr, chief counsel for District 12 and for the defendants, was a friend of Ed's, with whom he had many amicable arguments, Ed's thesis being that the law was the will of the stronger while Kerr maintained that law was ultimate justice, as perfect as possible in an imperfect world of imperfect people. Kerr had made sacrifices for the labor movement. "The Calumet-Hecla copper company ran him out of the upper peninsula of Michigan for defending the striking copper miners in the courts (1913), and confiscated all of his property by the simple device of threatening to boycott anyone who rented it or bought it." Ed remembered Kerr's "intense humanism." To save the men accused in the Herrin Massacre he had (words quoted from Kerr, in a letter from my father to me) "debauched the citizenry [jurors] of two whole counties," in betrayal of his loyalty to the law. He never got over it, Ed said, implying that it was the ultimate cause of Kerr's early death.[28]

Nearly six months after the massacre, *The Nation* published Edward A. Wieck's "Bloody Williamson County." The massacre is mentioned only in a prefatory note; connections are left to the reader. The dominant theme is the co-presence, the virtual confusion, of unionism and fundamentalist Protestantism. "Non-church-goers may be found in Williamson County but the non-believer is not there. The old-time revival and doctrinal debates are still carried on with the zeal and fervor of pioneer times. All through the summer months the revival tents can be seen on the vacant lots of the towns and great throngs attend nightly. . . . The same emotionalism that binds these people to their religion drew them to the union." Culture, not unionism, was the root cause of the massacre.[29]

In the concluding sentences I feel Agnes's presence more than Ed's; although in his style, the article was surely a collaboration. "The union is there to stay. It will fall as an inheritance to the next generation of miners, not only to cherish and to hold but to shape toward a task challenging the intellect and imagination. Once the tide of emotionalism, deep in these people, is turned to cultural aspirations, the history of this coal region will be re-written."[30]

Settling Down

From July 25, 1922, when her "Deportation" article was about to appear, until February 11, 1923, Agnes kept a diary. Of 204 legal-size typewritten pages just 45, beginning with page 68 and only intermittently continuous, survive. In these pages one important theme is developed at considerable length.

From Agnes's entry for November 12 (the beginning is missing):

> I shall not settle down to this, never! never! But tonight, when I stood looking at the soap I was keenly conscious of its significance—the price of soap, beans and flour determines for us how much music we shall hear at the symphony; the importance of bread and meat will keep us away from concerts all winter, I am sure. Further on I stopped at Dave Wallace's to inquire about the prospective baby at his brother's house. It had arrived. How different this! Inquiring about babies!
>
> When I reached Mayme's, Ed had David sleeping and as I peeped in on him I had the thought that it was for this little fellow that I had given up the freedom and the joy of other days, and that he was worth any sacrifice.[31]

Three weeks later the same theme is developed at length. Again the beginning is missing but the thought is essentially complete.

> But the old fire still burns within me. I know that I must give myself almost wholly to my baby, yet I am determined that David Thoreau's mother shall be different as I want him to be different from the great mass who live only to work. I do not know what I can achieve but I do know that I shall never be satisfied to merely exist. I shall never stop wanting to live. I sometimes ask myself if it is really I, this Agnes Burns, who sits with the women folk and joins in their gossip and trivial talk while the men folk sit in another room talking of labor and politics. Just after Ed and I were married, Mayme in her kindness and her desire to make friends for me, took me around to her relatives. After the first visit

of this kind I found my soul aflame with indignation, resentment, rebellion. I would not be content with this. Ed didn't want me to continue in my former work, owing to my health, but what was health if used only for this? Outwardly I appeared to enjoy the player piano, the phonograph, the conversations about the Royal Neighbors, the Moose, the Pocahontas, and working and sewing and babies, but inwardly I was saying to myself, as the men's voices carried snatches of interesting conversation, "I won't, I won't, I won't settle down into this, Agnes Burns, you who dragged those wives out of their kitchen in Johnston City and stood them, for the moment, alongside their husbands in the unions, here you are, back in their places. Why this segregation, the men with their politics and unions, the women with their lodges and babies?"

Now I sit with the women while they sew and I play the phonograph as I did today at the Yerebs. And I am no longer rebellious, not that this is what I want to do—it is not. The strange thing is, I am able to do it as if I had never known anything else.[32]

Her sister Amelia now appears in the diary as an even sterner conscience. First, however, Amelia should be allowed to tell of her life as housewife and mother as she recounted it in a letter that Agnes incorporated in the diary a few days later. Melie, now thirty-four, is still living down there in Johnston City. It is winter and the mines should be working. Gordon and Gil are the younger brothers Agnes "raised"; unlike the men in Melie's family, they've got plenty of work but the working conditions are terrible: "you speak of Gordon looking bad, you ought to see Gil he looks like a walking skeleton."

Sis I think if I was keeping a diary now I could sure relate some experiences. I am having some of them now. Just think, three men [husband and older boys] making $42 on the [semi-monthly] pay. . . . You can bet they are not getting any of Gil and Gordon's work. But you won't know us either before long, but it won't be hard work that will change our looks. It will be hard luck. . . . But really I don't know what we will do, you can't get work where they are working and we are not by ourselves. . . . I haven't got good sense sometimes, winter here, no work, no clothes, nor nothing at all. You can bet if you were in my place you would worry. All last summer no work at all [the national coal strike] and hardly able to do anything even for myself but had to do it just the same. How I could do if I just had to do it with. . . . Yes Sis seven kids don't give a woman much chance for anything else but I believe if I had to have one every 10 or 11 months or even 18 months like some women, I'd take the shortest way out. Life isn't worth living at best for poor people but some has it even worse than others. Poor Ora [a friend] I feel sorry for her, but that don't do her much good. . . . Lillian Faye is awful good, sleeps all the time and is growing fast.[33]

Lillian Faye is a month old. Her birth is itself a story. Amelia wrote to Agnes, announcing it: "I have sure been a misery to myself for the last nine months but I staid with it. I think this will surely be the last one." "The reason I didn't tell you before it happened was because I hated it myself so bad I didn't want you to worry about it. [Sister] Mag didn't know it either until two weeks ago last Tuesday."[34] No doctor knew either. For Lillian Faye, Amelia asked for, and of course got, some of my baby clothes, including clothes first worn by my slightly older cousin Dorothy, my one Wieck cousin, daughter of Elvin and Ruine in Staunton.

Back now to the entry of November 28 and Amelia as conscience:

When Amelia came to visit me, before the baby was born, she said, I can't believe this is you. You, spending your days in a house, doing the same thing over and over. Why, when you were back home, you wouldn't let housekeeping shut you off from the other things. You taught school and kept house at the same time and even then you weren't satisfied—you had to have something else. It was the labor movement, the labor movement—all we could hear you talk—and after you started organizing the women down there, it seemed like you wanted to get out of a house forever and never get back. You told me and you told all the women that we were foolish to spend our lives at nothing but housework. When you went away to Chicago and all over the country you never did want to settle down back home again. You hated the towns down there—I know you did. You wouldn't stay only long enough for a visit and I know you was mighty glad when your train pulled out and you got away from it all again. Now what is there in this town? I can't see anything but little old fashioned houses and slow poky people. Why, we've got paved streets now, electric lights all over town and that new movie theater, I'll bet it's as big as any you've got here. There's mines there and there's mines here, so what's the difference? What has changed you, what makes you different?[35]

Ed is here of course, she had answered. They go to St. Louis for concerts occasionally, visitors come through, they read books together, go to meetings together, talk and don't care for movies. And then, "the baby is coming, I want him above everything else.

But we won't stay settled always—I am not changed as much as you think. . . . In a few years I can devote myself to some sort of work but David will always be the biggest thing in my life." The baby is a year old now and she can imagine Amelia saying that Mayme is right, "You have become just like the rest of us." Agnes's answer: "But I am not. I am glad that married life has set me down into this day to day existence of other women. I have learned much, much that I can make use of in the future—the future into which I am always projecting myself."[36]

Agnes dealt with the same topic a few weeks later, two days before Christmas, in the form of a withering portrayal of life in her neighborhood. It's "lives of quiet desperation," without much sympathy evident.

> Settled! Is that life's goal? I have admired the spirit of restlessness and dissatisfaction in Mrs. Davison, though she knows not what she wants. I have enjoyed our back porch chats—her longing after life has quickened my own spirit. All the other neighbors are settled. For the men all ambitions have been realized in home and children. For the women romance and adventure died when marriage was achieved. No purpose in their lives, they now live from day to day. They stare blankly into the straight road ahead of them. Like the men at their jobs in industry the women's work has put an eternal sameness in their lives—every Monday the same washing, and each successive day a duplication of that day the previous week. On Saturdays when I can observe them at their work outside I am reminded of a factory—invariably down on their knees scrubbing porches, on ladders shining windows, sweeping yards, and at a certain time in the afternoon the emergence through back doors of shiny-faced children fresh from their Saturday bath. Monotonous, mechanical lives, devoid of imagination.[37]

Once again, in the very next paragraph, her baby comes into the picture, this time somewhat ambiguously.

> In the days when we waited for David to be born we used to sit on the back porch in summer evenings dreaming of the happy, joyful times in store for him—in fancy sharing with him the adventures of his childhood. Shall we change, too? Will the advancing years, the problems of existence, put an end to our dreams, our longing after life? I shink from such a future. When Mayme's boy first left home she grieved for days and often now I find her weeping. I laugh at her and tell her that we want our baby to roam, to seek always after knowledge and experience. "You

think that now," she says, "but wait. You'll be like all the rest. It will break your heart, too." Ed says he intends to take David hoboing at an early age. He wants him to know life. Mayme laughs. I wonder.[38]

Mayme's Mikey, son of a previous marriage, had taken off for Hollywood in search (presumably) of fame, fortune, and love. (Eventually he would travel further, to Alaska, where in time Michael J. Haas became labor commissioner under Governor Gruening.) Although Mayme professed a no-children ideology, she could argue both sides.

For help in publishing the diary Agnes turned to Robert Morss Lovett. Graduate of Harvard, professor of literature at the University of Chicago, his life had, once for all, been changed by America's entry into the war, which, as he put it in his autobiography, drew him out of "academic seclusion and a passive attitude of good will." He had believed in Woodrow Wilson's "Fourteen Points," "Peace without victory." War once declared, he accepted it as a fact, but when he joined with others who still believed in peace without victory and in negotiations to end the slaughter and produce a general disarmament and renunciation of war, he found himself denounced as disloyal. A crowd assembled in front of his home, hanged him in effigy. His outrage at the brutal treatment of dissenters and conscientious objectors during this "war to end war" in which his only son was killed in France started him on a second career. He continued to teach at Chicago—he loved teaching and the list of writers whom he taught or gave counsel to is lengthy—but from then on he lent his energies freely to the cause of social justice, a militant liberal grandly indifferent to sectarian quarrels. For a couple of years he and his wife had been living at Jane Addams's Hull House, far from the university campus. An associate editor of *The New Republic*, he knew of Agnes from the Yereb case and had done his part in the campaign to free Yereb.[39]

Lovett was enthusiastic about the diary and tried all his connections. Without luck. One publisher wanted a more typical miner's wife. To Lovett an incensed Agnes wrote:

When I began the diary I remarked to Mr. Wieck that after all it would not be the diary of the average miner's wife, but I added that the average miner's wife isn't given to writing diaries. I have a sister whose diary would doubtless impress Mr. [Benjamin] Huebsch far more than mine but what time has she for diaries? (Then, too, is she not exceptional in her gift for expression, though her world is no bigger than her own community?) Who then is to write the much-talked-of-story of the workers? . . . Education for such as us—be it ever so little—would appear to have its penalties.[40]

The truth, I'm afraid, is that Lovett looked right through the words of the text into the passions of an unusual woman. I imagine he was moved by her willingness to confess the shame that poverty engenders, for she had told in the diary that she had made excuses rather than allow friends to pay her fare to go to a nearby town to hear a dear friend, Lillian Herstein of the Chicago teachers' union, speak.[41] As to why the diary I have is a mere fragment, I just don't know. Perhaps it is a thinning out in response to one editor's complaint of diffuseness and slowness of pace.

Agnes had wanted to educate a public that did not understand the world of coal miners or of working-class women. She had also hoped to help out the household economy. (But I would be amazed if the $35 she got for her "Deportation" article stayed in our house.) The short but severe depression of 1921 and the 1922 strike meant hand-to-mouth living. The "Work" "No Work" notations at the head of each Monday through Saturday diary entry were there for good reason. Fortunately they both were frugal by habit and they furnished their small flat minimally, with orange-crates for bookcases, their only luxury purchase being a really good rug. It wasn't until the summer of 1923, when work picked up, that Agnes and Ed felt they could afford to subscribe to the *New Republic*.[42]

Alias Mrs. Mason

In the time of the diary or not long after Agnes wrote a story she titled "For the Glory of the Order," in which she dealt once more with the life of Belleville women. The burden of the piece is a nicely drawn contrast among three kinds of "marching" that "Mrs. Mason" has done. The first: "Blessed with a strong and vigorous body, she is well equipped for marching. Whether with broom, dust-cloth, or dish-rag, she marches about the house in a most amazing fashion. She marches right through a big week's washing in the time it takes the ordinary woman to get started. To wash, scrub, scour, shine, bake bread, can fruit, prepare supper for a houseful of unexpected company, and be marching off to the lodge by seven is no trick at all for Mrs. Mason."[43] The description of the march through the house fits my Aunt Mayme to a tee; I can still see her marching and you had better not get in her way.

But at the moment Mrs. Mason is going to Chicago for a national convention of her lodge. As a member of the drill team of the local women's auxiliary of the Order, she will march, "the climax of an entire year of practice and preparation." "Marching, merely marching, just as little children march in pretty drill exercises at school. . . . Their military caps of white and gold provide the necessary martial flourish, while the large American flags they bear aloft attest the patriotism of women whose husbands have been guilty of defying a noble judge," a reference to the 1919 national strike that "Julia" celebrated.[44] In Chicago she

> will meet many of her kind to whom this convention trip is the first vacation of a life-time at the cookstove. But these submerged housewives talk not of economic freedom. Nor will they join as equals in the convention of the Order. An auxiliary is an appendage of "just women," and when grave matters are at hand the Loyal Ladies will retire from the convention. In the quiet seclusion of their Auxiliary they may gather as the Loyal Ladies' Aid. . . . She has never known anything but hard work—and her lodges. She would be lost without either.[45]

But Agnes added one more dimension:

> Mrs. Mason once had an opportunity to go marching in a real crusade. Leading a band of striking miners' wives she marched down a railroad track at an early morning hour to round up certain women whose husbands had not struck. To the mother of eleven children she thus addressed herself: "Are you satisfied with the livin' you're a' gittin'?" To which the woman, a match for Mrs. Mason in physique if not in repartee, shot back, "Yes, I am!" "What are you raisin' your young'uns for?" demanded Mrs. Mason. "Can you give 'em the kind of an education you'd like to?" "My kids go to school, I'd have you know." "Oh, yes, we've still got free schools, but what about a musical education? Out of a dozen, like as not you've got one that's turned that way. Could you educate her in music if she had talent?" "We've got a graphophone in our house, and we can have all the music we want." "Oh, I see!" said Mrs. Mason. "You believe in gittin' your music out of a box instead of havin' it brought out of your children!"[46]

That would be the 1919 Wildcat, in which wives of Belleville miners are known to have taken just such a part. The voice is distinctly Mayme's.

Frieda Kirchwey at *The Nation*, where Agnes's piece was published under the title "Mrs. Mason Marches," "insisted that I make my point. The point was I wasn't trying to make a point, merely telling a story."[47] Agnes yielded and tacked on an if-only ending whereby Mrs. Mason would be marching for LaFollette (by then the 1924 presidential campaign was under way) instead of merely voting for him at her husband's lead, were it not for "her lack of training and for the fact that the women's organizations somehow have passed her and her class by."[48] Certainly, Agnes would have liked to see Mrs. Mason march for "Fighting Bob," who had the formal endorsement of the A.F.L. and the active support of much of the rank and file, but she knew that a pat didactic ending did not do her topic justice.

Again, Williamson County

The dead of the Herrin Massacre were not a year in the ground when a different madness gripped Williamson County, as the Invisible Empire made visible appearance. In order to wipe out the stain of alcohol in that pretty much wide-open county, and perhaps remove the stain of blood, the Klan, which enjoyed the support of the churches, engaged the services of a gun-handy former Prohibition agent. The easiest targets of his campaign were the "foreigners," especially the numerous Italians who persisted in making wine. Some of them did exchange wine for dollars. But there were deadly serious large-scale bootleggers also, several of whose protectors later became famous in the annals of Illinois crime. Soon the county was in a state of civil war.

In the midst of these new troubles there was a disaster in the East mine at Johnston City, an explosion; Jim, Amelia's youngest boy, was killed. Agnes knew her sister's anguish, the ordeal of her long wait at the pit head to know whether her boy was dead or alive. Agnes's article in the *New Republic*, "Ku Kluxing in Miners' Country," perhaps the finest she ever wrote, begins by telling of that late January day.

JOHNSTON CITY. Mines. The miners at work—quitting time not far off. Their wives stirring their fires to start supper. Suddenly a whistle blows—long—again and again. The East mine—gas! Women run from their homes. Screaming children follow. A hush on Main Street—a rush of automobiles, trucks, people. Soon a thousand souls are at the East mine shaft. A thousand more are coming. As the cages bring men at the top, every woman looks for her man, her boy. Some look in vain. The rescue teams. Ropes stretched. Frantic women held back. How long this work of rescue! The mine manager and a face boss, both dead. No one in charge familiar with the air circulation. Hours pass. A telephone message from below—many entombed are still alive. But what of the others? Trapped. Dying. Night comes. Doctors are down below—lives may yet be saved. Brave miners strive to reach the stricken entry. Midnight. Cold, so cold—below zero. Women's bodies shiver but they are conscious of only one thing—their eyes are never off those moving cages. At last the bodies—whose? Ambulance after ambulance carries away its load of bruised, burned, charred, unidentified bodies. They yet may live, men tell these mourning women, and in some breasts comes the first faint hope. But others wail in despair. "They're dead! They're dead!" Yes, dead, thirty-two. Father and son. Brothers. And nine for whom death might have been better. Mine disasters the town had known before but never one with such heavy toll of human life.

The tragedy of this little town cast its shadows over the entire county where in the name of law and religion the people have allowed themselves to be divided into warring factions. Only the week before mobs of religious folk had terrorized home after home. Women were abusively treated, crucifixes were smashed, homes looted, property burned. State troops were necessary to prevent bloodshed. Now in the presence of death Ku Kluxism is quiet.

A joint memorial service is held for the thirty-two dead. Catholic and Protestant homes alike are sorrowing. Do the men of God use this opportunity to preach the lesson of religious tolerance? They preach religious salvation. Do they exhort the people to join in a mighty demand for the rigid enforcement of mine safety laws? Men predict that the most appalling disaster known to mining will some day come in this region of gaseous mines. "Prepare for death! Make your peace with God while you yet are spared!" With this warning to the living, the thirty-two are committed to God.[49]

As the funeral processions move through the town, "crowds of miners line the streets. The native American face predominates— kind faces these. For the time there are softened hearts, sobered minds, solemn thoughts. But in their breasts are deep-rooted prejudices, for theirs is the blood of God-fearing pioneers who believed all men should worship God and in one way. . . . The armistice is brief indeed."[50]

> The next week through the same streets are herded one hundred and twenty-eight men and women, branded as wicked, lawless, immoral. They are transported outside the county for arraignment. . . . Some are boot-leggers; some, makers of wine and home brew for use; frequenters of boot-leggers' places; church members but of the wrong church; Protestants who are "back-sliders"; Protestants who have black faces; sinners, downright, outright sinners—but believers in God, all. Williamson County is a county of believers and joiners.[51]

Another week and there is a shoot-out in Herrin as "the Flaming Cross meets the Flaming Circle," the latter composed of persons with materialistic reasons for subduing the Klan. A Klansman is killed and his fellows besiege the Herrin hospital to get at a wounded enemy and his friends. "Doctors and nurses seize patients from their beds and stretch them out upon the floor; bullets are whizzing through windows." The Klan is in control of the town until the troopers arrive once more. These wars would go on for a fair while, to be succeeded by pure and simple bootleg wars as support for the Klan waned.[52]

Important for our purposes is Agnes's message to the folks of Williamson County, with which she closes her article. (The message will be delivered by reprint in the *Illinois Miner*.) She names the cause of these events by the name she thinks it deserves: "Only last spring when a religious revival was on were its first rumblings heard, but the Ku Klux mind has always dominated this section of the country." "Generation after generation came up in the belief that the purpose of life is to prepare for death."[53]

> To those people there is only one right way, their way. You must be a Protestant and being that, it follows that you don't drink, dance, play cards or believe in evolution. If there is a single teacher in that country who believes in evolution—or understands it—I venture that he or she holds that belief in strictest privacy. And woe unto the teacher who would dare to dance! Education and the teacher's conduct, like religion and politics, must be strictly orthodox. From the schools of theology, the normal schools, the state university, there has come in this section neither the spirit of tolerance nor the promise of culture. . . . Like church, like school—the Ku Klux mind is firmly entrenched.[54]

The Klan's roots are in the old "settler" culture, strongest in the county seat of Marion; the coal towns, Herrin and Johnston City, are struggling toward a new culture and if the Klan has a following among the miners this is due to the churches and the inaction of the local labor leaders. "The youth of this generation are unwilling to follow the beaten moral path."[55] If that's not quite so, she will try to persuade them to new ways by telling what the union, in which they believe with religious zeal, stands for; a new idealism to supplant the old. Agnes's concluding paragraph:

> The brief industrial era of this coal country has wrought remarkable changes in the character of the present generation who are now miners. While their conception of the origin of life and the destination of the soul remains the same, their outlook on life is changed indeed. To them the labor movement has brought a new philosophy of life. This philosophy insists on a better living here on earth; on brotherhood, regardless of race, creed or color. It brought the seed of tolerance where tolerance was sorely needed. Opportunity, brotherhood, tolerance—these have been the gifts of the labor movement to a people who knew them not. And for a quarter of a century these sons of the old settlers have lived at peace with the Dago, the Hunkie and the Jew clothier. In their hearts they have believed these foreigners on the wrong track toward God but until the coming of the Klan the old prejudices, like the old ways of life, were slowly but surely passing. Now poison is added to prejudice and the way becomes hard indeed. The leaders of the miners, to whom have come the larger opportunities, must assume the responsibility of the hour. They are leaders of the church as well as the union, and they have no easy task. But what the union has brought to them and theirs must not be destroyed by prejudice and poison. Opportunity, brotherhood, tolerance—these things they must preserve.[56]

There are ambiguities in that triad; the kind of brotherhood and tolerance that Agnes has in mind goes beyond acceptance as union members. She is exploiting those ambiguities. Readers of the *New Republic* might take her to be describing what is. To her people, she is preaching.

Another Housewife

Shortly after her "Ku Kluxing" article, Agnes wrote a story, "Condemned uv God," about the troubles of a woman in that church-ridden Ku Klux culture. A true story, she said about it, "told in my presence by an old school-mate."[57]

Daughter of a later migration from Kentucky than the Burns family's, Hallie had always had a hard life, starting with being sent out to work as a "hired girl" at age twelve. When she got married, that meant "a-slavin' in her own kitchen for her board and keep." "But Hallie's days of working out were not yet over; when her sixth child was two years old, she was 'goin' out washin' an' arnin' for other people." She could talk and work at the same time, both full-speed, and "each new place was the occasion for her relating in detail the story of her Holy Roller husband who had to leave her 'to keep from bein' condemned uv God.'"[58] I quote key paragraphs, beginning with Hallie's plight:

> Hit wuz that crazy Holy Roller religion what done it. . . . Yes, ma'am, he jes' up and lef' me, with six uv his young'uns to feed. Says the church tells him he'd be a-livin' in adult'ry if he kep' on a-livin' with me. Course, I know he never waited the year out after he wuz divorct from his fust wife, but nobody never said nothin' till he went an' j'ined them thar Holy Rollers an' give it away on hisse'f, an' now they tell him he'll be condemned uv God if he stays with me. 'Pears lak hit wa'nt wrong 'fore he got religion, but now that he's got it, hit's a sin. So he has to go off to that dirty, little old ba'ch an' live to hisse'f. I declar' if I kin see how the Lawd wuld uv give him so much—sanc'ification an' the Holy Ghost an' that unknown tongue—if the Lawd a-thought he wuz livin' in sin all these years he wuz livin' with me. Kin y'all figger that out?[59]

Now, what Hallie tried:

> I might-nigh beat the life out uv that man uv mine las' week. He got up thar on that hill behind the South Side schoolhouse an' wuz a-rollin' an' a-rollin', jes' lak a hog, till I had to git me a club and beat up on him. The cops, they had to come git him and lock him up an' the nex' day he comes home an' wants to know if I'll wash his dirty, stinkin' close, an' I said yes, same as I would fer anybody else, if he paid me, but I wanted him to know I didn't aim to wash six weeks' dirt fer the same price I would one.
>
> Some folks say I orter have him sent to the 'sylum. I know he's fit fer it but I'd never git nothin' out uv him thar. I had him 'rested fer not s'portin' his fam'ly an' they put him in the county jail an' hit cost me twenty dolla's fer a lawyer an' never did me nary bit uv good.[60]

Hallie's last hope:

> What's needed is somebody that kin mek him pervide fer his fam'ly an' that's what these here Koo Kluckers air doin'.[61]

Hallie doesn't approve of everything the "Kluckers" do, but—

> Y'all orter go to some uv the Koo Kluck services at the churches an' see the purty work they put on in thur white robes an' that big cross, though I admit it meks a body feel sorter trem'ly at fust sight. They shore bury thur members purty. I seen Clarence Turner's fun'ral an' hit stretched plum from the Free Will Baptis' church to the graveyard. They all marched in thur white robes an' the main ones wuz on the big white horses.[62]

It comes down to this:

> Floyd Bailey shore talked nice to me 'bout Elmer. He said they take up sich cases as his'n in man-to-man fashion fust, then if that fails, wall, he couldn't come right straight out with it, but the nex' time they'll try somep'n what will work.[63]

If I am right that the ending is Agnes's, then it reflects her ambivalence about Hallie. She allows Hallie to get the comeuppance of learning that the person whose ironing she was doing and to whom she has told her tale is a Catholic, as is her husband, manager of the mine where Hallie was hoping her Elmer could get a job with steady work and so be able to give her support money. The wife compliments Hallie on her work but won't be calling her back; her husband is eager to fire anybody who belongs to the Klan, as the union constitution now demands. Agnes couldn't like Hallie and could only find more reasons for feeling sorry for her. Who was going to help this woman who lived in a monologue?

Mencken, Lovett reported, would have taken the story for the *Mercury* if his quota of low-life fiction were not entirely full. (Agnes didn't find a publisher.) There wasn't much fiction in it and I don't think Agnes meant to satisfy appetites for "low-life" fiction. It was just some truth about a woman's life.

Staff Writer

There is a truth in what Agnes wrote to me many years later, on her wedding anniversary: "It's funny, Dave, but I believe you will admit it, too, in your old age, how we can do more when pressed for time. I was thinking back today to when you were an infant and I managed all the housework, took care of you, and turned out a lot of writing. More than at any time since. And look at the writing your father did in those days—yes, even when he had to do it of a night, after a hard day in the mine."[64] And their work was attracting attention: it was becoming known to a steadily widening circle that the Wiecks were people to see if information on the miners' union and the coal industry was wanted.

In the fall of 1923 Ed started a diary of his work as a pit committeeman, a duty to which he had just been elected; it ended up as 193 typewritten pages, "Six Months on the Pit Committee." In July 1924 the *Atlantic Monthly* published selections under the title "A Coal Miner's Journal."[65] (The possibility that the *New Republic* would take the diary for its Dollar Book series vanished when that series got into financial trouble.) The well-chosen selections do give a wonderful picture of a pit committeeman's work, and of Ed in this lawyer role. Evelyn Preston, a young woman who had visited the Wiecks during the course of her studies of the coal industry, advised Carter Goodrich, an economist who was doing research for his book, *The Miner's Freedom: A Study of the Working Life in a Changing Industry,* that he should by all means make a stop in Belleville.[66] Goodrich saw mechanization, which would introduce factory organization and factory psychology, as the future of underground mining; the freedom of the workplace that Ed so prized was due to disappear. Besides spending several days with the Wiecks—they hit it off splendidly—he got permission to go down in the mine and work with Ed; Carter was not content with facts and figures. As it turned out, Goodrich's forecast of the pace of mechanization and its consequences was far closer to the mark than Ed's, whose review in the *New Republic,* while praising the book, indicated his doubts that mechanization could proceed so swiftly or would pose so grave a threat to the union.[67]

My mother used to tell me that as a very small child—my third year, in fact—I sat on the laps of several professors. Besides Goodrich, there was Alexander Meikeljohn, philosopher, recently fired as president of Amherst College, the trustees of which found his educational views to be unacceptably radical. And there was Lovett of course! Fixed in my parents' memory was the image of "the tall dignified professor of Harvard background, at ease in a coal miner's kitchen, drying the dishes and smoking a great big cigar at the same time."[68] For professors, those who allied themselves with the labor movement, Agnes felt a certain deference; more confident of his education and knowledge, Ed treated them with the respect due equals.

In the summer of 1924 Oscar Ameringer began to make serious overtures to Agnes—he could use her talents. An eight-column eight-page weekly with a $1500 a week budget, quite a nice sum in those days, the *Miner* was a real newspaper. (Among official union publications, I haven't seen a peer.) Through it, mining families in the scattered towns could keep in touch with the world beyond. Ameringer had a highly professional staff and he made good use of the Federated Press, so that besides District 12 official business and other Illinois miners' affairs, there were reports from other coalfields and news of labor struggles in other industries and on other continents. During the fight to save Sacco and Vanzetti there was a news story every week. In my scanning of microfilm of the *Miner,* articles about Nicaragua catch my eye, one in particular (reprinted from *The Nation*) about Augusto Calderòn Sandino. There was political news, sports news, and items concerning some of the more scandalous doings of the upper classes. There was Oscar's highly popular column, under the name Adam Coaldigger, full of Oscar's Germanic wit and humor. There was a page for children and young people, a co-op section, sports news. And there was a woman's page. Oscar was careful; he knew his constituency. But he wanted to be insidious, which in a mild way at least he was.

From a collection of "Digs" from Adam Coaldigger's column, these specimens:

> The good book says "It is easier for a camel to go through the eye of a needle than it is for a rich man to enter the kingdom of heaven." Well, suppose it is. But why should a camel want to go through the eye of a needle? What is there on the other side that a camel can't see just as well by standing in front of it? And why in the name of common sense should a rich man try to worm himself into heaven to mingle with folks he's been trying to get away from all his life?
>
> Unless there comes a great spiritual awakening and an earnest search in the dark continent of the human mind, civilization will blow its fool head off some fine morning. No, I am not a bit afraid that reds and

radicals, short skirts and bare arms, boozers and bolsheviks, will destroy
civilization. What makes me shiver in my boots is to see millions of half-
baked cave men fooling around with home-made earthquakes.[69]

A dialogue:

"How's the Old Man today?" — "Fine."
"Making any money?" — "Betcher life I am."
"What became of your gal Sally?" — "Married a fellow down at Rose-
    dale."
"Making any money?" — "Nope. Just a living."
"What's he doing?" — "Raising flowers and canary birds."
"No money in that." — "That's what I tell him."
"Won't he listen?" — "Not a bit. The fool says flowers and birds give him
    more pleasure than filthy green backs."
"Something wrong with that guy." — "'Fraid so."
"How does Sally take it?" — "Oh, they're just crazy about each other."
"Too bad." — "Yep, and Sally's got two of the finest babies I ever laid eyes
    on."
"Poor kids." — "That's what I say."[70]

Agnes became editor of the woman's page and a column, "When
We Have Time to Think," by Mrs. Lotta Work, began to appear
weekly with the issue of November 1, 1924. The name would
be kindred to "Adam Coaldigger," although easier to decipher.
(But Lotta was not a humorist: Agnes did not have Ameringer's
Nietzschean-Olympian perspective.) A series of seventeen articles,
"Mother and Child," signed "Agnes Burns Wieck," began two
months later; shortly she began to write other articles under her
own name. It would appear that Agnes wanted through "Lotta
Work" to communicate sister-to-sister, in contrast to the teacherly
style of "Mother and Child."

The offices of the *Miner* were at District 12 headquarters in
Springfield, ninety miles from home. I have what might be a
memory from my fourth year, Agnes's first with the *Miner*, of a trip
to those offices and that memory may stand for a number of such
trips; she may have been able to do most of her work at home. In the
spring of 1925 we moved to a small brick cottage near the center of
town; it must have been income from Agnes's work that made it
possible. (If I interpret a letter correctly, her salary also allowed her
to be relieved of the heavier burdens of housework.) We were now

next-door neighbors to Walter Nesbit and family, he the secretary-treasurer of District 12 and (I believe) our landlord. Nothing fancy, our cottage, very small: "modernized," my mother wrote on the back of a snapshot of it, "to extent of furnace and shower bath," but decidedly an improvement on the Fifteenth Street flat. In my memory the Nesbit house on the corner is a house of many rooms, mansion-like, splendidly furnished, with a great lawn. Which surely it was, by contrast.

Agnes's work for the *Miner* reflects the times, the "return to normalcy" of the Harding-Coolidge era. Across the nation the postwar "open shop drive" was having very considerable success. Although on a lesser scale, the state "criminal syndicalism" laws carried on the work of the federal sedition statutes of wartime; California's law was applied on a large scale in the violent suppression of the San Pedro harbor strike in 1923, one of the last big Wobbly-organized strikes. Even with union endorsements, LaFollette's candidacy against Calvin Coolidge and a Democrat whose name would be known only to masters of trivia drew but a sixth of the popular vote (he carried his home state of Wisconsin); so died the idea of a "third party." About the miners' union, there was reason for alarm. By 1925 corporate feudalism had regained virtually the whole of the West Virginia coalfields. The United Mine Workers of America was on the way down, precipitously.

It will not be surprising that there was nothing noticeably radical in Agnes's writings for the *Miner.* She had an audience that she very much wanted to reach and she felt she knew the level at which she could begin to reach them. There were too many women like her sister who were ashamed of pregnancy, so she would try to educate them. In her "Mother and Child" articles she supplied the best information she could, by advanced standards of the day, on nursing and bottling and milk and rickets and teething, and tried to persuade women to practice prenatal care and hospital birthing. (The era of "scientific pediatrics" had arrived, its ambiguities unrecognized until many years later.) Agnes was "modern." In her first year or so she wrote her Philadelphia stories and the Leiter mine story, advertised the Pioneer Youth movement of the Socialists, made clear her views on war and very clear her views on R.O.T.C., explained the role of foreign warships in China's waters and reminded her readers of the treatment of Chinese immigrants, flayed the public schools as "factories," gave advice to young women in search of careers and much more, including instructions on dealing with such fundamentals as bedbugs and cockroaches. I would say that above all she was seeking, while educating, to instill in her readers "pride," in an affirmative sense of the term.[71]

Beginning with one of Lotta's first columns, she also tried to broach the topic of a women's auxiliary. A letter from a reader who expressed her concern about mine safety offered an occasion. Unlike Agnes, who set an example of good, clear writing, Lotta indulged sometimes in a slightly folksy, grammatically casual style that no one would take as condescending.

> I believe all of us miners' wives feel the same way about protecting our men folk down in the mine, only we don't know how to go about it. Don't you see, we women need to organize. Now, this Woman's Page is the first connecting link between all the women that's back of the 100,000 miners in Illinois. And now that we've begun to get acquainted through this page, maybe we've taken the first step toward an organization of Illinois Miners' Wives or some such name. We'd have plenty to keep us busy.[72]

But Illinois was quiet, the Illinois union was still secure, and there was no indication of response to Agnes's invitations.

The year 1925 was a full one. With considerable inspiration from Brookwood Labor College at Katonah, New York, the middle twenties were a high point in "workers' education." Among the photographs on a flier put out by the A.F.L.-sponsored Workers Education Bureau in New York, there is one of "A Class in Labor Problems among the Illinois Miners."[73] Tom Tippett, a former miner, had come back from Brookwood to run an educational program under the auspices of the Taylorville-Hillsboro subdistrict. The program for a banquet, climax to a "history course" held in a number of mining communities, lists "Agnes Burnes Weicks" as guest of honor, speaking on "Why the Shorter Workday."[74] Along with nationalization or public ownership, the six-hour-day was being put forward as rational solution to the coal industry's woes. Students presented reports, and two women gave talks on women and history. "Earnest, yet possessing a keen Irish wit," the publicity says about Agnes, who followed up with a lecture-tour.[75] More than writing, speaking was her medium.

Also that summer of 1925, on the Fourth of July came the occasion for Agnes's reminiscence of Gene Debs in Harrisburg: There was a labor picnic, the crowd predominantly socialist, in St. Louis' Triangle Park, and Debs, now in his seventieth year, was the honored guest. In a little over fifteen months he would be dead; for Agnes, as for many, no one would ever replace him. The crowd understood that this would probably be their farewell.

To greet him, a parade of children had been organized. "The little girls, fairylike in their appearance, bedecked in leaves of green, a symbol of Peace Everlasting," Agnes wrote in the *Miner*. "The little boys, arrayed in the national colors, proud of the honor accorded them. . . . Old comrades affectionately embraced him and ushered him into the park. Cheers and cheers and shouts of 'Debs! Debs!'. . . . The children's voices were raised again in song. 'My country, 'tis of thee, Sweet Land of Liberty, From every mountain's side, Let freedom ring.'" It was an authentically patriotic song that Agnes, who abhorred the militarism of the "Star Spangled Banner," would gladly sing.[76]

"Two little girls presented a green, growing plant, presented it to Debs. This, he was told, betokened the ideal for which he had paid so great a price, the ideal of Peace Everlasting." Debs (quoted by Agnes) responded as his audience knew he would; sentimentality did not offend them. "In my darkest hours I have always been heartened by the memory of the friendship and love I have won from little children. And when I pass into the sunset I shall carry with me the beautiful memories of such wonderful friends as you precious little children!"[77]

> Debs, facing that multitude . . . , was a splendid picture of triumph!. . . . Here was not the old and broken man many of us had feared we would behold—the strenuous career and the cruel prison sentence had left no visible imprint upon him. There was no evidence of weakness of the spirit! Nor was there any trace of bitterness in the heart of this man who had paid so cruelly for his convictions and his courage. In his infinite sweetness of spirit, in his love and affection for humankind, in his passionate devotion to life, and in his unwavering faith in the righteousness of his ideals, he was the Debs that we had known before the war.[78]

"When he has passed into the Sunset," she concluded, "it can be truly said of him, he was a man who lived not for himself, and not alone for the generations of his time; he lived for the centuries."[79] The prisoners of Atlanta Penitentiary, from which in 1920 he made his last campaign for the U.S. presidency, would have said "Amen."

That night Agnes wrote, for herself and probably for her son, a lengthy account of the family's day in St. Louis. As Ameringer's guests, the Wiecks had come over with him on the Inter-Urban, traveled by taxi to his hotel, lunched at a Chinese restaurant, and spent a good part of the afternoon browsing in used-book stores where Oscar found a couple of Dreiser's novels he hadn't read, Agnes bought *Jennie Gerhardt* and Eugene Field's *Western Verse*, and Ed picked up a German-English dictionary that he was going to need. Thence to Triangle Park, where an organizer of the Children's Parade enlisted, with Agnes's consent, young David, only recently turned three-and-a-half. David "became so proud of it, once he heard the band music, that he strongly protested any attempt of mine to keep hold of him. . . . He raised his feet in time with the music and clung tightly to his partner, Carl somebody whose daddy is a cabinet maker." David, she noted, was "the only representative of the coal miners" in the parade. Last lines: "When my boy is carrying on the fight, as I hope he will, I know he will be proud that his Mother and Daddy took him to look upon old 'Gene Debs."[80]

That was a busy year for Ed, too. In the early spring the *New Republic* published his "Gambling with Miners' Lives."[81] (The death toll of the mines had reached a peak of 2,452 in 1923.) In July he was in Dayton, Tennessee, for the "monkey trial," as he and other scoffers at fundamentalism termed the trial of John T. Scopes, a school teacher who had tested the state law that prohibited the teaching of evolution. Clarence Darrow had been a hero of the labor movement since his defense of Debs thirty years earlier; Ed and his Belleville companions, not to say Ameringer, who could not pass up such an occasion, enjoyed Darrow's demolition of William Jennings Bryan, who had eagerly accepted the invitation to conduct the prosecution. (Did Darrow kill him with his cross-examination, or did he unwisely, in that hot weather, overeat? I remember later overhearing not-very-sympathetic speculations.) Ed got acquainted with Easterners down for the trial including Joseph Wood Krutsch, with whom there was a shared interest in Thoreau, and Mencken, who remembered Agnes's "Condemned uv God" and wanted to see more from the Wiecks. That encounter with Mencken led to Ed's getting his "General Alexander Bradley" into the *American Mercury*. Highly pleased with this recognition of Belleville talent, Fred Kern reprinted the article on the editorial page of the *News-Democrat*. [82]

That article had a verve rare in Ed's writings—but his enthusiasm is easy to understand. Alexander Bradley had gone to work, at nine, a not abnormal age in those pre-union days, at a mine in the Belleville field. But "the rebel in him sent him, during the summer months of slack work, away from the drabness of the coal camp to the colorful jungles of the open road. With other youngsters he came to know the fascination of Hinky Dink's place in Chicago's Clark Street and the big schooners and free lunches of Tom Allen's saloon in Market Street, St. Louis. He came to know, too, golden hours along the Lazy Wabash or the Kaw or in the shadow of the railroad water-tanks." [83] (Ed had known Hinky Dink's and Tom Allen's and he knew the hobo jungles.) At twenty-five the future "general" was one of the first recruits to "General" Coxey's hobo army in its hard-times march to Washington. Three years later, during the strike of 1897, this "inspired mule-driver" led the miners of Mt. Olive down to Belleville and pulled the St. Clair County miners out on strike. He went over to St. Louis and came back decked out in a shiny plug hat, stiff collar, bow tie, Prince Albert coat, boutonniere, rings covering his left hand, broad belt-buckle, and huge umbrella. He also came back with a roll of bills, "bribed," he told his troops, "to sell the miners out." The cash he distributed "to git you some shoes," supplied with which, the army marched on to further adventures. [84] The strike won, the general returned to his drifting ways, but the miners always looked out for him, and buried him in the Miners' Cemetery at Mt. Olive with appropriate honors.

For much of the last half of that year 1925, Agnes and Ed were apart. Toward the end of September a German trade-union delegation arrived in New York. With the help of their counterparts, they hoped to learn lessons from American industry and the American economy that might help them deal with Germany's economic catastrophe. John L. Lewis named Ed as escort and translator for Friedrich Husemann, president of the German miners, and the union economist and Reichstag deputy, Dr. Georg Berger, who accompanied him. Ed was excited to learn that Husemann, a socialist, had begun his labor career very young by leading a strike of weed pullers in the beet fields; Ed's first strike had been at ten or twelve when he and another youngser, hired to weed an onion field, demanded a wage increase. When the delegation split up, Ed took Husemann and Dr. Berger on a tour of the coalfields from the Pennsylvania anthracite to Colorado, with a stop for a meeting in Belleville. In the volume, *Amerikareise deutscher gewerkschaftsführer* (Berlin, 1926), general thanks were given to the translators and guides, with an exception on which Husemann must have insisted, "one we cannot leave unnamed, . . . generous with wise counsel."[85] But Dr. Berger surely would have supported that, and not only because Ed knew where to find good *Kognak* in "dry" America. In the booklet in which Husemann and Berger made their own report to the German miners' union, a photograph shows E. Wieck ceremonially welcoming the visitors.

A postscript. Within weeks after the Nazis came to power in 1933, Husemann was arrested. In the *New York Times* of April 17, 1935, an Associated Press dispatch reported his death—shot while "attempting to escape."[86] A set of bookcases, a parting gift from Husemann to my father, stands in my study.

The New "Antis"

In Agnes's files I found just one letter from Margaret Robins, a note, very affectionate, dated July 8, 1922. After fifteen years at its head, Robins had just retired from the presidency of the National Women's Trade Union League. A check for twenty-five dollars for Mrs. Yereb was enclosed; apparently, Agnes had written her about the case.[87] In 1924, after a lapse due most likely to the priorities of poverty, Agnes rejoined the league, but although she recognized its value in support of the organization of women workers, she did find it to be "regrettably out of touch with the vast army of housewives of our nation."[88]

In a two-column article in the *Miner* in the summer of 1925, under the heading "Labor Women of Great Britain Gather in an Inspiring Conference," she pointed to a contrast between the United States and England. Of the one thousand labor women who, according to the report she summarized, "packed Birmingham

Town Hall," not all were union members; the conference was "largely representative of housewives." Agnes also drew attention to the fact that "our British sisters" "have their women's sections within the British Labor Party," whereas when the U.S. labor movement "hurriedly got itself together for action in the last presidential election . . . we housewives had no share in the councils of that campaign." In short, "Without organization our votes count for little."[89]

There were other differences. Besides "political and labor questions, British sisters discussed purely feminist subjects, among them birth control," and resolved to support a campaign already underway to permit dissemination of birth-control information by publicly funded medical services to married people requesting it. As for the United States, again, "Those two million married women working outside the home may be regarded by the extreme feminists as an evidence of the freedom of women." "Freedom! Ask the garment workers' and textile workers' unions whose members are walking the streets while the employers are thriving on the cheap woman labor of remote communities."[90]

The point of Agnes's reference to "extreme feminists" becomes fully clear in an article, "The New 'Antis,'" which she wrote for the *Miner* six months later. The Women's Trade Union League, with union support, had always lobbied for laws that would protect women workers, especially laws setting maximum hours of work and prohibiting employment in hazardous industries. (The exclusion of women from work underground in the mines of the United Kingdom, in 1842 was esteemed a great victory for labor. No women worked in the mines of the United States, and Agnes could not have imagined that any woman would freely choose to do so.) When the National Woman's Party followed up the victory of the suffrage movement with a campaign for an Equal Rights Amendment, it struck at the league's "protective legislation" program and battle lines were drawn.

The "old" Antis had opposed woman suffrage. The "new" Antis were the women of the Woman's Party "who have walked right into the camp of the open shop employers." Their slogan was freedom but "the working women of Illinois are enjoying the freedom to work ten hours and most of them being unorganized, they enjoy the further freedom to work for any wage the boss chooses to pay."[91] In a later article, after acknowledging that "something daring and spectacular was needed to force the politicians to action" on suffrage, and that the Woman's Party supplied it, she explained the why of their stand on labor, namely, "that these are middle class women whose time hangs long on their hands and who know no more about the labor movement than I know about astronomy."[92] In remarking on another occasion that she had "never taken much stock in the feminist movement," she was expressing the view of many political radicals, both men and women, who saw "feminism" as the individualistic self-interest of career women, who felt no bond of solidarity with women of the lower classes.[93]

Changes

The earliest memory that I can fix with fair approximation is of departure with my mother, in the fall of 1925, on a Pullman train from Union Station in St. Louis, destination Oklahoma City, where Ameringer's plant was located and the *Miner* printed. At Christmas Freda gave me a copy of *The Happy Prince and Other Fairy Tales* by Oscar Wilde; "with love from all the Hogans, including Skeezix, Beans and Fluffy," those named specifically being, naturally, dogs. My father was in New York City writing his report on his tour.

I remember that Christmas Eve as a sad one despite the Christmas stocking and wooden train and Indian doll. (My mother believed that children should have their Santa and Easter Bunny along with other fairy tales.) I should not have been unhappy—I had playmates among the Hogan family, and not only the dog members. It might be that the tone of sadness is a mask for my flood of tears when my mother read me "The Happy Prince," whenever that was; a story that stayed with me. It would be obvious that I was missing my father, except that this very natural explanation is the last to occur to me. There may have been another reason: my mother.

There is a letter, just one, from that period, a letter from New York, the second sheet only. The contents indicate that it was written in December. Except for meeting with a publisher to discuss his idea for a multi-generational novel of the mines, Ed had wound up his business. "Now drop all of your hesitancy, put on the glad rags and let me meet you."[94] The paragraph that follows tells all that I really know about the family's problems.

> But whatever you decide I know that hereafter there shall be no more of the misunderstandings in our life that marred it in some of the past months. If there was no other reason — and there is — Davy would not be given a square deal if we were not together. He needs us both and I think we should see that he has us both. The other reason is that we need each other — at least I need you. I think I can say now that life would not be much for me without the two of you in it. I was very glad to have you say that you preferred the three of us in a house to regular hours of a job. My efforts will be directed to making it a better house than it has been for all three of us.[95]

A host of questions suggest themselves. Five years of marriage, the romance of it over — not unheard of. Agnes, for the sake of a career, prepared to separate — that seems almost to be implied. Did her strong disapproval of separation by parents of young children, which I remember, reflect her having made a sacrifice at this point? The Wieck brothers did like their home brew, at the making of which Fod excelled; consuming it made for pleasant evenings. But I only once saw Ed with too much to drink. I have something approaching a conviction, with no memory to support it, that Agnes tried once to sound out how I would feel about living with her. But nothing is explicit except "regular hours of a job." Another kind of jealousy, a rational jealousy at any rate, is difficult to credit.

Agnes did go to New York and she and Ed returned to the cottage on West Lincoln Street. But for reasons unrelated to conflict within the family, 1926 and 1927 were not good years for the family. Here was Ed back from his mission, a job well done, finding, erelong, that his mine was working three days a week — work time that was shared with men whose mine was idle — and rumor had it that this mine too would soon shut down.

"It behooved us," Agnes wrote to a correspondent, "to find additional means of support." The family bought its first car, an old Model T, and moved to a country place not far from Scott Field. "Here with our one acre of very fertile ground we hope to wrestle more successfully with the High Cost of Living and eventually go into the business of raising dogs." With luck they would "emancipate" themselves from coal mining and have more leisure for writing. It didn't work out that way — not at all.[96] Before long Ed found himself emancipated from coal mining for good: he was fired and unable to find another job. If memory serves, he was fired, on a pretext it may be, for something connected with union activity, perhaps as pit committeeman, and did not receive the support he expected from the union. He found himself blacklisted, something hard to prove when more and more Illinois miners were without jobs as cheaper non-union coal from the South competed successfully with Illinois even in its regional markets. The Wiecks now had "to scramble our living out of the soil."[97]

Except that the country might be good for the boy, and that the country was pretty, I cannot imagine for Agnes an affirmative motive for being there. She had no hankering for that kind of simple life: coal-oil and gasoline lights, the latter something of a luxury, an outhouse for a toilet, drinking water carried from a well at a considerable distance from the house, and so on. Above all, she needed to be among people. It wasn't good, either, for the writing in which they had invested so much hope. Ed wrote a couple of reviews for the *New Republic*, but no more articles.[98] Agnes continued writing for the *Miner*, but after the first months of 1926 there were fewer items that I find myself pausing over in my scanning of the paper. Lotta Work disappeared and for a considerable period Agnes's weekly pieces were unsigned "Odds and Ends."

There was one significant exception: a Belleville story, in the fall of 1926, for which she enlisted the help of Mary Anderson, a league friend from Chicago days, now chief of the Women's Bureau of the U.S. Department of Labor. On the front page of the *Miner*, Agnes's article bore the title, "Low Wages and Disease-Breeding Shops Caused Belleville Enamel-Workers' Strike; Men, Girls Balked at Breathing Dust and 'Spitting Lead.'" In the *Belleville News-Democrat*, on Fred Kern's editorial page, the heading is just "Belleville Stoves"; a splendidly simple title, for the good citizens of Belleville were immensely proud of the stoves produced in the locally owned foundries. The men sandblasters were getting silicosis, the women enamelers, lead poisoning; the women were working nine-hour days, eight on Saturday.[99] (In my diary, the following spring, I wrote: "Mother went to the funeral of a striker. He was a sandblaster."[100]) Belleville's good citizens were not significantly different than business classes everywhere; they weren't shocked, they just wouldn't believe that the deaths and illnesses were due to conditions in the foundries.

If there was in our family a depression of a certain kind, of which a five-year-old was only confusedly aware, happenings in the miners' union added to its weight. The morale of Illinois miners received a hard blow in September 1926 when John Lewis was able to deliver proof that District President Farrington had signed a contract to work for the Peabody Coal Company upon expiration of his current term; Farrington, of course, was forced to resign. (Such self-advancement was far from unusual. Thanks to the union, men such as Farrington had something to sell.) The reasonable, almost unavoidable, hypothesis that the coal company had supplied Lewis with a copy of the contract as soon as signed offered no solace. Farrington's successor was no more than a competent vice president in charge of a political machine that had lost its brains but not its determination to hang on.

In December, John Brophy ran against Lewis on the Save-the-Union ticket. That movement was of Communist inspiration but Brophy's long service as president of the Central Pennsylvania district had earned him respect; colorless he was, but not self-seeking. Ed just didn't like the company he kept; the Save-the-Union movement would do more harm than good. It didn't matter. Lewis piled up "votes" in districts, now plentiful, where the union was dead. Then there was the news from the union convention the following month. Powers Hapgood, a friend of Brophy's, was lured into a hotel room and beaten by a crew of Lewis officials and set upon again on the convention floor. A Harvard graduate, Powers had chosen to join the working class in its struggles, not as an intellectual ally but as a coal miner and organizer; in 1922 he had been "up against the gat" as an organizer in the non-union fields of Pennsylvania. Back then he had visited the Wiecks—Agnes was immensely fond of him and had written a story in the *Miner* about him.[101] What was going to save the union?

In the fall of 1927, back to town it was. I had just started school in Shiloh village. The convincing reason for the move was Agnes's belief that the school would not be good enough for her son; Belleville had an up-to-date school system. It was not an irrelevant reason, but perhaps was secondary to her need to get out of the country. She never learned to drive and was fearful of cars; besides, the Model T had to be cranked to start and that took strength she didn't have. (In those times, of course, and long after, the "woman driver" was regarded as a menace.) But the move was truly "over-determined": whether an invasion by termites could have been fought off I don't know, but that horde did eventually bring the house to its very knees. In choice of living quarters in town, rent must have been the deciding factor—we were really poor.

Along about here, though, there was a bright spot: Agnes's shared in the preparation of a ninety-six-page magazine-format booklet, *Visions: For the Boys and Girls of the Illinois Miners,* published by the *Illinois Miner* (1928). On the cover a boy and girl, hand in hand, are walking into a subtly colored brighter future. It was an anthology with a wide range, containing fiction, verse, art, biography, labor history, science; Anatole France, Tagore, Oscar Wilde, Romain Rolland, Tolstoy, Van Loon, Louis Untermeyer; sketches of Sandburg, Thoreau ("he was something of an anarchist"), Villon, Mark Twain (strongly recommending Huck Finn), a piece about Sam Gompers and of course John Mitchell, but also an article about Gene Debs ("He taught, 'love one another'; preached brotherhood and in prison proved that his beliefs were not idle words or empty dreams"); Agnes's "The High School Graduate," Ed's sketch of Husemann. The collection's principal virtue was respect for the intelligence of the young.[102]

Before the school year was out, spring 1928, our fortunes changed again. The general bad luck was, in a narrow sense, our good luck. For the past five years, Illinois miners, those who still had jobs in a declining industry, had been doing pretty well. In an article in the *Miner,* Agnes had noted the prosperous look of towns in Franklin County, now the coal center of Egypt.[103] The new bungalows might be a bit cheesy, and people were going heavily into debt for them; but installment buying had been invented and if there weren't too many mouths to feed, miners' families were able to furnish their homes decently. Everybody had a car. But the future no longer looked bright. In the summer of 1928, Illinois miners had to accept a 20 percent wage cut. To try to protect Illinois coal and Illinois jobs, an Illinois Coal Sales Association was set up that spring, with the support of the union and of businessmen and, by approval without participation, the coal companies. (Agnes's brother Gilbert was one of the initiators.) Ed became secretary-manager; he was a natural choice, in terms of ability and experience, but his abstention from union politics as well as his friendship with Walter Nesbit, still a district officer, did not hurt.

Ed must have understood the futility of the "Buy Illinois Coal" enterprise. Across the country too many mines had been opened and mechanization of mining was rapidly increasing productive capacity, while oil and gas were cutting into demand. Of the major producers of bituminous coal, Illinois alone was still unionized. The industry that the union had temporarily stabilized was now hopelessly destabilized; coal was in trouble from which only another world war would temporarily recover it. Factors of the very same kind would soon bring down the whole economy.

Ed now had an office in an East St. Louis office building. He always carried himself in a dignified manner. In business attire he wouldn't be taken for a miner. Both he and Agnes always liked to "dress up," but never ostentatiously. Cleanness, politeness, dignity—the middle class should not believe that working people were incapable of such. The same was true of our family's coal-miner friends.

We moved across town into a middle-class neighborhood and enjoyed a couple of years of modest prosperity. I should emphasize "modest": when, after a while, Dad needed a better car for his job, my very small bank account paid part of the price of a brand new Model A. We had, nevertheless, changed class. This probably affected Agnes more than Ed. He had a job, he could support his family; he could perform quite well, none better, the role he had accepted; just maybe he could do some good. Not that Agnes had forgotten the folks "down home," or the labor movement. Relieved from pressure, she wrote for the *Miner* more regularly. But her role was now more emphatically "mother." My father was away every day and away also on overnight or longer trips to Chicago and other points. (I remember my fascination with the "time tables" he brought home from his train travels.) In recollection, that household was primarily mother-and-boy.

We had a flat in a rather nice two-family house with a yard. Agnes spent a good deal of time with her flower garden. She was studying plans (leaning to Dutch Colonial) for a home on the order of one that Lotta Work had fantasized; we had the lots, on a side street way out on the western end of town, toward East St. Louis. In 1928, when I learned the difference between electrical volts and electoral

votes, the talk in the household was of Al Smith, chiefly because he
favored the repeal of Prohibition, but he was also regarded as pro-
labor. Ameringer, who like everyone else had no trouble in supply-
ing himself with beer and schnapps, refused to believe that there
was a real difference between the folks who paid the way for Smith
and those who paid Hoover's bills, and voted for Norman Thomas.
(One of Adam Coaldigger's "digs": "It is better to vote for heaven
and lose than to vote for hell and win."[104]) The family's social circle
underwent some changes and seemed to center more in Walter
Nesbit's house. I particularly recall the evening of gloom in that
house when the bad news came about Walter's race, on the Democratic line, for congressman-at-large.

For the son whose future was much on her mind, Agnes wondered about a career as lawyer, with Darrow as model of course,
while a local congressman friend (and lawyer for the union) suggested the possibility of an appointment to West Point some day.
No, I am *quite* sure that Charlie Karch's suggestion was not to the
liking of either Ed or Agnes. But her pieces in the *Miner,* a good
many of them, reflect these changed circumstances. Yes, she was
very pleased to be able to write that there were several Negro
children in her little boy's class and that he liked them and was
friends with one.[105] (In the joshing way in which she encouraged
and discouraged, she must have encouraged that friendship. None
of the other kids had anything to do with the blacks.) Her deepest
beliefs had not altered. But she saw no place for idealism to be
active, and I am strongly tempted to say that she saw her own work
as essentially over. Agnes had settled down at last.

Mother and Son

Writing in the *Miner,* fall 1925, a couple of months before my fourth
birthday, Agnes recalled her wish that her younger brothers would
escape the mines and go on to professional careers. Now, about her
son, Agnes felt a little differently: "As a mother I am more
concerned with creating character in my boy than with seeing him
attain a 'position' in life. I want my boy to believe not only in the
dignity of labor but in the rights of labor. . . . I want him to hate
militarism and war, to be free of race prejudice, and to believe in the
brotherhood of man. I hope he may have an active and a critical

mind, to be able to do his own thinking and always to have the courage of his convictions."[106] This was of course her way of saying "integrity." She could have had Ed in mind.

Agnes had good ideas, beginning with "a spirit of love and comradeship rather than fear."[107] A boy should have dolls, male and female and not all caucasian. As playthings he should have blocks and other materials that stimulate imagination. (I don't know how much thought she gave to the fact that she, for the most part, was my playmate.) He should have games that teach geography. No war toys, of course. Fantasy and fairy tale would stimulate imagination. He shouldn't be pushed. Whether or not she said it to herself, she had the right idea, of following where my curiosity led. In this way she did much informal "teaching." But she was also anxious. Rationally, but excessively, she worried about the contagious childhood diseases, which were more serious then; that this would be her only child, she must have understood fairly early. (And the killer 'flu of 1918–1919, which struck Belleville hard, was on everybody's mind.)

Intentions are one thing, circumstances are another. For some months in the latter part of my fourth year, my father was absent; I cannot but have felt the crisis discussed earlier. If one takes the Oedipus complex not as a human universal, as Freud did, but rather as symbolic description of a familial pattern of particular cultures, it is pertinent to this classical male-child-only family where the mother was very loving, very protective, by far the more reluctant to discipline, and more seductive in her attentions than she realized. It will not be surprising, then, that I persevered after the reuniting of the family in primary attachment to my mother.

Writing and reading were of course major activities in this home. Some time in my fifth year, after our move to the country, Agnes discovered that, bored with pounding the bell of an old and otherwise inoperable typewriter, I had taken to coming downstairs after my parents were asleep, to "monkey around" with the good Oliver machine. She decided to teach me the sounds of the letters, which would allow me supervised access to the real thing, but only if all fingers were used appropriately, with no two-finger "hunt and peck" like my father. Agnes liked to say that I taught myself to read. But the English code is hard to crack. I remember my guesses at "neighbor," "knight," and "seize" and the family joke that was made from combining those words, pronounced analogically, in a sentence. What she should have said was that the initiative was coming from the pupil—learning rather than being taught. When the boy insisted that he wanted the very cheap farm-machinery that a mail-order catalogue was advertising, it was ordered and when it turned out to be toys, as his parents had predicted, he got a bitter lesson in the deceptiveness of advertising.

From here on, however, circumstances became increasingly more powerful than intentions. The move to Shiloh Valley brought me into a world I enjoyed exploring. The activity in the barns and sheds of the landlord's farm a short distance down the dirt road, and in the fields opposite our house, was a source of wonder and delight. First entries from a diary, typed on the Oliver machine at the Shiloh Valley farm when I was a few months past age five (with some consultation about spelling, no doubt):

> Monday, March 28, 1927—Today was a bright sunshiny day. The first thing this morning a woodpecker was in our hackberry tree and a robin was on our fence. Daddy planted lettuce and spinach. I worked in the garden too. I hoed some weeds out of the ground. In the afternoon I went to Muelche's with Wilmer in the car. I watched Bill Muelche sow alfalfa and oats and Wilmer harrowed while Bill sowed the seed. I walked home and on my way I stopped at the flower house and brought my Mother some flowers.

> Tuesday, March 29—Today was a nice day but it was blustery. After I went to Ohlendorf's for the milk I saw Wilmer in the wheat field with the new rotary hoe and I went into the wheat field and he let me ride on the seat of the rotary hoe while he walked behind driving the horses. It was fun.[108]

There were no small children close by, that I recall, but I had a play-learning environment. Agnes's fears—she became terrified when I slid off a gentle horse onto whose back one of the farm-boys had lifted me—could be countered by my father's influence and others'. But school was a problem to which there was no good answer. An active and curious child had to be transplanted from a real world into an artifactual child-world of formal, teacher-centered, grade-differentiated classes. I won't take up space with the vicissitudes of my schooling: four schools in four years, the fourth so that I could be in a new experimental class; through all that I was the same fidgety boy.

In town, the nuclearity of the family became more significant. We did not have the lodge or church community of most Bellevillians. My parents were on no more than speaking terms with their middle-class neighbors. Uncle John and Aunt Mayme had no children at home; my nearest cousin, Dorothy, was forty miles away in Staunton. Ed and Agnes knew a great many people in Belleville, but their circle of friends was rather small; only one of those families had a youngster and Rita's Catholic mother was raising her very strictly. As to sex, Agnes accepted the then-modern doctrines of education of the young but the advice she read assigned the task to the same-sex parent, who never managed to do it. The only "sex education" I received came at age eight from a little book, *In the Beginning,* whose chief result was to produce utter bewilderment about female anatomy. I don't know what the books were recommending but Agnes was and remained careful to keep her body clothed, a taboo she never renounced; a taboo reenforced, if it needed that, by Ed's firm commitment to "modesty." In later years, Agnes blamed herself for "mistakes." What I see is circumstances. She planted seeds carefully; though in truth, many were more like "seeds beneath the snow."

A Fiasco

Meanwhile, for coal miners and their union there was more trouble. In the fall of 1929, almost simultaneously with the collapse of the New York stock market, John Lewis revoked the charter of the Illinois district with the intention of installing "provisional officers," only nominally such, who would be loyal to him and answerable only to him. (The prize was access, without accountability, to the district's substantial treasury.) Lewis had exercised that power freely in other states but neither union constitution nor precedent supported its application to a self-sustaining district. A temporary injunction directed Lewis to keep hands off.

In the "war" that followed—"war," truly in quotation marks, even if there was some rough stuff—the *Illinois Miner* had a leading role. As part of the counterattack there appeared immediately a report by Agnes Burns Wieck of a conversation among outraged women, followed a week later by an anti-Lewis blast of her own. In the third week of the campaign, under the page-one banner, "Miners' Wives

Urge Membership to Kick Lewis Out," Ameringer printed a long article by Amelia Cobb of Johnston City.[109] Amelia was not a writer of
articles and the style is not the style of her letters; possibly, Agnes
took shorthand notes from a conversation with Amelia, who certainly
had no need of a ghost. In the fourth week, the *Miner* carried on the
Woman's Page an article by Agnes, its contents fully described by
its multi-deck heading: "Women Urged to Rally to Aid of Illinois
and Help 'Clean House' in U.M.W. of A. Must Rebuild Union with
neither Lewis nor 'Red' Leadership. 'Illinois Will Not Go Down'
Should Be Watchword of All, 'Rule or Ruin Lewis' at End of Rope,
but Must Not Be Allowed to Take Last Union Stronghold Down
With Him; Time to Rebel When Homes Hang in the Balance."[110]

Consistent with the *Miner*'s status as official organ, Agnes had
heretofore refrained from comment on union policies. Now to all appearances she was committing herself to an all-out war in an
idealistic cause. But the cause was not, by a long stretch, so idealistic
as it seemed and Agnes's commitment turned out not to be firm.

What was going on, in truth, was a fight between two union
machines, between Farrington's old Illinois machine, now managed by his heirs, and Lewis's. During a half-decade of truce, when
Lewis faced opposition only from the Left, he had perfected his
control of the national union — or what remained of it, for outside of
Illinois and the anthracite districts in northeastern Pennsylvania all
the major coal regions had been lost to the union. On a superficial
view, the district officers were protecting not only their jobs but
also union democracy. But Illinois miners, especially those working
in the highly mechanized mines of the larger corporations, had
many grievances; the union was not doing its job about working
conditions and piecework rates in the mechanized mines. (By the
following year, one-half of the coal produced in Illinois would be
machine-loaded.) There was a hard core of Lewis loyalists, and a
substantially larger hard core of the Illinois faithful; the rest of the
miners were prepared to believe what each said about the other.

Less than two months after Lewis made his move, the Communist controlled National Miners Union, recently founded, issued a
strike call with recognition of that union its principal demand.
Agnes and Ed saw the Communists as helping to destroy, for their
political aims, whatever solidarity remained; hence the reference to
"Reds" in her article. Despite the last-minute defection of the

N.M.U.'s national president, as many as ten thousand miners, counting those who honored picket lines, may have stayed off the job. Franklin County, northern neighbor of Williamson, was now the number one coal county in the state—big mechanized mines, big companies. The strike call drew a strong response there, as it did in Christian County, adjacent to Sangamon, where picket-line battles led to the calling of the state militia. The strike was short-lived—more than anything else it was a vote of no confidence in both U.M.W. factions. Something else was present, also: a growing awareness that "business unionism" was impotent to deal with the consequences of economic crisis, that harmonious cooperation between capital and labor benefitted only capital, and that something more radical was needed. Insofar it is not wrong, despite the considerably smaller role of Communists in the latter, to see continuity between the N.M.U. strike and the rebellion three years later that led to formation of the Progressive Miners of America.[111]

I don't think that Ed and Agnes were reading very well these signs of deep discontent. Ed through the Coal Sales Association, Agnes through the *Miner,* were too close to the District 12 official family. But I have merely phrased what I understand to be their retrospective view of the events described here.

Left to themselves, the Illinois officials would simply have put the fate of their jobs into the hands of lawyers and judges. Ameringer, who had become in effect a member of that official family, seems to have been chiefly responsible for their decision to take the offensive by forming, on what they hoped would be national scale, a "Reorganized" United Mine Workers of America, minus Lewis and all his "provisional" officers. Even Oscar had a personal stake in the outcome of this officers' fight, for Lewis would have liquidated his paper at the first opportunity. But he may have felt some guilt for having closed the paper to all criticism of Lewis during the more than five years of peace between Lewis and the District 12 officers and for letting go unchallenged the always optimistic official pronouncements about the state of the union.

The Reorganized, as the new union was commonly called, was a terribly bad joke, carried out with full seriousness. To its founding convention in the spring of 1931 came Lewis's old (non-Communist) foes from other districts, men who represented no membership. Farrington was forgiven his trespass (the contract with Peabody), became a strategy advisor, and aspired to office once more. The Franklin County miners manifested their indifference by abstention. After many months of much sound and fury, worthy of not the slightest attention here, all was settled by a judge: Lewis must not touch Illinois but Illinois must acknowledge his presidency, which it did by choosing not to appeal. In the *Miner,* renamed *The American Miner* to serve as organ for the Reorganized, Oscar hurled a last thunderbolt in a front-page editorial, March 14, 1931, "Rather Death than Compromise and Dishonor," and walked away. In Oklahoma City once more, he would publish all through the thirties the weekly *American Guardian,* which achieved a certain national circulation and was always welcome in our home. Of the post-Ameringer *Illinois Miner,* nothing need be said.[112]

Long before Ameringer's departure, Agnes had done her last writing for his paper (July 26, 1930). (Since her first contribution, published November 1, 1924, she had written some 250 articles and columns.) After that initial barrage the previous fall, her participation in the *Miner*'s crusade had diminished rapidly; her contributions to the anti-Lewis cause were limited to printing, under her by-line with brief introductions, a handful of letters and a few reports of conversations. Fearing the worst from the very start, that war between Lewis and District 12 would damage the union seriously, Ed had tried unsuccessfully to mediate between the two sides. When the "war" was over, Agnes wrote to Mary and Powers Hapgood that the District 12 officials, who claimed to be defending the union, had merely been looking out for their jobs. "I haven't had a great deal of enthusiasm over the whole thing, anyway, knowing labor leaders like I do. Now I am thoroughly disgusted."[113] Shocked that Farrington might become secretary-treasurer of the "Reorganized," and disturbed by charges that what we now call "creative bookkeeping" was being practiced in that office—something he could not abide, Ed had announced his own candidacy. Before the election could be held, the judge's ruling had cleaned the slate and the farce was over.

Hard Times—and Rebellion

Pretty soon there was no more Coal Sales Association. We did gain something by that, the office furniture and equipment and a supply of stationery that lasted a very long time. These goods came into our house as part of an effort to save the association by economizing on office rent, and stayed, permanently, in lieu of back salary. If I look around my study now I can see, besides Husemann's gift, six shelves of sectional bookcases and a steel filing cabinet from that East St. Louis office.

In the spring of 1931 it was back to the country to survive; but there were no termites this time and we were only about four miles from town, on the Old Collinsville Road. With shame, I recall my shame before my recent schoolmates at our return to a roof over our heads, but with no electricity and no plumbing. In the fall I would be going to a one-room schoolhouse, a mile cross-country, with seventeen other kids. Ed put in a large garden with which I helped as I could, and he started a flock of Rhode Island Reds. Financed by one of Walter Nesbit's sons, he tried raising dogs, beautiful fine-pedigree Llewellyn Setters, wonderful playmates for a boy. I remember vividly the frantic struggle to save Polyanna (!) of the Silken Ears from distemper and the subsequent birth of nine splendid pups, not one of which was ever sold. Ed was bringing back from town the produce that he tried to market house-to-house. When eggs dropped below ten cents a dozen in the spring of 1932, we stopped selling eggs. He tried peddling advertising for the *Miner.* A friendly coroner helped us out by calling Ed for duty on his jury as often as he could. A case where a fellow had blown his brains out with a shotgun was a visual memory Ed had trouble getting out of his mind; even years after, he would refer to it. The store bill mounted and so did the back rent. How long would grocer and landlord be patient? Not that our situation was uncommon: an awful lot of people were having it far worse. We ate our chickens and eggs and our vegetables and berries and there were fruit trees.

For Ed, ascetic by temperament, not needing a great deal of human company, the garden, animals, woods, and fields provided compensations. With time on his hands he built, mainly for Agnes, for whom a stinking privy was the symbol of defeat by poverty, a remarkable "Chic Sales" to replace the ramshackle shit-house we found, a two-holer with a drawer underneath so that the waste could be dragged away for burial. Agnes had neither the physical strength nor the physical endurance for this life; nor the spirit. Her temperament did not allow her to be "philosophical," and she felt helpless.

Just how desperate? I know that in the spring of 1932 my parents were trying to find out whether a skilled worker like Ed might find welcome in Russia. My memory of this is vague and I don't know how far the matter was pursued; I don't know if they were thinking of a permanent emigration, or whether the idea was more Agnes's or Ed's. How much worse could life be there than under capitalism, where people were starving and Hoovervilles were springing up all over the country? In any case it seems that the Soviet government was now looking only for specialized technicians.

Of the direction my parents' thinking was taking, a diary I kept that spring, in the early part of my eleventh year, provides a few other indications. There are notes about our going to several socialist gatherings in Belleville; an effort was being made to revive the party locally and I believe that Agnes joined at that point. But several items about myself say even more about the family. April 15: "Wrote composition 'Why I am a Socialist.'" Presumably it was for school, but the idea definitely wouldn't have come from the teacher. April 20: "I won the debate on—resolved: The Phillipine [sic] Islands should be free and independent? I was on the affirmative." May 4: "I am reading two books. Golden Days of Soviet Russia and The Road Ahead. The Road Ahead was written by [Harry] Laidler. It's a primer on Socialism and Capitalism." June 8: "On June 6th was a revolution in Chile. They have set up a Socialistic Government. That's what may happen in the U.S." I was following closely the fighting in Shanghai between the Chinese army and the invading Japanese—I was "rooting," of course, for the Chinese. I didn't record it in my diary but I embarrassed terribly my very young and terribly naive country-school teacher, who had explained to the class that overpopulation had obliged Japan to seize Manchuria, by protesting that birth control was the solution to that problem; which ended the schoolroom discussion.[114]

Unfortunately, my diary, which I discontinued after school let out—and so did not record General MacArthur's military victory over the bonus-marching war veterans in the battle of Anacostia Flats—tells little about the troubles that led up the Progressive Miners movement. April 1 [1932]: "Ill. Miners on strike. 36% reduction demanded by operators." Follow-up, May 9: "The times are so bad down in the Southern Illinois coal fields that people are getting along on government flower [sic] free."[115] (So bad were the times that Agnes's letters "down home" cost six cents: one stamp on the envelope and another enclosed.) The district officials, meanwhile, fearful of rebellion, were going up and down the state pledging that there would be no reduction.

Soon the pace of events accelerated. In June, inspired by auxiliaries that had sprung up in the southern Indiana field, also on strike, a "ladies' auxiliary" was formed in West Frankfort, its main function, a soup kitchen. (Auxiliaries had appeared several years earlier in the "outlying fields" in the course of long strikes; few in number, they had disappeared along with the union when the strikes were lost.) Later in the month, the district officials, John Walker now president, thinking perhaps to distribute the blame for a wage cut, decided to throw in with Lewis and brought him into the deadlocked contract negotiations. (They survived in their positions as figureheads into the following year, when Lewis had had his use of them.) In mid-July, by a five-to-two majority on referendum, the union membership voted down a contract that would have given the companies one-half the reduction they demanded. The news spread that in the Taylorville field the Peabody Coal Company, leader of the Coal Operators' Association, anticipating trouble, had hired several hundred armed guards.

Three weeks later, the miners' officials resubmitted a virtually identical contract, a brazen act of contempt for their membership. The "theft" of the tally sheets served as pretext: in this "emergency," announcement was made, the contract, "which in our judgment was approved by a majority vote," was "executed."[116] Anyone could see that all this was planned in advance—for if the tally sheets were truly stolen, duplicates from the local unions could have been procured within twenty-four hours. At issue now, far more than dollars and cents, was deprivation of the miners' right to determine their own fate.

In Christian County (the Taylorville field) and in Franklin County, the companies owned the law and had their private armies. Letters from Amelia to Agnes tell of the fears, the mutual distrust, that sent the miners in the south back to work; including the men of her family, who hated themselves for it, felt like scabs, but were going to hold onto their jobs until a new strike movement could get underway. There was a moment of uncertainty in Christian County but miners from the adjacent fields, who came in by the thousands prepared to picket, easily persuaded those miners to rejoin the strike; north of Egypt virtually all mines remained shut down. In Franklin County terror ruled, the sheriff its commander; a small army of deputies and special deputies, armed with machine guns as well as smaller arms, was ready for action. The great unarmed caravan of support from the central and northern fields was decoyed and blockaded and broken up at the Franklin County border, the road left littered with smashed-up cars. The union, the companies, and the law, working in cooperation, had won the battle.[117] Amelia said they were worse off than the scabs in non-union Kentucky, who didn't have to pay, by the check-off of dues, for the privilege of scabbing.[118]

Agnes had kept abreast of all these events. Lovett, still teaching at Chicago, living at Hull House, and working with the League for Industrial Democracy, had written Agnes in July on behalf of a group of socially active students who were much concerned about developments downstate and eager to be of assistance. Agnes gave him a thorough report (of which I have been unable to find a copy). Then came the news of the "stolen" tally-sheets and of the fate of the Mulkeytown March. Younger, single, or not a mother, Agnes would have leaped in immediately. Of what was going on in her mind I have only a rough picture. Life on "the farm" was hard for her; she felt submerged in it, overwhelmed by it. She tried to maintain a certain gaiety but she was deeply depressed and her health was very poor, possibly due to early and problematic menopause. She could see no future for herself, for her husband, or for her son. A man like Ed, nearing fifty, didn't stand the chance "of a snowball in hell" in getting a job in the mines again, even if Illinois were not aflood with out-of-work miners. How were they going to pay the taxes and not lose those lots on which she still hoped some day to build a house and which represented our only asset? (Given the real estate market in 1932, they were hardly a current asset.) Emotionally, Agnes was part of the developing warfare: her whole life history involved her in it. But a job for Ed, or for her, anywhere, was a priority they could not neglect.

I am sure, though I have no direct evidence for it, that Ed was discouraging involvement, and not just because Agnes was needed at home and should not neglect her family. He felt contempt for the union officials who had dug their own hole by their stupidity and cowardice and were dragging everyone else in. (Walter Nesbit, once our friend, and still secretary-treasurer of District 12, had done the bidding of John Lewis and John Walker.) There was no more question for him than there was for Agnes about which side he was on: the membership may have been wrong in resisting the wage cut, which I believe Ed thought, but the union signified "all stand together" whichever way the vote went. But he didn't idealize the rank and file—the Wieck brothers, Ed and John and Elvin, had no great confidence in the "general timber" that would make up any new union that might be formed. Nor do I think that Ed, who never had a high opinion of southern Illinois, had much sympathy for those miners who had worked on the day the marchers came down and the day following and any day after when the whistle blew "work." That was not how the old union was built.

The period immediately following the founding of the Progressive Miners of America was fairly quiet. North of Egypt, the smaller companies, and one larger, were willing to recognize the new union in exchange for acceptance of the U.M.W. wage scale. The only issue now was union-of-choice, a union the miners could trust. The auxiliary idea was spreading rapidly; the first issue of the *Progressive Miner*, September 16, 1932, initiated an auxiliary column, with its own editor, and a news story reported a meeting of Ladies' Auxiliaries from a number of central Illinois towns. Along with his local, Ed had become a member of the P.M.A. I am sure that Agnes joined as soon as an auxiliary chapter was organized in Belleville; whether she was among the initiators, I don't know. I have an image of her straining at a leash, but with nothing so simple to cut as an actual physical constraint.

For the October 12th anniversary of the battle in 1898, the *Progressive Miner* published an article by Agnes, "Remember Virden!" and reprinted Ed's old *American Mercury* article about "General" Bradley and his army and the strike of 1897.[119] The present moment was tense: the Peabody Coal Company was trying to reopen its mines in the Taylorville field, with strikebreakers recruited from its Franklin County mines and working under the protection of the state militia. But Agnes had no idea, surely, of where this year's October 12th pilgrimage to the Mt. Olive cemetery would lead her; no idea that within a few weeks she would become president of the State Auxiliary. But after the women, Agnes among them, took the tear gas at Taylorville and "hurled their defiance" at the militia, Agnes knew that she was in this fight for good, and the women knew Agnes.

A letter she wrote to Lovett, after the State Auxiliary's founding convention in early November, conveys a great deal: "I was certainly down in the depths when I wrote you."[120] That would have been in September, after the P.M.A. was formed, with Agnes still on the sideline.

> But getting into this strike has pulled me out of it. I was stuck out here in the country, tied down with canning and preserving, and shut out from the world that I belonged in. We left the "farm" long enough to make our annual journey to Mt. Olive on October 12 and the sight of all those thousands of marching women and then the news from Taylorville of the attack of the militia—well, I was off and the "farm" was forgotten and I haven't stopped since! And now I am state president of the Illinois Women's Auxiliary of the Progressive Miners of America! Isn't that a grand and glorious title.[121]

Plainly, there is ego in this, the ego needs of a person who has come to feel useless, if not to feel that her life is over. (Lovett had sent a check for fifty dollars, a fortune when three-cents stamps were precious. "As much as the money meant, and we certainly didn't expect that, it was the big lift it gave us out of our mental depression—to know that you're still considered of some importance in the world is a tremendous inspiration.") Here is what gave her joy and hope: "Everybody has jumped into this thing as a crusade and this movement of women seems to be going of its own momentum."[122]

Agnes's role at the convention was considerable. Not only did she deliver the opening-day address and end up as president—she had a hand, more than a hand, in writing the constitution. In the same letter: "But what a strange constitution I drafted for a labor organization—no salaries! Not even expenses, other than clerical for the District Secretary. I just didn't want the fine idealism spoiled by paid workers."[123] That constitution, like the union's, included a no-self-succession rule, a principle in which Agnes believed strongly; two-year terms in the case of the union, one year only for auxiliary officers. An auxiliary officer could advance to a higher position but the president must retire.

You would laugh if you should read our constitution—it begins with a revolutionary preamble and winds up with a burial service that attributes death to the pleasure of an all-wise Providence! I let it go—I didn't want to try to uproot too many prejudices at one time. I had a time of it getting them to be the Women's Auxiliary instead of the *Ladies!* One after another got up in the convention and said there was no reason why we couldn't be ladies just because we were miners' wives. The argument about parasites, etc. influenced a minority but to get it over I had to use the Bible, wherein, I reminded them, the word *lady* never is used! This moved a very religious woman to get up and say that the mother of our Lord was called *woman!* But the funniest thing was when we came to the resolution against women swearing! The only experience any of these women had had in organizations has been in the lodges. This strike has made even the church women swear on the picket line and it is reflected in some of the meetings—hence the resolution. It was finally laughed down.[124]

Agnes was probably the only woman who could create a feeling of harmony and solidarity among women from nearly forty local auxiliaries and of quite diverse backgrounds, more than a few of whom were way to the "left" politically, some of whom had hardly a political thought. Of the politics of the convention she didn't tell Lovett anything but there is always politics and the more radical, the more militant, of the women surely understood that she was the president, the leader, that the auxiliary would need: experienced in organizations, widely known, articulate, and above all able, because of her roots in the southern field, to bridge the gap between north and south.

When I look more closely at the date of the letter, I understand something else about the tone, something she does not mention. Within a matter of days, a week at the most, she was going to take the lead in an invasion of Franklin County—not a march this time, but what might be called a "raid." Her silence could not possibly imply mistrust of Lovett. Surprise was going to be crucial and I can imagine that strict secrecy was agreed on. The risks she knew well and she may have preferred to entertain Lovett with the "swearing" question and give emphasis to her longer-run hopes that the auxiliaries, "when the strike-excitement dies down," would have a powerful educational influence,[125] rather than think about what she was going to face.

There is already the blood of martyrs: Joe Colbert and Dominic Laurenti in Franklin County in August, and Andy Gyenes killed at Taylorville by a national guardsman, shot dead because he did not obey an order to come out of a neighbor's yard and submit to arrest for calling a man a scab, on the day Agnes joined the fight. At Gyenes's grave she had delivered a eulogy that was a pledge. It was not the last eulogy Agnes was to deliver. "Dry your eyes, you women of the auxiliaries, hold back your tears, make strong your hearts for the great task that is ours. To this widow and her children, sitting here beside this grave, we owe a debt that we must pay. Hold up your hands and in their presence here declare that we will carry on to victory the great cause for which our brother died! Our men folk need strong women at their sides in this dark hour."[126] These are the words that have been spoken in too many wars, but I can't read them so stonily as I would in another context. I was not there and I don't know whether she spoke exactly the words on her typewritten copy, from which I have quoted the central paragraph of a very brief speech. (They might be—she would remember what she had spoken.) What I know, because in my imagination I can hear the voice clearly and all the emotion of it, is that she meant, absolutely, every word she spoke and did not forget her pledge.

Husband and child would have to take care of themselves. Because of the closing of the country school it had been arranged earlier that I live weekdays with my Uncle John and Aunt Mayme, so I could go to junior high in town. Ed may still have had his own thoughts about what was possible, but with Agnes now in the movement, he gave her all the support and counsel he could, and he was happy to discover among some of the more radical young men, and many of the women, an idealism and a dedication that he had probably not expected to see again. The capitalist system had disintegrated in self-destruction—old Karl Marx had foretold it— but no wisdom, conventional or otherwise, could say what "the road ahead" would be like. Might a socialist world come to birth? Or would there be another war? I know that was in my mother's thoughts. What I heard told me that we were at a crucial turning point and in my eighth-grade class in Belleville's junior high school there was one vote, that November, for the Communist William Z. Foster for U.S. president. I had heard Norman Thomas on the radio and judged him too tame for the times.

But the focus of the story is no longer the family. By the end of her auxiliary year Agnes would write to the president of the West Frankfort auxiliary that she no longer worried as she once would have that an epidemic of encephalitis reported in the Belleville area might reach her son. Too many had suffered in this struggle, too many had died. In another letter, to the mother, in Italy, of Dominic Laurenti, one of the first victims of this civil war, who had been killed on the picket line at Zeigler, killed savagely, his neck broken as he lay on the ground, his body full of shotgun pellets, she wrote: "I have a son eleven years old; and as I have seen one man after another dying in this miners' struggle, I have well realized that the future may claim my son, too, as a victim of humanity's long struggle. I say this because I teach my son to believe in the principles of unionism, of liberty and justice, and to be ready, if need be, to die for these principles."[127]

This Heroic Struggle Has Come to Naught

In a history of labor unions in the United States, the Progressive Miners of America would receive an agate-type footnote at most.[1] If the history were encylopedic, such a footnote might read:

> In the fall of 1932, when the United Mine Workers of America, of which John L. Lewis was president, was near extinction nationally, a large number of local unions in Illinois seceded and formed the Progressive Miners of America. The miners alleged that they had been "sold out" by imposition of a wage-reduction that had not been ratified by the membership. The new union won recognition from coal operators in a number of counties but nearly all major companies aligned themselves firmly with the U.M.W.A. Except for Franklin County, where law officers and agents of Lewis' union guarded the territory, strikes by Progressive union members paralyzed operations at U.M.W.A. mines throughout the state for a considerable period. But the large number of unemployed miners in Illinois and adjacent states provided a reservoir of strikebreakers and the struck pits were gradually restored to operation. Violence was widespread and a number of persons, the greater number from the Progressive side, were killed. The new union successfully documented systematic violation of civil liberties but the public sympathy that the union gained had no effect. The fate of the rebel union, which made only token efforts to expand beyond Illinois, was sealed in mid-1933 when, by a bold campaign, Lewis's union organized the miners of almost all states from which it had been driven in the 1920s. Administrators of the Roosevelt government's National Recovery Administration, in which Lewis participated on the side of labor, rejected the claims made against the United Mine Workers by the Progressive union. For its later history, see: The Progressive Mine Workers of America.[2]

Then there would follow—or should follow—a note to the effect that the most striking feature of the Progressive union, during the first year of its existence, was its Women's Auxiliary:

> In the view of the union officials, the Auxiliary interfered unwarrant-edly in union affairs. But a contemporary report tells of the Auxiliary women "setting up strikers' soup kitchens, making quilts to raffle for relief, producing labor plays, singing labor songs, conducting labor educational classes, . . . shivering in the dawn at the mine tipples" on picket lines, "marching from one county to another in unemployment and strike demonstrations"; being "clubbed, tear-gassed, insulted by thugs, thrown into jail"; going, ten thousand of them, "to the state capitol to demonstrate before the governor for civil rights in the coal camps."[3]

After November 1933, the P.M.A.'s Women's Auxiliary passes into the domain where only scholars of minutiae forage.

That November, right after the convention with which her term of office expired, Agnes wrote to her friend Tom Tippett. He had returned to Illinois to set up and direct the Education Department of the Progressive Miners' union; now he was living in the East and writing his novel of the mines, *Horse Shoe Bottoms*. Agnes's letter begins:

> It is all over! I feel as if I had lived a hundred years in one, so crowded with events has this past year been, so full of struggle, sacrifice and death! When I finally got back to the "farm" in the dead of the night, and looked out into the starlit space, looked through the branches of the big trees, now bare of leaves, I wondered if all those terrible things had actually happened. I thought of a year ago when I left the "farm" for the first convention, with no thought in the world of assuming the fearful responsibility of leadership, and now, here I was back, after a year of the most appalling experiences. The hush of the November night brought a deep sense of sadness.
>
> I was not regretting that I had gone. But god, to think that this heroic struggle has come to naught! To think of the magnificent army and the lost opportunities! This time last year Tom, we had Peabody licked—in December Peabody began to talk terms. And what results![4]

For a portrait of Agnes in that time, and a brief summation of how she saw the auxiliary, I go back a month before that second convention, to an interview by a reporter for the *East St. Louis Journal*'s "Illinois Magazine." Agnes was good copy. The full-page

spread, under the heading "Agnes Burns Weick [sic] — 'Coal Field
Hell Raiser,'" was a treasured memento of her auxiliary year. The
headline writer fumbled it but the reporter, Charles M. Swart, had
done his homework well and got her name right.[5]

A seven-by-ten photograph shows Belleville's auxiliary, wearing
their white uniforms and red scarves, in their meeting hall. They
are facing toward Agnes, who is out of the picture. The white was
standard auxiliary; the red flashing, a statement of the militancy of
this "Mother Jones Post." "The red," Agnes told another reporter,
"doesn't stand for communism. Our women like the word militant,
they don't like communism. The red stands for the blood of our
dead."[6] Militancy would be the common denominator, but there
were a lot of women there, including Agnes, for whom red stood for
more than that. On the floor in a row in front are girls too young for
membership; in some localities there were "junior" auxiliaries.
Here and there, babies in laps. Except for some of the youngsters
who may not have caught the joke, whatever it was, and a few
women who may not have liked it, Agnes's audience is smiling and
laughing; they know her and trust her and are proud of her.

An accompanying full-length photograph, front view, shows a
"small black-haired woman in a brown street suit," carrying a
bulging briefcase that serves also as purse; she was just on the point
of leaving the meeting hall for her train. (She may not have told
Swart that she was wearing her only outfit, freshly washed out.)
"Her bobbed hair showed a single gray hair here and there." As the
photograph confirms, "her brown eyes were sharp and challenging."[7] She stands proudly erect but what seems like an effort at a
smile succeeds only in turning the corners of her mouth slightly.
She had returned just the day before from Harrisburg, where the
Peabody Coal Company was trying to reopen its mines with strikebreakers, and after a day at the "farm" and before taking a midnight
train for Chicago, three hundred miles away, for a scheduled
speech, she has stopped to give her home auxiliary a report on her
trip and on the state of the Progressive union.

"Guarded by strong capable women," sergeants-at-arms, the
heavy entrance door of the hall stayed shut while the meeting was in
session. Like the reporter, husbands waited in the anteroom;
taking turns, they caught peephole glimpses of the meeting. "In the
silence, a strong feminine voice cut through the closed door in

sharp staccato stabs. . . . Now and then a whole phrase could be understood. 'Harrisburg—our men—get back their jobs—more hell.' Again and again applause stopped the speaker." On the way to the train the reporter has his interview; with a cup of coffee at the depot, Agnes revives and she is eager to tell the auxiliary's story. "Her voice was low. She was slightly hoarse after her long harangue. But there was a pleasant vibrant quality that made it difficult to imagine her a 'Hell raiser,'" a person sometimes compared with Mother Jones, or a user, in the tradition of Mother Jones, of "fighting four letter words," the question with which the reporter framed his story. Like the miner-husbands, he concluded that when occasion demanded she would. But he also remembered "her lilting laugh."[8]

The writer, sympathetic, took good notes. He got down her life history about as she would have told it. Then comes her view of the auxiliary:

> Mrs. Wieck has been, not so much a Joan of Arc as a leader of Joan of Arcs. She has been leading women who have learned to be leaders of men in a cause which they have cloaked with idealism.
>
> Women who a year ago would have hesitated to have engaged in more than monosyllabic conversation with strangers now unhesitatingly mount improvised rostrums and take their turn at spellbinding.
>
> She sees two important results of the auxiliary already bearing fruit. In the old days, women of the mine areas were a hazard to the success of any strike. The men knew that a complaining woman at home could drive the most militant union man back to the pits without victory.
>
> Now the women, organized under the auxiliary, glory in the privations they suffer. They would not let the men go back if they wanted to go, unless the return was a distinct victory. That, says Mrs. Wieck, is why there never can be a compromise between the Progressives and the U.M.W.A. in Illinois.
>
> The second factor is that as an organization the women have taken an important role in the actual hostilities. They have picketed and they have marched in demonstrations. They have held meetings in the face of orders forbidding meetings. Where they might have starved singly, they have learned through organization to raise money for food, clothing, and strike expense.[9]

Agnes knew that the cause to which she had devoted a year of her life was lost. But the story she wants to be heard is what had been, or had almost been; a legacy she wanted preserved.

"The Sheriff's Gonta Kill You!"

From the start it had been clear that aggressive strategies were going to be needed if the Progressive movement was to achieve its goals. In the geography of Illinois coal, Egypt, more specifically Franklin County and its neighbors, was crucial. With the defeat of the Mulkeytown March, open resistance ceased. If the state's biggest coal-producing region could not be won, the Progressive rebellion would succeed only in dividing Illinois miners into mutually hostile groups, to the permanent benefit of the coal operators. For Agnes, strategy and emotion agreed.

As auxiliary president, Agnes conducted three major campaigns. About the first, the southern campaign, she had this to say in her end-of-term Annual Report:

> The work of winning "little Egypt" to the new Union and thereby strengthening the strike upstate was the first undertaking of the State Auxiliary. The word "Progressive" could scarcely be whispered in the south when your President planned to invade this territory. Auxiliary women of the south aided her in carrying the Progressive cause right into the local unions of the U.M.W. Rank and file "militants" of the men's union came from the north to direct the underground work, for the "law" was with Lewis.
>
> Encouraged by their women taking the lead, the men of the south worked day and night to establish the new union. In DuQuoin and Dowell (Perry and Jackson counties) the men soon took an open stand. But in Franklin County, where the "law" was vicious and thousands of miners were involved, the work did not bear fruit so soon.
>
> The sheriff of notorious Franklin County tried to check the women's activities by barring the Auxiliary president from that county; but meetings went on secretly and one Auxiliary after another was organized.
>
> An Auxiliary is a branch, but in this situation, the tree grew from the branch. The rank and file leaders of the south were proud of their courageous women. The P.M. of A. officials were merely permitting this work to be done, after much persuasion of the "militants" for an expansion program.[10]

Franklin County, bordering Williamson on the north, was the key. It contained modern, high-tonnage mines. One of them, New Orient, tied in with U.S. Steel, was said to be the largest soft-coal mine in the world; two of Peabody's dozen Illinois mines were located in the county, and three more were nearby. From that same era, the story of Harlan County, Kentucky, is still remembered; differences between Harlan and Franklin counties are differences of detail except that in the latter case the United Mine Workers' union was in open collusion with the coal companies and the law.

Agnes was aware of the danger but she was known down there— not only from her articles and speeches but as a "native." This was especially important because, besides "Red," the Progressive union was being labeled a "hunkie" movement. (My impression is that the P.M.A. did draw a great deal of support from "foreigners," Italian especially.) If Agnes could get to talk to the miners and the women, they would listen.

Of that campaign in Franklin County, Agnes wrote to Tippett shortly afterward:

> I got in some good licks in Franklin County before Lewis' order to the sheriff barred my meetings. I caught him at a time when his mind was on Cincinnati [a reference I cannot interpret] and the Peabody negotiations with the Progressives. It was a daring and perhaps a reckless thing to do but I walked right into U.M.W. meetings, got the floor for five min-utes—they knew not what for—and then made a P.M. of A. speech. Right across the street in [U.M.W.] sub-district headquarters the gun-men were on duty but after I had captured one local, they were in confusion until Lewis took the thing in hand. Anyway, I have a fine bunch of women organized down there.[11]

Not very long after these events, the Wiecks had a visitor from the East, Edmund Wilson. From New York he sent them a copy of what he wrote about that visit and they got very upset. They thought he had made them look ridiculous, "outlandish." He thought that they appeared dignified, even heroic. But he yielded and in the *New Republic* there appeared, instead, an objective report of the kind that his hosts had hoped for.[12] Fortunately, what he wrote to them, "Your household is one I will long remember," turned out to be literally true.[13] In his *Travels in Two Democracies*, two years later, there appears, with the title "Illinois Household," the story as he wanted it (except that the speakers go unnamed). And it turns up again in his *American Earthquake* (1957), in which a postscript identifies the members of this "rather remarkable fami-ly."[14]

"Illinois Household" is all dialogue, with "Wife" as principal speaker. Wilson asks no questions. "Husband" adds remarks here and there. "Boy (eleven)" thinks his mother is leaving out something important — "They killed Laurenti on the picket line!"[15] And he has to be sure that Wilson understands: "Gotta fight John L. Lewis' gun thugs!"[16] Wilson also gives him the last line: "While you're down there in Franklin County, Ma, you're not doin' anything for Taylorville!"[17] Strange as it sounds, I have no recollection of that day. Maybe it didn't seem unusual that a journalist from New York would come to us to find out what was going on in Illinois.

Wilson set the scene neatly: "A picture of Lincoln, a desk, a dictionary stand. Outside the countryside of central Illinois is large and flat and covered with snow."[18] But his *Notebooks* for the thirties, now published, provide many other accurately noted details, beginning with Belleville's long Main Street, the "strong compact German houses," "time-yellowed white on brick," "fine ornamental doors." Then our place: "Farm house on a little hill with a dip in the ground just beyond it, beyond which you saw a field dry russet-color against the snow — and beyond that the thick stacks of corn." "The house in excellent taste — Mrs. Wieck referred to the overstuffed furniture which had been sold to people during the boom — bare of everything but necessities."[19] "Big [coal] stove that gave a lot of heat — the dictionary on its stand — the desk — bookcases and magazines — oilcloth in green and white squares on kitchen table — green [cooking] stove — rather rich pattern of linoleum on the floor." "Blackboard: ethnology, etymology, philology, entomology." (Vocabulary lesson for the boy.) Lunch: Good "Belleville Dutch" food, "potatoes, pork sausages, German cheese made out of buttermilk, delicious liverwurst which seemed to me richer than what you get in delicatessen stores in New York." The dogs: "In chicken-wire enclosure, shivering in the cold, jumping up against the wire." And last, "the way the little boy talked — all in a loud outpouring that ran the words together."[20]

Wilson began with Agnes's recapitulation of the story of Mulkeytown and the breaking of the Franklin County strike. Then:

WIFE. . . . . — They told us it was no use going down — that the Law said there never would be a Progressives' meeting held in Franklin County —

but we held about six meetings with the gunmen right across the street. We had meetings in people's houses with miners on guard outside and in U.M.W. halls—it's against the Lewis constitution to let anybody else speak there, you know, but they let me. I taught school five years in the next county and all my family worked in the mines and the people know me down there. And I'd come at the psychological moment—they were mad about the special assessment. I'd say to them, "They're assessing you men to shoot people up in Taylorville!—there are six hundred deputies and gun-thugs up in Taylorville alone!—they've even got a thug up there who was mixed up in the Kincaid robbery—a man who killed his own brother and stuck him in the strawstack!—and that's what they're assessing you men to pay for!" And I said that I'd heard that some of them from down there had gone up to Taylorville to scab. That's what I can't understand—their being so shameless about scabbing! I told them the boys were saying that any miners that went up to Taylorville were gonta come back in boxes! They say they sent one man back with an S branded on his cheek.—At one of the meetings there was a Lewis man there and he got up and tried to oppose me—and then somebody pulled out a razor and said, "You're not going to insult a woman here!" And then the Lewis man tried to stop me on a point of order—he said I was going beyond the five-minute limit and so they took a vote on whether I was to have all the time I wanted and everybody got up except the Lewis man.[21]

The man who pulled the straight-razor had worked with Agnes's brother Gordon at New Orient. "Red" was a real union man—a sufficient recommendation for Agnes.

Agnes went on to tell Wilson about a second foray into West Frankfort the following week to organize the women. "We are having Auxiliary meetings in house after house," she had reported in the *Progressive Miner.* "We eat 'sow belly' and flour gravy and biscuits and talk Progressive."[22] Now she was going to try to hold a meeting and formally issue charters. Women would be coming from all over the county. From "Illinois Household," again:

They told us that Lewis would never let us speak there—that's where Orient No. 2 is. But we went down anyway—we said, "Those women expect us and we're going!" We'd written to the state's attorney, and he'd promised that we could hold a meeting—he said he'd give us an escort out of the county if we had any reason to believe we were in danger. Well, when I went to go to the meeting, the street was full of people and the hall was dark. The sheriff and the gang had been after me in people's houses, but they hadn't found me—and I walked down the street in plain view with a roll of charters under my arm. But when I got to the hall, the women said, "Come here, the sheriff's gonta kill you!" I said, "That's hot—the sheriff's gonta kill me!" They said, "They're walking up and down the street—they're drunk—you better get away!—you can't go up against the law."[23]

The U.M.W. trustees of the building, perhaps Progressive sympathizers, reaffirmed their agreeableness to the meeting's being held but that wasn't enough. In the passage below, Wilson made a small slip. It wasn't the sheriff who threatened to take away the trustees' union cards—that was Ray Edmundson, a Lewis tough and gunhandler and future "provisional" president of Lewis's District 12.

The sheriff [*sic*] stood over [the trustees] and he raved and he threatened and he told them, "If you try to have her speak, you got no more [union] card, you got no more job! I'll bar the door, and if she tries to speak, her life ain't worth a damn!" They used clubs to drive out the women—there were about a thousand there. One woman who was there with her daughter tried to go to a movie to meet another woman, and a deputy chased her and hit her on the back of the head and knocked her down— and the girl tried to scream and he slapped her—but she screamed, "Oh, my God! don't kill my mother!"—Then the sheriff [correct, this time] came in and he said that I'd have to get out of town right away—and what do you think he had in his hand to identify me? He had the letter the state's attorney had written me promising to give me protection![24]

Perhaps not on this occasion—perhaps because of this occasion—Agnes carried a small-caliber automatic in her briefcase on at least one of her dangerous missions. In the same circumstances a man might well have been killed or taken a serious beating; gender was, however, only a limited immunity. If Agnes was not (I am sure) above taunting a man for being man enough to beat up a woman, she did not play a feminine role, no more than had Mother Jones. It goes without saying that a woman not publicly known would almost certainly not have left unharmed.[25]

It had been a whirlwind campaign—Agnes's, of course, only in the sense that she was suited ideally for the lead role, for she depended not only upon her fellow "invaders," men and women, but also upon the existence in Franklin County of (what we would call) a network, also of both sexes, of individuals who were wholly on the Progressive side. The reception she got at local union meetings demonstrated that although there were Lewis loyalists and men who would go up to Taylorville to scab, it was fear that kept the mines running. Just beyond the borders of Franklin, Agnes had been instrumental in swinging two big locals to the P.M.A., one of them at a Peabody mine; those miners were now on strike for recognition of the new union. One of the locals at which she spoke in West Frankfort was a Peabody local. No wonder she felt they had Peabody on the run. If Peabody surrendered, the rest of the companies would fall into line. But in Franklin County the law and Lewis's "gun thugs," momentarily caught off guard, tightened their grip once again.

Left Wingers

About the Franklin County campaign I quoted Agnes as writing in her Annual Report that "The P.M. of A. officials were merely permitting this work to be done, after much persuasion of the 'militants' for an expansion program." "Officials" versus "militants" and "left wingers": this will be a constant theme.

By the time of the auxiliary's first convention, the P.M.A. had successfully negotiated contracts with the companies who were willing to break the united front of the Illinois Coal Operators' Association. The miners who were now back at work had endured a long strike and were assuming the burden of providing financial assistance to the families of the thousands still on strike. There is no sure way of judging, but the officials of the new union may have represented the sentiments of a fair number of the miners who returned to work by choosing to believe that a legal strategy of seeking invalidation of the U.M.W. contract, rather than trying to spread the strike, was the wisest course. The hope, based on the advice of a lawyer with no experience in labor relations, was a fanciful one; there wasn't a court in the land that would find any fault with a labor agreement satisfactory to powerful corporations.

From the start, Agnes's friends and strongest supporters, both men and women, were the "left wingers," the "militants," labeled "Reds" and "Communists" by Lewis and the coal companies and company-dominated local newspapers, and eventually by the Progressive officers. A considerable number were Socialists, Communists, syndicalists, and anarchists, but in those days, amidst that terrible economic depression, you would hear "there's got to be a revolution" voiced by many who never imagined they would think such thoughts. (The circle with which Agnes was associated most closely might be described as "non-Communist Left.") I often heard it said that in the mood that prevailed at the founding of the union the left-wingers were strong enough to elect officials from their own ranks but had chosen to elect men of a neutral political coloration: this would be a genuinely "rank-and-file" union with a severely democratic constitution, in which office holding would be unattractive. Unfortunately, there is no way to make office holding unattractive.

As I see it, the left wing, the auxiliary, and in its inception the Progressive rebellion, expressed something fundamental in miners' tradition. Miners had long been in the vanguard of the labor movement. Conditions of work and geography, my father liked to point out, were conducive to independence and self-reliance and also to solidarity, a solidarity that extended almost as reflex beyond the mining regions. The miners especially, those who actually dug and loaded the coal, were highly skilled workers with enormous pride in their work; their lives, always at risk, depended on their judgment and the reliability of their comrades. Typically, mine workers lived in coal camps or one-industry towns or villages. Militants had been plentiful among both coal and hard-rock miners everywhere and ever since (I sometimes think) there have been miners and employers of miners. The coming of mechanization, which stole "the miner's freedom" and made factory-type speed-up possible, was felt as a violation of dignity.

In Agnes's mind, certainly, was the strike of 1897, a strike desperate against all odds and won by boldness. But she was not an adventurist; she wanted to help in building something solid. "Leaders too far ahead of their army" was an expression I heard in our house many times. Illustrative, thoroughly characteristic, are her remarks about Gerry Allard, the *Progressive Miner*'s first editor, in the letter in which she told Lovett about her becoming involved in the movement.

Born in France, Gerry came from a family of coal-miner revolutionaries; all the Allard boys and girls had been given French revolutionary names, one of them "Germinal." A red flag made by his mother, it was told, draped his cradle. In 1912, when he was four, the family emigrated to Johnston City, Illinois. It became a joke between Agnes and Gerry that she just missed being his first-grade teacher. Agnes loved this "kid"; he was enthusiastic, idealistic, a fiery speaker, full of laughter, a bit cocky. Not much taller than Agnes, he was all energy. He was active in the National Miners Union strike in 1929 and the Communist Party had thought well enough of Gerry to send him to its Workers' School in New York City; but his revolutionary ancestry had more than a touch of the anarchist and he was not amenable to party-line discipline.

Agnes, to Lovett, about Allard:

> Expelled from public school, before he could get a high school educa-
> tion, for being unpatriotic, into the mine [in Franklin County] before
> the legal age, into activities in the miners' union and also the CP and now
> only 24 (or 25) and the driving force in this revolt! The conservatives are
> handling negotiations and naturally he opposes all compromise—that's
> his youth and his community teaching, but he is so very sensible and I do
> think that the long talks Ed and I have had with him are a tempering
> influence, although not for the world would we want to lessen his
> fighting spirit or dampen his revolutionary ardor.
>
> We want him to see the importance of getting this new union rooted
> in the industry. He was thrown out of the CP, even before this new union
> was formed, is a Trokskyite, but is beginning to realize that radicals
> sitting in conferences and drawing up blueprints aren't accomplishing
> much; that you've got to get into the moving masses, sometimes ahead of
> them, sometimes behind them, but always with them.[26]

Time, however, was not on the Progressives' side.

Marching Women

Possibly, the PMA officials believed that Agnes and those who supported her campaign in the south were interfering with their negotiations with Peabody, which fell through. (It seems probable that Peabody's purpose was to buy time.) But "Boy, eleven," in Wilson's story, who must have reflected what he had heard from his elders, was right that success or failure of the strike in the Taylor-ville field, in the central part of the state, was crucial. The four big mines there were Peabody's. In her letter to Tippett, after her return from the south, Agnes wrote that "our officials in Gillespie [union headquarters] were very optimistic the last time I talked with them but I confess I am not. We need to launch an offensive, in my opinion. Lewis has recruited hundreds of 'card men' scabs in southern Illinois to fill the Taylorville mines."[27]

On New Year's Eve the Belleville auxiliary hosted a "reunion." From the north and the south, in bitterly cold weather, hundreds came in open trucks over long distances. It was a festive occasion, as I recall, with music and dancing; Pat Ansboury, one of the Franklin County leaders, did an Irish jig at which I was wide-eyed. The occasion was as festive, that is, as festive could be in the shadow of an explosion that left fifty-four dead in a Progressive mine, just seven days before, on Christmas Eve. In her Annual Report, Agnes wrote: "When the strikers from the Peabody mines in Christian County and the working miners from Peabody mines of the south sat down to eat together, the reality of the reunion was most vivid."[28] Nine months now those miners of the Taylorville field had been on strike. To what was talked about behind the scenes, I was not privy.

In Christian County, a few days later, outnumbered pickets engaged company guards, sheriff's deputies, and strikebreakers in "the Battle of Kincaid," a pitched battle in semi-darkness that lasted ten minutes or more. A mine guard who led the attack was wounded fatally. In my father's history of the rise of the Progressive union, he wrote that "in their retreat the Peabody men riddled nearby strikers' homes, and in this fusilade [sic] a shot killed Mrs. Emma Cummerlato, a striker's wife, mother of three children and a loyal member of the Women's Auxiliary. She was standing on the porch of her home holding open the door as her husband entered for shelter from the gunfire."[29] Indictments for murder were brought against more than a dozen Progressive miners, two of whom, including the chief of police of the village, were brought to trial and then acquitted. But the militia, withdrawn temporarily, had been returned immediately after the battle. In her Annual Report, Agnes wrote: "At her [Cummerlato's] funeral the military power of the state and Federal government was an insult to the dead. Guardsmen surrounded the Cumerlatto [sic] home and the words of the minister were interrupted by the roar of huge army planes zooming down at the little house. . . . The streets were unsafe. Homes were invaded. Terrified children hid under beds. Homes were bombed. Soup kitchens were locked. Soldiers stood by with bayonets while thugs clubbed men over the head. Family after family fled."[30] I heard many corroborating stories. The scene in Christian County and the scene in Franklin County were nothing unique in labor history, not even for the union that allies itself with the corporation against the workers, a de facto company union. But these miners had not imagined that this would happen in the coalfields of Illinois.

Agnes literally trembled at the thought of violence, but the history of class struggle had always been "a bloodstained trail." The "Virden Martyrs" were killed in gun-battle with armed guards protecting strikebreakers. "Virden," and "Pana" in the following year, had erased any thought that Illinois coal operators might have had of trying to undo the union's victory of 1897. Miners are not pacifists, and these miners felt that West Virginia had come to Illinois.

Under pressure from the left wing and the auxiliary, the P.M.A. officials threatened a general strike if "civil and constitutional rights" were not restored throughout the state.[31] As she put it in her report, Agnes felt that "the south could be won to the Progressives if only the right to hold meetings could be secured."[32] The hope behind the threat was that the newly inaugurated governor, a Democrat (Henry Horner) succeeding a Republican and reputed to be liberal, would do something about the sheriffs' and Lewis's gunmen and allow the miners to be represented by the union of their choice. In 1898 it had been a sympathetic governor who had ruled, in the face of the Virden and Pana "riots," that importation of strikebreakers from out of state would not be permitted. Agnes did lead an auxiliary delegation to the governor that persuaded him to authorize reopening of strike relief stations in Christian County.[33] But this governor, as is the common habit of governors, temporized.

At this juncture Agnes sent forth a call to the auxiliaries to bring all their members to Springfield on the 26th of January. Their "march" to the state capitol would put pressure on the governor and take the Progressives' cause to the public. Specifically, the auxiliary would petition for "immediate and full restitution of civil liberties in the coal fields," increased state aid for the jobless, and unemployment-insurance legislation.[34] The P.M.A. officials, who were viewing Agnes Burns Wieck in much the same light as Lewis and other

officials had viewed Mother Jones—as a disturber of the peace—
were apprehensive about this march, apprehensive that it would
confirm the dreaded "Red" image.

In Agnes's letters to the local auxiliaries she wrote, "Won't that
be a splendid sight, thousands of miners' wives and daughters,
marching in white?" The Mrs. Masons would be really marching
now. She hoped for five thousand; press estimates ran to ten
thousand, perhaps more accurate than usual because the women,
from fifty-one auxiliaries, from as many towns, marched through
the streets in orderly ranks in their white uniforms, except for
members of families of the Moweaqua explosion, who at Agnes's
suggestion wore black.[35] It was an impressive show of strength. I
remember vividly the great crowd in the state armory and before
the Capitol singing over and over "Solidarity Forever," the Wobblies' song, inspired by the Kanawha Valley strike in West Virginia
twenty years before, which the auxiliaries had adopted as theirs, as
the auto workers would a few years later. It was the third verse,
supremely fitting in the year 1933, words that often come back to
me, that was favored:

> It is we who plowed the prairies, built the cities where they trade,
> Dug the mines and built the workshops, endless miles of railroad laid,
> Now we stand outcast and starving mid the wonders we have made,
> But the Union makes us strong.

There were wonderful speeches, of indignation and of hope. The
spirit was irresistible. It was, to use a word that Agnes liked, a
"grand" occasion. The governor accepted the women's petition,
written of course by Agnes in her most vigorous Declaration of
Independence prose. I wonder what the governor was thinking as
he read the concluding paragraph: "Not only is our welfare at stake,
but our faith in the ability and willingness of the Government to
protect and serve us, is menaced. Dare you fail us now?"[36] Well,
yes, he did. Marches to capitols, I learned young, are likely to affect
most the people who march. Under pressure from the Progressive
officials, Agnes and Tom Tippett had gone so far as to tear up ultra-
radical banners that some of the women had brought, even so not
quieting the alarm of those officials. But the governor surely did not
need banners to tell him what the march was about. For his part, the
governor assumed the role of mediator, but there was nothing to

mediate. John Walker is said to have exclaimed that it would be suicide for his union to accept the Progressives' proposal of referendum, statewide or by locality, to determine which union would be recognized for collective bargaining.[37]

Agreement was reached that there be a truce. Presumably the governor would see to constitutional rights—he said he would. Ten days after the Springfield March, the West Frankfort auxiliary tried to hold a public meeting but clubs broke it up and a number of women were injured. The next day Agnes had those women at the governor's office. He was very busy. Agnes succeeded in making him look at the women—after three-and-a-half hours he had to leave for dinner and they had twenty minutes of his time outside his office. That was that.[38] For some days, while the worst-injured stayed in a hospital, one with a seriously fractured skull, Agnes stayed also. Then she went home utterly exhausted, with terrible headaches and laryngitis/tonsilitis so bad that she could barely talk. Ed insisted that she not go out again until thoroughly rested, which took, disregarding brief outings, two or three weeks. So ended Agnes's second campaign.

Knowing something of Agnes's illnesses, I suspect that more than physical exhaustion was involved. Under the "truce," only innocuous picketing was permitted in the Taylorville field, patrolled by soldiers; if the Peabody mines didn't already have full crews, the company and Lewis's union were free to recruit scabs. "On the curb stone of the mine town streets sat sullen miners on strike since April 1, 1932."[39] Peabody was restarting its mines in the Springfield district, in the same way. More people were going to be beaten and killed. I can imagine the heavy responsibility that Agnes felt for those women who had been clubbed at West Frankfort. But of course it was her duty to keep going and she could not shirk that.

Hiding Behind the Skirts of Women

Agnes went forth again, in early March, once more incessantly active. I have no log to tell the miles she traveled. Harrisburg would appear on the log, for the county had "gone Progressive"; county authorities would not allow the importation of strikebreakers and the two Peabody mines remained closed. She was in demand at meetings and picnics; on some days she spoke in two or three different towns. She visited local auxiliaries and local leaders whenever possible. There were board meetings and strategy sessions. She had no money—by the end of the year our landlord was talking eviction—but there were always people to drive her, homes in which to eat and sleep, people who would share what they had. The "farm" was a place she passed through. What she said in October to the East St. Louis reporter held for most of the year. How did she manage to keep a home together? "I don't. You should come out and see the place. It is like a cyclone has just gone through."[40]

Her main job that spring, the object of her third and last major campaign, was to publicize the terrorism that the Progressives faced. In Franklin County, where a strike was called finally at the end of March, the conditions that Agnes had met in December persisted. The strike call could be distributed only by airplane drop of huge leaflets.[41] The streets were not safe, meetings could not be held, people looked to the skies for news, and the plane, it was said, drew fire. It was now or never. What is amazing is that some thousands in Franklin and in Williamson did answer the strike call.

The strike couldn't keep the mines closed. If a man stayed home or identified himself with the Progressive union, he could lose more than his job. Here is a letter, written by the president of the West Frankfort auxiliary to an auxiliary sister, dated April 24, 1933, a month into the Franklin County strike. (It was included in a pamphlet, "The Struggle for Civil Liberties in Illinois," issued by the American Civil Liberties Union.) I surmise that the writer had no confidence that a letter to Mrs. Wieck would get through the local post office.

> Four carloads of U.M.W. thugs went to Orient and beat my father, nearly killing him. . . . One fellow hit him in the face with a pair of knucks and they beat him and took him and drug him out in the yard saying they were going to take him off and kill him . . . and they knocked him in the head with a gun, he was unconscious, they kicked him and kicked him injuring his arm and kidneys, his arm is broke in the shoulder. . . . They beat up more men there that same night in their own homes, and over 30 men in West Frankfort. For God's sake, get a hold of Mrs. Wieck and tell her to let's hurry and get to Washington so we can do something. . . . We slept in the garage last night and the

thugs come and yelled and beat on the door of our house and flashed their lights in our bedroom. They told my father they were going to civilize the people here.[42]

For months, until the men came out on strike, this woman had refused to pack her husband's lunch bucket.

To Du Quoin, where the strike had been solid and peaceful, the terrorism spread as the reopening of the mines began. Grim news; grimmer still, that in Du Quoin five young men went out to avenge the beatings of men and women on the picket line and a shot fired from a moving automobile into a mine guard's home killed a fourteen-year-old girl. To insist upon the innocence of "the boys" caused Agnes no qualms; she understood the rage that fired the gun. The "Du Quoin boys" would be sentenced to long prison terms and grief was added to grief.

At the urging of the League for Industrial Democracy and the ACLU, the Social Justice Commission of St. Louis, its chairman the highly respected Rabbi Ferdinand M. Isserman, agreed to look into the warfare in Illinois. A citizens' organization of liberal cast, it commanded respect. Agnes had plenty to show them. A letter to Tippett, early May:

> I took a delegation to the Social Justice Commission . . . yesterday. Among our people was a man frightful looking from a terrible beating; a woman who had just been beaten, the poor woman whose skull was broken last Feb. and who still has terrible headaches, a man who had been beaten in his own home and dragged to the river and thrown in for dead, and more and more and more. The clergymen and the professors looked their amazement. The St. Louis Star is running a series of three articles, featured big, on acts of terrorism.[43]

As a result of these preliminary hearings, the commission invited the Progressives and the United Mine Workers to meet with them. To everyone's surprise, John Lewis agreed. At the meeting in the parish house of Temple Israel, in the middle of May, Lewis was accompanied by his appointed president for Illinois and by a lawyer. Representing the Progressive Miners were president Claude Percy, the union's chief counsel, and Agnes Burnes Wieck. At Lewis's insistence, no press and no observers. Both sides were on their honor not to make public anything that went on behind the closed doors in what turned out to be an all-day meeting.

Lewis and Mrs. Wieck were in dramatic juxtaposition. Imagine Lewis as Ed Wieck had described him to Edmund Wilson: "He's sort of squat and wears his hair long and talks without moving his mouth. He walks up and down the floor and pours forth a torrent of eloquence. . . . People go to see him and come away as if they'd had a dose of hop. He never had that effect on me but he does on lots of people."[44] Add a habit of arrogance, a habit of sarcasm, a voice that rose to thunder and dropped to a whisper, a practiced theatricality, and when he pleased a practiced courtesy and deference.

Robert Morss Lovett, who had done much to interest the commission in the "civil war in Illinois," was present as a guest. "At the conference," Lovett wrote in his autobiography, "Lewis treated the group of perhaps twenty leading citizens of St. Louis to an oration of over an hour, delivered with a sound and fury that befitted an audience of twenty thousand."[45] Those out in the hallway, including Allard and my father, had no difficulty hearing him. Allard felt free to report what he could hear. Besides mentioning Lewis's claim, which astounded the commission, that because they were trying to "steal" his union's contract with the coal companies the Progressives had no right to picket or hold meetings, Allard (in the *Progressive Miner*) quoted Lewis as follows: "They have left their father's home. And now there is no mercy for them. The thirteen original colonies, if they would have been defeated, and King George would have triumphed, history would tell us that our revolutionary forefathers were traitors, who necessarily had to be smashed. Possibly you and I would believe that story. If the Progressive Union were successful they would be the heroes of tomorrow. But they have failed in their plans and thus must pay the consequences."[46] Small wonder he earned the epithet "King John," which indeed he may have found amusing.

Lovett adds a little more: "Among other charges, he [Lewis] asserted that the leaders of the Progressives were disappointed office-seekers who left the U.M.W. in order to enjoy salaries and release from toil by holding office jobs. Someone inquired of Lewis what his salary was. He replied twelve thousand, with, of course, an expense account. When Pearcy was asked he answered twelve hundred, but added pleasantly, 'Of course I don't get it.' And expenses? 'There aren't any.'"[47]

Then came the turn of Mrs. Wieck. In her Annual Report she said merely that "the Auxiliary president dealt with the conditions in the coal industry that led up to the rebellion and presented the plight of the women and children. She directly charged Lewis with the responsibility for the violence and the tragic fate of our people."[48] But there was more to it than that. Lovett: After Lewis was finished, "then there arose to her full five feet Agnes Wieck. . . . for twenty minutes she excoriated him. Finally, Lewis sprang up like a tiger and rushed at Mrs. Wieck, shouting, 'I won't stand for that.' His two-hour oration was completely shot."[49]

It wasn't by recital of statistics and legalisms that Agnes had provoked Lewis. Allard: "Agnes Burns Wieck provoked Lewis into a rage when she told the conference of a miner's wife dying with a new born baby in the strike torn village of Kincaid. As she lay on her lingering death bed from lack of food, Mrs. Wieck said, her last words were curses for Lewis."[50] There was fear in the chamber and in the corridors that Lewis might attack Agnes physically—I think he did close his fist—but Lewis was not such a fool as that, however murderous his feelings, and when Rabbi Isserman, presiding, told him to sit he sat. I believe Lovett that Lewis's oration was completely shot. "Lewis's vehement tirade against the Auxiliary women as active participants in an industrial struggle," Agnes wrote in her *Report*, "his ridicule of men 'hiding behind the skirts of women,' prompted the *St. Louis Star* [May 18, 1933] to remind him editorially of the first woman Secretary of Labor and of the black skirts of old Mother Jones." But Lewis was no admirer of Mother Jones.[51]

The Conservatives Rebel

The verdict of the metropolitan press was favorable. The commission was impressed. But such a commission, by its very nature, could not conceive of a solution other than "conciliation." Everything would go on as before.

Amelia was president of the Johnston City auxiliary. Williamson County was not quite so dangerous as its neighbor but meetings were forbidden. Early that summer, a group of women tried to have a picnic outside of town. (That may not have been utterly innocent; they probably were in fact holding a kind of meeting.) The police chief of the town, who had no jurisdiction, "and all the little cops and 15 or 20 thugs, came with machine guns, clubs, blackjacks and no telling what else. . . . What the hell you damn women doing now. . . . I'm tired of people running to me all times of the day saying you are having a meeting." Did the churches and schools have to get his permission for a picnic? "Get them damn lunch buckets and go home and I mean go." Leaving, they passed by a bunch of youngsters swimming and a bunch watching them. Why didn't he make them go? Before the chief could answer, "old Josh the night cop hit me over the head and shoulders with a whip of some kind." The force of it threw Amelia down a hillside; from the whip she got a bad bruise on her breast. "They had beat a man almost to death before they got to us—a poor innocent foreigner who happened to be around there." The state's attorney to whom Amelia reported the incident had no idea such things were going on—"even if we were having a meeting they had no right to break it up or beat the women any time." He would be glad to present it to a grand jury. Next month. "What I didn't tell him didn't need to be told."[52] Earlier, Norman Thomas had gone to Franklin County to test civil liberties; his lecture went undisturbed.[53] No doubt, if he had returned for another lecture it too would have been undisturbed, but everything else would stay the same.

Much more effective than the Social Justice Commission's recommendation of conciliation was the verdict that the P.M.A. officials rendered shortly upon the left wing and the auxiliary. If the union was to be received favorably by the National Recovery Administration and gain acceptance of its long-standing position that only a referendum could resolve the Illinois coal mine problems, it would have to erase the "Red" tincture for which the left wing was held responsible. Either way it was a vain hope because Lewis was always known as an arch-conservative (being a Communist was ground for expulsion) and now could get excellent recommendations from Illinois coal operators. More important, a single national union whose president could speak for all miners, at his absolute discretion, fit perfectly with the near corporatist ideology of the early New Deal. That ideology was industrial peace, harmony, and "recovery" through the cooperation of organized capital and, when inevitable, properly organized labor, "company unions" by preference.

It would be several months before the N.R.A. game was played out. Even sooner would vanish the hopes of the women, which I think Agnes shared, that Frances Perkins, the woman secretary of labor in Roosevelt's cabinet, might be responsive to their appeals, which she might have been, were she not secretary of labor. (Agnes toyed with the idea, around the time of the St. Louis hearings, of calling a special auxiliary convention and inviting Perkins to speak. She wondered where. In the state armory at Springfield? In the Christian County soldier-patrolled war zone? In Progressive territory? In Franklin County?[54]) To play the game out, the left wing would have to be silenced.

At a joint meeting in mid-June of union and auxiliary boards, a unique event requested by the union officers, the latter made their resolve quite clear. The women did not come there in the best of moods. Fresh in memory was a battle, just a few days earlier, at Peabody's Peerless Mine, close by the state capital. From Agnes's Annual Report:

> At a mass meeting [the day previous to the battle] the Auxiliary women had challenged the men to go to the picket lines. These desperate mothers of hungry children declared they would rather lose their lives fighting for their men's jobs than to be slowly starved to death.
>
> The Peabody Coal Company was ready for the pickets. Rifles were leveled from the mine tipple. Machine guns were set up in nearby homes of strike breakers. Sawed off shot guns and automatics were pointing from the car windows of the United Mine Workers on their way to the mine.
>
> The pickets stood their ground and fought. The Auxiliary women stood shoulder to shoulder with their men. When the gunfire was fiercest, women lay flat upon the ground but not a woman ran for cover. With the same deadly aim of their men, they hurled their brickbats. A woman tore off strips from her clothes to bind up the wounds of Thomas Urbon, who died in the hospital. A woman ran through whizzing bullets to bring a car to transport the wounded. Another woman fought off two soldiers and held them down with feet and fists. The wounded on both sides numbered over fifty. The soldiers now took up their military occupation along the Peabody front in the state capitol.[55]

Among the rhythms of Agnes's report is the rhythm of "fights": Taylorville in October, Kincaid in January, the Peerless mine in June, Harrisburg in October. There is also celebration of the rank and file, of the women especially.

Besides making it clear that union policies were none of the auxiliary's business, the union officers also made it clear that their tolerance for left-wing criticism of their policies and of their trust in lawyers was at an end. These officials were not the evil men that I then took them to be; they were ordinary men, lacking in vision, subjected to what they no doubt thought to be unfair criticism, and expecting, as office holders generally do, to be respected for their position.

Realistically, the Progressive rebellion had from the beginning stood hardly a chance of ousting Lewis from Illinois. The demonstration is virtually mathematical. Demand for coal in 1932–1933 was at nadir; unemployed miners were plentiful; in more than a few mines, work was divided to share the poverty, but this meant that five hundred strikers could be entirely replaced by half that number of men. It mattered not that in a free vote of Illinois miners the new union would have been the choice of a large majority; votes are not taken in the midst of civil wars for the benefit of a rebel union. The big companies could afford to reopen their mines one by one, with miners recruited elsewhere. The only answer was mass picketing, to enforce the shame of scabbing and block access to the mine; but then the militia came. Within just a couple of years, automobile workers in Toledo and rubber workers in Akron would begin to experiment with an effective answer, occupation of the plant, which would culminate in the great sitdown strikes of 1936 that shifted the balance of power for a time, and whose revolutionary implications the U.S. Supreme Court was quick to recognize, by outlawing this assault on corporate power. But that tactic is difficult to apply to mining.

Present in the founding of the Progressive union was the hope that it would become the base for a new national union. Stymied in Illinois, must the union give up that hope? Even if the probability of success was slight, could not the union dispatch organizers into other states to "organize the unorganized," many of whom had had bitter experiences with Lewis's union? Such was the program of the left wing, supported by the auxiliary officers. The issue came to a head shortly before the union-auxiliary joint meeting when Gerry Allard published an editorial, "Toward a National Drive," in which he charged the officials with being "lax in their duties" because they had made no effort to implement a program of expansion beyond Illinois.[56] This editorial raised, of course, the secondary issue of union democracy. The officers claimed the authority to oversee and control what was published in the paper, i.e., power of censorship: Allard could remain only if he would accept that control. (He had until then been remarkably patient, Gerry being Gerry.) But if this was a "rank and file" union rather than a union that was constitutionally democratic but, as customary, controlled from the top, what right did the officers have to shield themselves from criticism? Allard would not prevent Pearcy from defending himself, as Pearcy did in the very next issue.

At the joint meeting, through long hours of debate, the auxiliary's executive board was a unit on these questions: on Allard's impending dismissal, on censorship of the *Miner*, on a campaign to expand to other states, and on the worthlessness of the union's expensive legal staff, upon which the officers seemed to rely for advice. The women also asserted their right "to voice our opinions on Union policy." "The Auxiliary women were sharing in the suffering and sacrifice to build the new union; therefore, the women were justified in the expression of opinion or even in making protest, if they believed that the fate of the Union was at stake."[57] A position that stands in another light nowadays, when we might ask immediately what right would men have to intervene in the affairs of women workers who happen to be their wives; but such questions are not easily separable from the social context in which they are raised.

Allard's job was the test. The officials hesitated, then saw that they could survive the clamor. Instantly, a paper full of inspiration, vitality, information, collapsed into nullity; a worthy successor to the now-defunct post-Ameringer *Illinois Miner*. From now on, the *Progressive Miner* was going to be a purely official organ—and go from bad to worse.[58] From now on, Agnes's name would be found in its pages only (perhaps) among a list of speakers at a mass meeting. In the announcement of the auxiliary's second convention, neither her name nor any other's appeared. As for expansion of the union, by the time of the joint meeting Lewis's organizers were already sweeping through West Virginia. The National Industrial Recovery Act had been passed and Lewis had seized the moment.

What was left for Agnes was to refute charges that she and her friends were responsible for the problems of the union and to continue to advocate what she believed in, while being careful to do nothing that would allow her to be depicted as a destroyer of the movement. She accepted every speaking engagement she could but there were no more campaigns unless her refusal to back down, her continuing to speak her mind, be counted as such. For Agnes the story of Franklin County ended on a quiet note. The near cheerfulness with which she tells about it is revealing. It was, in the beginning of August, one more test of civil liberties in the Buckner coal camp, home of the women who had got the worst of it at West Frankfort six months before. "The men who called the meeting"— who had, I suspect, been pressured into doing so—didn't show. The law said, no meeting. From a letter to an auxiliary sister:

> Pat Ansboury refused to call it off and I refused to call it off and when the Sheriff and his gunmen with all their artillery invaded the hall and made their demands, they found me leading the audience in singing and because we didn't stop and everybody didn't run out when they saw all the guns, the Sheriff was pretty much bewildered. Our women were magnificent! They, the sheriff's crowd, pleaded with Pat but he said the men called the meeting and only the men could call it off. I had a great time kidding the sheriff. Then when I kept the singing going, he gave me my choice, either stop or go to jail. I wouldn't stop so he took me to jail.[59]

They didn't keep her, but there was no meeting.

"All the Educational Things We Hoped to Do"

Agnes thought the Education Department of the P.M.A. was a casualty of the struggle over Allard and the *Progressive Miner,* and perhaps it was. She was looking beyond the winning or losing of the union cause to something for which there was in those days only the hackneyed term "education." The term "consciousness-raising," if relieved of some of its modern feminist connotations and connected with "class consciousness," can describe what she understood by education; but I would not divest it of feminist connotations entirely, for she wanted women to achieve a real citizenship through developing their abilities and claiming a place outside the family. In this present struggle many had emerged from the kitchen, but miners' wives on the picket line or marching after a Mother

Jones were nothing new. She wanted them to know why they were picketing and marching and she wanted them to develop themselves as persons, something in which Mother Jones had not the slightest interest.

In her long letter to Lovett at the beginning of Agnes's term, from which I quoted earlier, there is an important passage. After telling of how "everybody has jumped into this thing as a crusade and this movement of women seems to be going of its own momentum," Agnes continued: "All of the educational things we hoped to do, when Ameringer was running the Illinois Miner, we now can do, for economic pressure has turned their [the women's] minds from bungalows and cars and radios to the serious things of life. I used to despair of ever doing anything with our working-class wives." She was thinking of it as beginning after "the strike excitement dies down" but those educational things were going to have to be done in the midst of it all.[60] The union was committed to supporting an Education Department. Tom Tippett was the one she wanted for that. Most recently, he had been working with and raising money for the independent West Virginia Mine Workers which had tried to bring unionism back to the Appalachian field. The prospect of working in his home state, and with "Agness Burnes Weicks," was attraction enough for Tom.

In a circular letter to the local unions and auxiliaries, inviting participation, Tippett wrote: "Our notion of an educational activity is anything that will enable us better to organize our strength as a working class." That meant "classes and discussion groups" to "study and discuss the general economic problems facing workers" and to "analyze and discuss the important questions now appearing in the daily press which affect the lives of coal miners." "We should like also to set up classes in public speaking, in the writing and production of labor plays, in singing songs of labor, and we want to bring in outside speakers."[61] Tom only had, it turned out, less than three months. But before he left Illinois he had one tremendous success.

Tom had been an organizer in North Carolina during the textile strikes of 1928, about which he had written a book, *When Southern Labor Stirs*. He had also written a play, *Mill Shadows*, based closely on the Marion, North Carolina, strike.[62] "It turns upon the story of how six men were shot to death, as they stood on the picket line, by

Deputy Sheriffs," the *St. Louis Post-Dispatch* reported. "The play ends on a somewhat uncertain note, with Granny, a heroic mountain type, vowing to stay on and carry on the labor conflict in which she had seen relatives and friends die."[63] The play, directed by Tom, was presented in a number of mining towns, and then triumphantly in St. Louis, where Agnes's curtain speech made clear the reasons why the members of the cast, miners and coalfield women, identified so easily with the characters and understood the action of the play. I wouldn't have been a good judge of the play's artistic qualities, but I thought it as at least as good as labor plays I saw in New York City not much later. There were no artificial Heroic Proletarians; there were people, very much as Tom had found them, Granny included. As I recall it, the cast was marvelous and the chorus, led by my Aunt Mayme's daughter Myrtle, sang wonderfully. Irene Allard, Gerry's youthful wife, was a very believable "Granny."

For the audience, the author and director was one of "theirs," the son of a miner, a miner in his youth, who had not lost his identification with them, a self-educated man who wanted to help others educate themselves. The cast was acting out a drama in which they could feel themselves projected in their weaknesses as well as their strengths. "It has no love interest, no hero—the strike itself is hero," the *Post-Dispatch* reporter wrote. The audiences, except in St. Louis, knew many of the players. For the sympathetic middle-class audience in St. Louis, there was an emotional equivalent to the "civil war in Illinois" about which they had been reading in the papers. It wasn't perfect; strife developed within the cast, perhaps due to intra-union politics or to any number of things, including the very nature of theater and acting.

Mill Shadows was the last act. Several weeks before the final performance, Tom was told that the union could not afford to pay his expenses and office rent (he received a modest salary from Brookwood Labor College, of which he was extension director). Agnes thought it more affordable than a high-priced and ineffectual legal staff. Tom had come under no false pretenses; he had told the union officials that his best friends were all radicals and that he admired Agnes Burns Wieck. He got his notice at the same time as Allard, at just the point when "radicals" and "Reds" would be an embarrassment harmful to any possibility of a kindly reception by the N.R.A. in Washington.

The Women's Auxiliary

To explain the militancy of the women, generalities are fine—the women experienced quite directly, as the husbands' pay shrank, the problems of making ends meet, the problems of food on the table, shoes for the kids. For strikers' wives, this meant making-do with such strike relief as the miners in the Progressive fields could afford. It wasn't shoes just for the kids either. Before the Progressives' strike call in the south, which he answered, Amelia's husband, she said, was "double-shifting" his shoes—wearing his pit shoes as street shoes.[64] What Amelia may have been walking on, I don't know. Maybe the soles of her feet.

Perhaps there are deeper truths also, a lurking sense of superior competence and courage, or a conviction that this terrible economic depression was men's doing. Real, certainly, was the excitement of practical sisterhood, of being needed for something more than keeping house and tending kids, feelings that built gradually over six months and achieved peak expression in the Springfield March. At that point Agnes was not wrong to see these women as sensing for the first time "the significance of their collective strength," as "recognizing "what organized action can do and what power lies in their hands."[65] (Not counting, that is, the important if small minority of women who came into the movement with their own radical political vision.) Of course, the excitement of such a march would not be wholly real, but the experience of a larger community was very real, in the feelings of many.

Agnes's role was nevertheless crucial. There were anarchist women, mostly Italian, in the movement and they respected Agnes, but most of the auxiliary women wanted a "leader." Entrusted with leadership, she was willing to accept that responsibility. Inevitable comparisons with Mother Jones—there were national news stories about "another Mother Jones"—are only roughly apt. She was not perceived as a mother, which would have been odd in any case, at age forty with hardly a trace of gray; "older sister" would not be far wrong.

She was educated and knowledgeable, an experienced organizer, not in awe of men, confident in her abilities. She understood working-class women, knew the lives of coalfield women. She didn't put on airs. She also had the guts to face danger, to walk in where men feared to tread. She was a highly effective "rabble-rouser," a phrase that proletarian radicals in those days applied to themselves defiantly, for they identified themselves as rabble. She could work up a crowd. At the same time she was teaching, always teaching, she had never really stopped being a teacher. (It is understandable that one of her close colleagues among the men remembered her, with the fallibility of "oral history" decades after the fact, as a "school marm" who had come to help out in the strike!) She possessed, in sum, a "natural" authority not based on office. As president, she also occupied a position of power, a hierarchical form of authority (which I distinguish from "natural" authority) from which she could claim to speak for the auxiliary's (perhaps) ten thousand members, and in doing so she could count on the support of an executive board that included several highly capable women.[66]

Agnes used this authority and this power to press the idea of the auxiliary to its limit. The auxiliary idea was by no means new. In the early twenties the *Illinois Miner* reprinted an article by Alice Henry, of the Women's Trade Union League, in which were mentioned, among others, auxiliaries of machinists and postal workers and of several railway unions, as well as a few in the coalfields. The majority were merely social organizations, lodges, but certain auxiliaries had recently been prominent in strikes both on the picket line and in publicizing strikers' grievances. Henry proposed going further: "Why not grant her ["the woman"] a say in the calling of a strike, in its settlement or calling-off? The women's auxiliaries seem to offer a way to reach women for just such expression of opinion."[67] Chiefly through force of circumstances, Agnes was found claiming for women not only consultation, which is what Henry seems to have been suggesting, but a kind of partnership.

It would be wrong to expect, in action in emergencies—in what was, within its bounds, a "revolutionary situation"—a perfect coherence of ideas. But I believe that an argument can be made for women's auxiliaries, in their time, similar to that which I offered in chapter 3 in connection with Agnes's claim of a place for housewives in "the labor movement." That argument presupposed a "class" conception of the labor movement, rather than a wage-earner conception. In the coalfields, very few wives worked for wages. It can be held that in hiring and paying miners the coal companies were at the same time hiring and paying for the services of the women who kept the houses and sustained the households. By that reasoning, the women had an "authority of interest," a powerful form of authority if backed by an "authority of competence." In fact, Henry's argument amounts to just about that:

> Women have always voluntarily or involuntarily played an indispensable part in the general labor movement, and in backing labor policies, as directed and carried out by men, for men's organizations. In every wage cut it is the woman at home who pays a large proportion of the price in an empty coal box, a shortage of milk for the baby, of clothes and of shoes for the children and herself. If there is an eviction, it is not the man alone who is turned out into the street.
>
> . . . If the woman at home has to pay so dearly, and if not only submission and endurance, but sympathy and active cooperation are expected of her, then why not grant her a say?[68]

The very idea of the auxiliary belongs, quite obviously, to a period when the two wage-earner family, especially in one-industry towns, was a rarity. (And no women worked in the mines!) The true importance of the auxiliary is the self-actualization that many women experienced through participation in it.

Agnes's motivation was certainly not abstractly idealistic. The counterweight to the working out of her dream of women's emergence was intense identification, empathy, always easy for her, and all the easier here because men in Amelia's family were among those who had reluctantly, bitterly gone back to work when the first strike in the south was broken and the Mulkeytown March had failed to rescue it—and were among those who answered the strike call in March and never worked in the mines again. A son-in-law of Amelia's, an impassioned union man, couldn't stand those months in between, when he was in his own eyes a scab. Amelia wrote to Agnes of his cursing the linoleum he was laying in his home: scab linoleum bought with scab money by a scab.[69] (But one-man strikes didn't make sense so long as it was possible that the other men would come 'round—that was the accepted view.) If Agnes needed another symbol of what she was fighting for, it was right in her own family. The fact that her older sister's family was stubbornly loyal to the United Mine Workers— or was it loyalty to the Peabody Coal

Company?—must have intensified, through the pain and anger she felt about it, her identification with the Progressive movement.

Agnes shared the hope of the left-wingers that this local struggle would contribute to a wider sense of solidarity and to that learning through experience for which idealists of the labor movement always hoped. By "coming out of the kitchen," to which, along with the church, Hitler was just then consigning German women, women would begin a new life, something that women's suffrage might seem to have promised. Of course they were not all by any means the Joan of Arcs that she claimed them to be, and she knew that; she knew that many were uncomfortable with the role in which she cast them. When it was all over, one of her strong supporters wrote her a letter of highest praise: that Agnes had again and again urged women to do for themselves what they knew they couldn't, which they discovered, those who tried, that they could.

If Agnes hoped, as I believe she did, to help build a movement of women that would cease to need her, there was also something else going on, the opposite of which would be amazing. She enjoyed the applause of audiences, her role at center-stage, her role as leader, this "trailblazing" venture, this realization of an army of women. She always liked to be at the center of conversation, and her conversation was sometimes a continuous sentence hard to interrupt. As early as her description of the convention that elected her, the first-person singular is obtrusive. Among the ten thousand at Springfield she was not one of the ten thousand, she was the focal point. She would lead the singing, she would make the big speech, she would write the petition, she would lead the delegation to the governor, she and Tom tore up those "too-radical" placards. It is true that she was not preempting space; it was created for her and if she had refused or vacated it, either she would have prepared the way, made herself dispensable, as she hoped, or there would be no point at which the sight-lines of those thousands of women intersected. At every natural opportunity she tried to push others forward. But the inspirational speaker, who can't even meet all the demands for her appearance and who brings essentially the same message wherever she goes, risks being convinced by the rhetoric her audience expects. I cannot say that Agnes was exceptionally vulnerable to such intoxication, or impervious to it.

These remarks, it may be evident, come from an anarchist perspective on authority, power, and organization, a perspective in which power is the root evil, truth is something of which each of us has a part, and consensus informally arrived at should be the goal. But it is also a perspective that has affinities both with a radical populism and, more clearly, with a feminism that recognizes that freedom from male domination is of slight significance if women succceed only in inserting themselves, some of them, into the power structures. Given the steadily increasing efforts of the Progressive union officials to isolate her, and given the expectations of her constituency, Agnes made the best compromises on these issues that she could envisage; foremost in her mind was the question of what could be done to rescue the Progressive Miners' cause from defeat.

Sister Katie

The strength of the auxiliary, of course, was in the coal towns. Agnes could have a role only because of the presence and activity of strong women who were inspirations in their localities. Some scores, perhaps some hundreds of local leaders, and others neither leaders nor followers, created the base from which and for which Agnes could speak and act and achieve influence. She knew it and she loved and prized these women—"trailblazers" she liked to call them. Catherine DeRorre will have to stand for others in various degrees her like. I knew her only slightly, visited her Du Quoin home on only one or two occasions, in times of quiet in that strike field, heard her speak, and have read her letters to Agnes. But for those who knew her even slightly, she was a famous person.

All the auxiliary women were "sisters" (as union men were "brothers"), and there were at least a couple of "Mothers," but only, to my knowledge, one "Sister."[70] Down south, in multi-ethnic Du Quoin, where a large number of blacks worked in Peabody's Majestic mine, Katie was the soul of the strike. As auxiliary board member her territory included the whole of Egypt.

Katie had come from Italy as a small child; she didn't have Agnes's schooling or experience in the labor movement or exposure to the world of intellectuals (to the world of socialist miners, however). In her early letters to Agnes she had trouble with grammar and spelling and she had to learn to speak in public. She was not an orator, she spoke what she felt, spoke it with passion; so she was, in fact, an orator. Her genius was to create a sense of community by her person and by her actions. Not that she was in the least "soft," as the "Good Samaritan" appellation, sometimes added, might suggest. She was a picket-line fighter, though a very small woman. And she could be hard: she regarded with contempt the men who had sworn never to work another day under King John and, when defeat became final, tried to get their jobs back, as none of her family or friends did.

A photograph from 1935 shows the old mill in which Katie and her friends were maintaining a soup kitchen, continuous from the strike days. At least a couple of hundred people, including many children, have posed in front of the mill for the photograph (there are "jobs" and "food" placards). In his eulogy at Katie's funeral in 1960, Gerry Allard remarked: "You will see in this picture the small faces of Negro children. Katie and her friends fed them too, and when it was suggested that social mixing the black kids with the white ones would be offensive to certain people and besides it just wasn't done in Southern Illinois, at that time, Katie dismissed this nonsense with a scoff and one scoff from Katie was more effective than a hundred sneers."[71] Yes, Katie had a marvelous scoff indeed.

In a letter to me ten years after the event, Agnes wrote about the origins of that soup kitchen. This was in the spring of 1933 when there was concern that the Peabody Coal Company might create racial divisions among the strikers at its big Majestic mine at Du Quoin. Racism was ubiquitous in Illinois; even in the central part of the state, "niggers out by sundown" was posted or understood in many towns. To "normal" white racism had been added, long before, the labor racism of "nigger" = "scab" engendered by the importation of blacks as strikebreakers in the early years of the union at Virden, at Pana, at Carterville, and at Zeigler. But for Agnes and Katie, practicality and principle coincided. The Thyra Edwards of Agnes's story was a young black woman, a Brookwood student, recommended by Tippett, who was preparing for work in the labor movement, with which she already had experience.

I sent for Thyra Edwards to help among the womenfolk of the Negro miners. . . . Of course ever since the mine owners, in 1898, had brought southern Negroes in as strikebreakers, the UMWA had taken in colored miners with absolutely no discrimination. But the color line was drawn in school and church and restaurants. . . . Thyra had landed in St. Louis from the east, without having eaten a bite. All along her trip she had been told she could eat in the kitchen, which she would not. When she and I took the bus south, a white woman and a colored woman traveling together had been unheard of.[72]

Then came the day when Katie

arranged for the colored women to meet the distinguished guest at her home. They stood back at first. Were very polite as they greeted her. They never dreamed that they were to sit down at Katie's big table, and when Katie announced that we were all to have coffee, they didn't move from their chairs in the livingroom. Katie quickly sensed it and told them, "Come on in, all of you and sit down, there's no white folks and colored folks here, we're all just folks" and then they fitted into the new pattern.

And then the gala affairs. Entertainments at the union hall, children's programs, women's programs, utilizing talent of both colored and white. And then Katie's famous Soup Kitchen. She had got an old empty house, got it heated up with a couple of old stoves the men had dragged in from god-knows-where, and then the Women's Auxiliary had sent committees canvassing the grocers for food donations and the countryside for milk, the men had built tables and benches of rough boards and the women decorated the place. Katie let it be known, by visits to public schools, colored and white, that any child in the community was welcome to a good hot meal at noon.

I'll always have that picture in my mind, the day Katie sent for me to pay them a visit, and I beheld her handiwork. When we arrived together, the children were all at their meal. Such a thing had never happened in that region before. No Jim Crow rows, no Jim Crow tables, just a lot of children eating together, perfectly natural, as though it were not a new experience.[73]

As they went in, Agnes noticed two white kids, "obviously hostile," in the back yard.

I instantly thought it was a case of PMA vs. UMWA but it wasn't. On the back porch a white woman and a colored woman were handling milk cans. When I asked what was wrong, the white woman said, "They want to eat here, but they want to eat on their own terms. They said they wouldn't eat with dirty nigger kids, and I told them we didn't have any dirty nigger kids here, that nobody eats here unless they've got clean face and hands and good manners. Just look at them." And they were a sight. When I suggested that they be given a chance to wash up, she was uncompromising. She said it would take a powerful lot of scrubbing ever to get them as clean as the nice little colored children inside, and besides they were trouble makers. So she ostracized them! I was thinking to myself how, only a short time before, had the question of color line been put before this woman, she would have said that she was for everybody having their rights but that colored people should keep their place.

Of course, on the side of this social progress was the influence of strong personalities. . . . Katie was absolutely free of racial bias and her heart was in what she was doing. Thyra was an educated, cultured person of rare charm. The community had never before seen a colored person like her. But through her they came to see the talents of her people in the community. They were fascinated by the sort of thing the colored people had been doing in their school and church which they reproduced in the social affairs of the auxiliary. It wasn't long before everyone was joining in the spirituals.[74]

It deprives Katie of no honor to say that there have been many such women, unknown to history, in the mining fields of many countries.

A Kind of Victory

During the late summer and fall the campaign against Agnes accelerated. The only victory she could win now was a moral victory. The *Progressive Miner* remained closed to her and her friends. The paper was filled with plenty of false hope that the N.R.A. would give the Progressive union a break; this was less, I judge, conscious deception than utter lack of political sense. The editor of the auxiliary section, herself not a member, followed the instructions of the new editor, a man whose background included service as a "provisional" officer for Lewis during the latter's earlier effort to take over the Illinois district. Not entirely without grounds did Agnes in a number of letters attribute attacks on her to "John Lewis agents in our ranks."[75] Without the *Miner* it became difficult for her to keep in touch with auxiliaries, now eighty-five in number, scattered over more than a score of counties and more than two hundred miles north to south of Illinois prairie.

On Labor Day, in a mining town near the union's Gillespie headquarters, the first anniversary of the P.M.A. was celebrated.

Agnes was the only "Red" invited. "The Sheriff of the county, in his speech, made a vicious attack on the Auxiliary President who preceded him on the program."[76] In that county, at least, the "law" was on the side of the union, but not of "the Reds." Agnes was now fighting for her honor; there was not much else left to fight for. The strikes were lost, although they would continue nominally so that the union's appeals to the N.R.A. Labor Board would not be without substance.

I pass now to the ninth of October, when Agnes, just returned from the Harrisburg battle zone, gave a report to Belleville's Mother Jones auxiliary post and an interview with Charles Swart of the *East St. Louis Journal.* Four days earlier there had been a gun-battle at one of the Peabody mines in the Harrisburg region, where Agnes had once served her apprenticeship as journalist. Initially, Saline County had remained with the old union like the rest of Egypt; early in 1933 the miners had "gone Progressive." The strike was solid but the county authorities, who had refused to allow the importation of strikebreakers, had finally yielded to pressures. Now the state militia had been brought in, "to restore order." "More hell."[77]

The campaign against Agnes was getting dirty. At the meeting of the Belleville auxiliary, she would certainly have had to refute malicious rumors, published in the union's official organ, that she and Gerry Allard were advocating secession from the Progressives and formation of a third union. "Of course these are only reports" from Indiana and Ohio, the anonymous author of the page one lead article had written.[78] There was something else about which she may have preferred not to speak with Swart that she would not have withheld from her auxiliary sisters. That news she told of in a letter written that very day to an auxiliary friend, president of the "Pat Ansboury" chapter in a town near Mt. Olive.

"I wonder if you know what the Mt. Olive Memorial committee has done. Both Pat Ansboury and I have received letters telling us that our speaking engagements have been canceled."[79] This is the Mt. Olive and this the annual Memorial (three days hence) from which, the year before, "in the moonlight of that October night, a long caravan of determined women moved northward into Christian County." Exclusion of "left wingers" from platforms and from the union's official organ had for some time been union policy; not

yet, however, had the auxiliary's president been barred from speaking.

> I have just come back from Harrisburg. . . . I spoke in the Harrisburg
> Auxiliary and woman after woman got up and told me how certain
> P.M.A. men had tried to poison them against me. It was plain to be seen
> that the president [of the auxiliary] had been poisoned against me, all the
> time pretending to be so true to me, but the rank and file of the women
> were not. Perhaps you don't know it, but they [the P.M.A. officials] have
> already got the officers of our State Auxiliary picked out for the
> women. . . . They pay the expenses of certain women to go around and
> speak in order to knock me and others whom they think might be
> running for state offices in the Auxiliary. The women all know that I am
> in for only one term and I have told them over and over that under no
> circumstances would I consent to any change in the constitution in order
> to run me again. . . . I cannot spare the time or the strength any longer
> than this one year. My health is already giving way. . . . But I will not
> permit these enemies of our Union to push me aside. I will serve my term
> out and do my duty to the end. . . . I have neglected my family and
> home and neglected myself. I have put this Union and the Auxiliary
> above everything else in the world, even my own child. And now certain
> people try to brand me as a traitor.[80]

She was going to do her duty to the end, and part of that duty would
be to tell the auxiliary women the truth about the events of the past
year. But she was not going to do that by means of the capitalist
press, no matter how sympathetic Charles Swart may have been.
She continues:

> It made certain people green-eyed when they saw the friends I had at
> that [October 1st Gillespie mass-] meeting and they know that they can't
> down my arguments with facts. They know I tell the truth and that I
> believe the rank and file have a right to know what is going on. That is
> why they are trying to throttle me.
>
> Well, if those Virden martyrs and Old Mother Jones and General
> Bradley could break their bonds of clay on this October 12th, and look
> about them and see the real militant fighters being crucified, you can
> imagine what they would say. If Mother Jones were alive, these same
> people would be against her, for she certainly told the truth and let the
> chips fall where they may.
>
> . . . . Well, Mary, you will see me fighting the battles of the workers
> when some of these people are forgotten. My name has been before the
> public and before the workers for more than twenty years and nothing

that any of these jealous-hearted enemies can do, will stand in my way. I
will go marching on, always and forever with the workers.[81]

She had received too much adulation, now too much hate, and the
attacks were getting to her. Publicly, to Charles Swart, she must
deny, because of her responsiblities as auxiliary president, that the
spirit of this movement was vanishing. But she was not through yet.

That women were being "poisoned" against her was no delusion;
she was the target of all shafts, for of the left-wingers only she
retained any power. She had been scrupulous not to sabotage the
union, while insisting on her right to criticize. For months her
triumphs had been the negative triumphs of self-vindication, of
receiving resolutions of support from local auxiliaries. She was hurt
to the quick and denying her Mt. Olive on October 12 was an act of
meanness. But it was also, in truth, an act of fear, for a "quitter"
Agnes was not, and she could move an audience, both by skill and
by sincerity, if that audience was not already convinced to hate her.

The tongue that lashed John Lewis could lash these less powerful
people. The day of the interview was October 9. Next day, she
would be speaking in Chicago. On the twelfth she would speak at
Virden, close by Mt. Olive (normally she would have spoken at
both places); the sheriff and his deputies would make sure that left-
wingers made no trouble at Mt. Olive. But on the eleventh Agnes
would be at Staunton, Ed's old home town, only a few miles from
Mt. Olive and a few more from the union's headquarters at Gillespie. At Staunton there would be an "emergency conference,"
called by the auxiliary board, of delegates from all the strike-field
auxiliaries. "They have even tried to prevent the Staunton conference," she wrote to Rudolph.[82] This was her counterattack and
vindication, and the reason, I suspect, why she was denied Mt.
Olive. She wanted these women to know the truth. The Progressive
Miners' president had accepted invitation to attend and he would
not be able to deny successfully that his policies, which had failed at
every turn, offered no hope for salvage of the strikes. The women
were going to see that Agnes Burns Wieck had not betrayed them.

In her Annual Report, Agnes wrote: "The Auxiliary was in grave
danger of being split by the false propaganda."

The Staunton conference gave the strikers' wives the truth about the
"left wing" and compelled President Pearcy to give these women a

report on how the strike was to be brought to a successful conclusion. To the dismay of the conference, Pearcy said a referendum would not settle the strike. And yet he had been advocating a referendum from the beginning. He said the Progressive case had gone to the NRA board. He gave the women no hope of success under the NRA, yet for months he had held out hope from the NRA. To all questions and suggestions of help from the Auxiliary, Pearcy shook his head. If the NRA failed us, he said our only recourse would be through the courts.[83]

Agnes was establishing the record.

When the second convention met in Springfield for three days, November 2 through 4, 221 delegates were present. Now Agnes could answer her critics directly. Her spirit had plummeted. Now it soared, for she could fight in the open. Her emotions resolved themselves.[84] About the convention it is best to go back to Agnes's letter to Tippett, quoted early in this chapter.

> The convention. Oh, how you would have reveled in the brilliant discussion of the women who have been developed this past year. But that contemptible gang gave us some stormy sessions and all but threw the end into a riot. That was their purpose, the despicable cowards, ganging outside the convention hall and using either guns or back fire to throw the women into a panic. Women did faint. But I held the gavel to the end, Tom, and won on every point of policy and held a big majority at the end.
>
> The militants could have held the leadership but my strategy was to prevent the split which they had planned, in case they lost, and also I wanted to throw complete responsibility upon that gang.
>
> . . . Some of my close friends were inclined to be critical at first but when I explained, they were convinced I had done the right thing.
>
> I am publishing a pamphlet history—our First Annual Report. Therein I show the tragedy of this Union. Now the cowards will shout traitor louder than ever, if this is possible—they have gone into the strike zones and told the women I had betrayed them, and women went home from meetings heart broken over it all. Damn them, the dirty cowards, they have wanted to see the strikers break ranks, to get the strike off their hands.[85]

So ends the first page of the letter. The continuation is missing from Agnes's files.

Agnes had turned defeat into a kind of victory. A month earlier, she seems still to have thought of Ruth Besson of the Taylorville field, her vice president and good friend, who would have been a splendid choice, as a possible successor, with Katie perhaps in Ruth's position. Now, at Agnes's urging, all her friends declined nomination. That the "men's union" would disown the auxiliary, if it could not control it, and charter a new one, was a virtual certainty. A parade of Progressive officials appeared on the opening day to warn the women that they must be more cooperative with the union.[86] It was alleged, truly I believe, that a hall was reserved for a rump convention, in case the "Reds" retained control of the organization. Did Agnes want to destroy what she could not continue to control? Questions about motives are hard to answer but I'm fairly sure that the answer is no. Disturbing, however, is Agnes's declaration that the strategy is "my" strategy, "I" had done the right thing. The last word on this point, I believe, is that personalization was, from the standpoint of power, a source of power and perhaps the only way in which Agnes could have endured all those "appalling" events.

Agnes's First Annual Report (the precedent was not followed) is of an altogether different tone. It is presented as the report of the officers. Agnes is referred to as "your president" or as "the Auxiliary president" and the president is no more conspicuous than a history of that year calls for. Here she transcends the self-centeredness.

Of the twenty-five-page report, Tippet wrote, accurately: "It isn't like a convention report at all. It is a pamphlet, cleverly illustrated and written as dramatically and as moving as the actual drama itself was."[87] It must have been something of a collective effort but the style is Agnes's, at its strongest. On the cover, a woman in auxiliary uniform, her scarf (it would surely be red) flying, strides across the foreground, holding high the placard "Women's Auxiliary P.M. of A."; in the background is a mine tipple; looking away from the viewer, the woman must be calling out to strikebreakers somewhere outside the incompletely framed linoleum-cut; she is holding the line. The frontispiece is a portrait of "Agnes Burns Wieck, Belleville, Illinois"; the artist, I'm not sure who, has caught the essentials of Agnes's face, strong jaw and dark eyebrows that emphasize a gaze that is directed at the viewer and carries through into a distance. On the title page, in black borders, were the twelve names of "our martyred dead," including the

auxiliary's Emma Cummerlato. Inside were illustrations of mo-
ments in the history.

Through this report, Agnes wanted everyone, not just the
women of Illinois, to understand the kind of movement this army of
women had been. Set against my knowledge of that year, my
knowledge of Agnes, and such documents as I have available, it is a
good and lively picture; partisan of course, simplistic in its counter-
posing of "rank and file" and "that little group who now dominate
our men's union," but she is thinking of the future and of lessons to
be carried forward. I have quoted from it freely throughout this
chapter not only because it expresses the way she wanted the
auxiliary to be viewed but because she felt a responsibility to
"history." I assume that the reader has corrected mentally for
partisanship.

Agnes sees this movement—she does not say it but neither does
she deny it—as now a part of history, gone. So the report's conclusion, above the names of Agnes Burns Wieck, Ruth Besson, and
Celina Burrell: "Deep in our hearts are the wounds inflicted during
this memorable year's struggle. We can only look to yesterday as a
road that we have traveled. From the yesterdays we extract the
invaluable experiences which steel us in our determination and
understanding, that we may perpetuate those ideals we inherited,
not a year ago, but from centuries of struggle through which the
common people have sought emancipation."[88]

In the report, Agnes's deep feeling show through, deeper than
"But who can say that we women have not kept the faith?"[89] (In the
quotations following, my italics.) At Taylorville, more than a year
earlier, before the state auxiliary was formed, "The women *hurled
their defiance* at the military power."[90] And then, at a last scene of
militant action, and one more death, in Springfield, just a few
weeks before the convention: "As ever [the rank and file, men and
women] *hurled defiance* at their oppressors, even with the Federal
government now against them. And they will rise again to *hurl that
same defiance*. For the very conditions that gave rise to this rebellion
still challenge their very right to live."[91] I would hesitate to say that
rebellion, the hurling of defiance, was not, for Agnes, a metaphysical as well as a social principle, though she would of course have
laughed at the "metaphysical" interpretation. I am mindful that
Agnes re-told often, every time with pride, that in the St. Louis

hospital where she brought me into the world, I yelled by far the loudest of all the new born; not infrequently this was glossed as my protest against coming into this cruel world. And in this rotten world we have to "steel ourselves," as the women of '97, of whom she wrote in her diary, "steeled their hearts";[92] for Agnes a basic metaphor, not surprisingly, for steel was certainly not her first nature.

Farewell, Illinois

We were broke, dead broke, and utterly without prospects. Ed couldn't hope to get a job in industry. Labor unions might be glad to get someone with Agnes's abilities and experience, but not a radical agitator with a record of association with a union outside the American Federation of Labor fold and enemy to John Lewis. But then, quite unexpectedly, we got a break: Ed was offered a one-year appointment in the Industrial Studies department of the Russell Sage Foundation in New York City, beginning January 1, 1934. We left the farm, my mother and I, and moved into a spacious flat on West Main Street near the center of Belleville. Between road trips Ed stayed at a residential hotel near the Foundation. In June, when it was pretty clear that he would be reappointed, my mother and I got on the bus to New York, leaving our furniture behind for shipment once we found a place to live. Agnes did not want to leave Illinois, where there was plenty that needed to be done. She understood that it was the right environment for her. But it was important that *Ed* have a job and the family be together.

We never returned to Illinois, except for visits. Before the scene shifts, there are certain events to be recorded.

• *November 1933.* Following the second auxiliary convention the Illinois Communists lose no time in denouncing Agnes Burns Wieck, betrayer of the masses.[93] The author of the leaflet, which gives a Belleville address, is a master of the vocabulary of Third Period Stalinism. "The sleek Socialist Party auctioneer" handed the women's auxiliaries to P.M.A. president Pearcy "just as if they were a bunch of cattle, . . . in a yellow socialist man-ner. . . . Wieck gave the Auxiliary to Pearcy just like the Ger-man socialists gave power to Hitler, to kill and maim the German

masses. . . . Every miner's door must be shut in the face of this
latest betrayal."

- *January 1934.* On the fourteenth of January dies Patrick Henry
Burns, "74 years old, veteran Williamson County coal miner and
father of Agnes Burns Wieck, militant labor leader."[94] The
Reverend Douglas Anderson, of Illiopolis, state chairman of the
Illinois Socialist Party, is "in charge" of the funeral. "Mr. Burns
died from a paralytic stroke Sunday night." For some while his
worn-out body hadn't been working. And he had been too poor,
near the end, to afford a regular supply of chewing tobacco. "He
had spent sixty years in the mine," Agnes would tell a New York
City reporter, "and he didn't leave enough to be buried on. They
took up a collection from the CWA men on the road—men
getting $10 a week—to get enough for his funeral."[95]

- The United Mine Workers of America meets in convention at
Indianapolis and John Lewis expresses pleasure at its negative
action on a proposal to organize women's auxiliaries of the
union.

- *February 1934.* Agnes is in New York City, at Town Hall, to speak
at a meeting of the newly formed American Workers Party, its
central figure A. J. Muste. A founder and for a dozen years
educational director of Brookwood Labor College, Muste, who
believed that in this time of world crisis Brookwood should raise
the level of its involvement in the labor struggles of the day, lost
out on a key vote (he had Tom Tippett's support) and saw no
choice but to leave.[96] Earlier a Christian pacifist, he is now
speaking the language of revolution. On the day of the meeting,
the *World-Telegram* gives two columns, interspersed with dramatic quotations from her Annual Report, to an interview with
Mrs. Wieck. "Tiny, dark-eyed, composed," writes Sutherland
Denlinger, "42, although she doesn't look it." In a "red skirt,
red and black sweater, fur coat"—but "the coat isn't really mine,
just borrowed it. . . . Called 'The New Mother Jones' by some
of her followers, Mrs. Wieck, whose auxiliary post in Belleville is
named after that Amazonian warrior, feels that she is not entitled
to that honor. 'If I were as free as Mother Jones—if I didn't have a
family—I might raise more Hell. All that she needed, all that she
had, was a hatred—I have that hatred.'" The solution for the
miners? Public ownership, but "we know that government own-

ership under a capitalist government would put us under a bureaucracy—we don't want to be on a level with the poor post office employes." The Progressive Miners? If she breathed a criticism of the union, it is off the record. Indeed, what Denlinger quotes she knows to be flatly false: "We are going to fight on. We are going to get that referendum." There are things you don't say to the capitalist press.[97]

•*March 1934.* The new auxiliary board member for the Belleville region and the new state secretary-treasurer come to a business meeting of the Mother Jones Post. Having no access to the auxiliary column of the *Progressive Miner,* the Belleville women mail to all the branches a mimeographed news letter describing the occasion. "Right in our meeting," the president of the Belleville chapter wrote, "a state officer of the Auxiliary threatened that charters would be revoked! Just like John Lewis." That wasn't all. The new state secretary "actually struck a member in the face! She struck the very woman who had led the 10,000 Auxiliary women, singing 'Solidarity Forever.' Mrs. Wieck did not strike her back." The newsletter also notes: "Many of our members have joined the Educational Classes now being conducted by Mrs. Wieck and open not only to Auxiliary women but other workers' wives interested in labor education."[98]

•*May 1934.* A leaflet advertises a May Day celebration in Springfield. Agnes heads the list of speakers. Also: Gerry Allard, Jack Battuello, Joe Burrell, Pat Ansboury, Catherine DeRorre, the old left-wing crowd. And Ralph Chaplin, of Wobbly fame, author of "Solidarity Forever." What orators![99]

•*June 1934.* Muste comes to Belleville. He has been in Toledo, where the "Musteites" have been very active in the Auto-Lite strike, the taking-off point for the 1930s surge of rank-and-file militancy that will lead to the unionization of the auto industry. A.J. is traveling with Hank Mayer and Jimmy Cross, young men active in organizing the unemployed. They stop to talk with pickets at a local plant that is shut down by a strike. Everything was quiet but, Muste wrote many years later, "Three policemen came over to us, asked who we were, looked at our C.P.L.A. [Conference for Progressive Labor Action] membership cards, which were red, in the fashion of those days, and announced that we were under arrest." Two charges: vagrancy and, far more serious, violation of Illinois's criminal syndicalism law. The preliminary hearing is a circus as a couple of hundred local people, including of course a large number of women from Belleville's auxiliary, jam the courtroom and a St. Louis defense lawyer succeeds in showing that these poor Belleville cops not only don't know anything about constitutional rights but are pretty vague about who Thomas Jefferson was. More to the point, A.J., an ordained minister, testifies that he is absolutely opposed to violence. But the judge thinks that a very good case has been made on the criminal syndicalism charge; the three are released on bail and a year will go by before the charges are dropped. In his memoirs, A.J. will not forget to give particular credit to Agnes Burns Wieck for her role in rallying the defense.[100]

•*November 1934.* The third convention of the auxiliary meets. From New York Agnes sends a greeting. It is known that she is ill (were I not in a hospital she would be). By a roar of "No" that drowns out the "Ayes" the convention votes down a motion to send an expression of sympathy. The auxiliaries, greatly diminished in membership, have with few exceptions quickly become social organizations. They are no longer a threat to anybody, not to the Peabody Coal Company, or to Lewis, nor are they an education for their members. Agnes cannot but have been hurt but the auxiliary in her memory was not *this* auxiliary. From "her" auxiliary she preserved a precious gift: a quilt, in natural white cotton, 72 inches by 80 inches, with a pattern of 3-inch red squares and a border of alternating red and white triangles. In large letters (I preserve the spelling of the original), TO OUR MILITANT LEDER AGNES WIECKS FROM MILITANT ADMIRERS OCTOBER 1 1933. The names of twenty-four women, sewn in, are spaced out over it. All the lettering is red. I recognize most of the names—"Reds" from the Gillespie area, including my Aunt Mayme's daughter Myrtle and Irene Allard and Bette Norman.

Beyond the New York Horizon

The reason we had moved to New York, one could say, was that Tom Tippett, determined to find a job for Agnes or Ed, had knocked on the right door.

The Russell Sage Foundation had a small Industrial Studies Department. Its director was Mary Van Kleeck, a Smith College graduate, member of the National Society of Colonial Dames, very much a lady in voice and carriage, and a social worker in a radically broadened sense of the term; perhaps "social economist" would be most accurate. Miss Van Kleeck had been connected with the foundation nearly all her working life. Women in industry were her first concern and during the war she had headed the forerunner of the Women's Bureau of the U.S. Department of Labor. She was no stranger to the coal industry; her *Miners and Management,* which argued for the socialization of natural resources, would be coming off the presses shortly.[1] Acquainted with Ed's writings and well informed about Agnes Burns Wieck, she agreed that these "soldiers of the revolution" should not be left in Illinois to starve.

Even for foundations time were hard, but Van Kleeck could think of an assignment for Ed that the trustees would endorse and for which he was eminently qualified. "His first task," the foundation's history says, "was to observe the operation of the National Industrial Recovery Administration in the coal mines and in certain other industries.[2] Ed received a one-year appointment, subject to annual renewal, as "research associate." After three years of unemployment, a $3,000 salary was a fortune; it wouldn't take long to pay Belleville back rent and store bills. Ed got a kick out of the fact that the foundation's endowment, and hence his salary, derived

175

from a fortune amassed by one of the most larcenous of nineteenth-century "robber barons." Philanthropy, which his widow took up in his name, was not Russell Sage's idea of a good time.

The day that my mother and I arrived, my dad took me way up in the Empire State Building—still very new, it was the "Empty State" in those depression years—for the magnificent view of the city and environs but also to philosophize about the tiny insects, so they seemed, on the sidewalks below. Not only were people diminished: on those streets no trees could grow, other than the stubborn gingko, imported because of its indifference to the noxious fumes.

Agnes didn't like apartment living. One of her articles in the twenties had contrasted, to cellular apartment houses where near-neighbors are mere mailbox names, the community that was possible, and sometimes realized, in a neighborhood of individual homes. Indeed, my parents' first thought, defeated by commuting distance, was of a New Jersey small town. Agnes found instead an apartment in Flushing, well within city limits but still a town at the end of a subway line, still bearing traces of its original Dutch settlement. This was our eighth "permanent" address, which we kept for two years.

For me the city was a wonder place—the Illinois prairie and the town of Belleville, with its "slow, poky people," I let go willingly. The tall buildings, busy streets, swift pace, the subways and els, the rivers and docks and great bridges, the multitude of languages, I loved immediately. Nothing excited me more than Union Square, then, practically speaking, Red Square, where at any time circles of listeners and hecklers surrounded impassioned polemicists skilled in merciless dialectic and in twisting their opponent's arguments into unrecognizability. I would surely have taken a different view of the city if my father didn't have work; the men in the square were a few of the great army of people who had no jobs to go to. New York was a city of poverty and of homeless drifting people, but except for gangsters furiously exterminating one another, it was a quiet city, where those who had anything to steal were careful to remain invisible. We were mighty fortunate.

Agnes, of course, was drawn to the cultural and political life of the city. If Manhattan was where my father worked when not on the road, for her as well as for her son it was a centripetal force. After caring for me in my recuperation from a frightening appendicitis in the fall of 1934, and after undergoing a deferred, at last affordable, surgery for hemorrhoids she had been living with too long, she was eager to become active again.

My memories of this period are revived by reading in Doctorow's *World's Fair* the story of a boyhood appendicitis; the setting is different but the drama is much the same. Against five o'clock traffic, with my mother, from Flushing, over the Queensborough Bridge, into Manhattan to the old French Hospital—treated as "a child"—"just an examination"—put under ether—"in the nick of time"—"fifty-fifty." From here on Agnes worried constantly about my health, her confidence shaken by learning that she had tried exactly the wrong remedies and had not taken seriously enough what were probably warning signs. But she was always a worrier and self-accuser.

Ed's work was yielding much satisfaction and the news he brought home added to Agnes's restlessness. On his first assignment he had driven our Model A into the mountains of West Virginia to find out how the miners were faring now that Lewis's union was back. "One organizer organized 47 locals in 17 days—big locals—from 200 to 700 members each. Did he organize them? I want the rank and file of these miners to have a little credit—it belongs to them."[3] Then it was on to Akron and Cleveland and Toledo and Detroit, with reports to write about the new labor movement that was arising and especially about the rank-and-file militancy, in the absence of which laws recognizing collective bargaining would be ink on paper, that came to climax in the sit-down strikes at General Motors plants in the winter of 1936–37.

In the summer of 1936 I accompanied my father on a trip through the Pennsylvania steel regions, from Bethlehem to Pittsburgh, with a stop also in Reading at a latest-model textile mill. By then the Committee for Industrial Organization had been formed, with Lewis at its head; the Steel Workers' Organizing Committee, with Lewis's vice president Philip Murray in charge, was just taking to the field. My father enjoyed talking with the organizers, many of them Lewis's "lounge lizards" whom he knew by first name. Obviously not very busy at, or talented at, or inclined to, organizing, Lewis's men kept tabs on the Communists who were doing the arduous and hazardous work. But Ed seized every opportunity to talk with mill workers, both because he enjoyed that—he had his

own "credentials" to offset his business suit—and because he could
learn more from them, about the economics and changing production methods of the industry, than from the company managers he
interviewed. He was being paid for doing something he thoroughly
enjoyed, and was amused when visitors to the Industrial Studies
Department presumed him to be "Dr. Wieck." No publications
came from his reports, perhaps because the pace of change in that
decade was so swift that last year's events were already "history." In
the archives of the Walter Reuther Library at Wayne State University, those reports are (I am told) valuable resources for students of
industry and labor.

My father wanted nothing to do with the "Left" politics of New
York City, where the Communists were ascendant. He had high
respect for individual Communists whom he regarded as genuinely
dedicated to the labor movement—Harry Bridges for example, an
ex-Wobbly in whom he saw something of a Wobbly still—but he
regarded the leadership as harebrained. He was now an interested
spectator, not just because it befit his job; and he was a student of
Man. He had read Gibbons's *Decline and Fall of the Roman Empire*
from beginning to end and probably more than once and had drawn
many inferences. He was trying, I suppose, to see human life in the
aspect of eternity as an atheist might, and with as much humor as
possible. About a "better world" he had long had doubts. But he
had not altered his conviction that nothing is given to the lower
classes without strings attached, and that life is struggle.

A Boy's Education

In the *East St. Louis Journal* interview (October 1933) my mother
was reported as saying that her eleven-year-old son was developing
some "cynical tendencies" under the tutorship of his father.[4]
Possibly there is some paraphrase there but I don't doubt that she
was troubled by my sudden exposure to the ugly adult world. As
best I am able to recall, Agnes, probably from belief that those
realities impinge on one soon enough, had until then successfully
sheltered me. There are certain names, Matewan, Logan County,
Mingo County, that are so deep in my memory that I wonder if I
first heard them in the cradle. One of our family friends was a
native of West Virginia and adult conversations often turned in that

direction; but I knew, from early school grades, the stories of the Persian Wars and Thermopylae and Marathon and couldn't have answered a single question about the Armed March.

I remember the summer evenings on the "farm" when my mother was away, when besides studying the constellations in the big midwestern sky, my father and I sang "The Red Flag" together, and "Hallelujah I'm a Bum" and "The Big Rock Candy Mountain." And he told me about the Chicago Anarchists and Governor Altgeld; and about Elijah Lovejoy, martyr to the anti-slavery cause and to the cause of freedom of the press, murdered by a mob in the city of Alton, upriver from East St. Louis; and about the Paris Commune and the Easter Rebellion in Dublin; and about why there were wars and depressions and revolutions; and about the class struggles that had been going on since time immemorial. He also talked about how the Socialist leaders of France and Germany, after vowing to call a general strike if war were declared, had, almost every one, caved in and supported their governments. And about Jean Jaurès, leader of the French Socialists, assassinated by the "patriots" because they knew he would stand firm against the war. I who had been at age ten an admirer of Sergeant York, was learning the tradition of internationalism and anti-nationalism. I had no sense of "ethnic" identity—though my mother tended somewhat to push "Irish"—and no sense of national identity except that America was my country and the rich and the rulers of one's own country were the enemy of the poor and oppressed.

I was also a student of the *Congressional Record*, which we received by courtesy of Congressmen Karch: an "independent study" course in civics with helpful interpretation by my father, quite unlike the civics the schools taught. I heard speeches of my mother's and other "fighters" and read radical periodicals in homes we visited. Some people had a very bad dog, kept on a heavy chain, named Mussolini, and I inquired about the name. In an "Eye-talian" home I asked about a photograph which turned out to be of Sacco and Vanzetti. Gerry Allard—youthful, playful, seriously revolutionary, so small alongside those big broad-shouldered or squat powerful miners, so quick with words—fascinated me. The Springfield March, my mother's stories of her Women's Auxiliary activities, *Mill Shadows,* the labor songs, spoke to me about the world. In the opening ceremonies of the auxiliary's second convention I declaimed "Spartacus to the Gladiators," a summons to rebellion. My real life was among adults who were very angry. I was angry. Other heroes of mine were those Midwest folk heroes who were stealing, with machine guns, not in true Robin Hood fashion I was aware, what the banks had stolen; for nothing was hated more universally in those days than banks and bankers. If my mother did say "cynical," that could have been in her mind.

We were in New York City hardly more than half a year, not long before the first national student-strike against war and fascism in spring 1935, when my mother stopped to talk with some young Communists who were distributing leaflets in Flushing. I hadn't yet made friends and she thought I would like these young people. They were older than I but my head was in their world. They were sharp and to my doubts they had answers. My Communist vote in eighth grade in 1932 had been a protest vote. Now I became serious.

For my converting rather quickly to Communism, reasons are not hard to find. The Communist Party was the party of the only successful workers' revolution; it was also the party of the Chinese Red Army, whose progress I began to follow enthusiastically. Only by fascism were the capitalists able — so far — to ward off revolution. Deeply moving was the uprising in Spain in the fall of 1934, in the province of Asturias, coal miners in the vanguard against a brutally repressive dictatorship, where thousands were massacred in the aftermath of defeat. Peaceful methods were useless; class struggle was becoming overt class war. "The final conflict" must be at hand.

The book with most impact on me was John Reed's *Ten Days That Shook The World.* Lenin's pamphlet, *State and Revolution,* I interpreted quite literally, not knowing that its near-anarchist vision of the coming revolution and of socialist society had nothing in common with Leninist practice. Son of my parents, I was too much a hater of autocracy to accept the idea of party dictatorship; but I could believe, as did so many, that the U.S.S.R. was truly a "dictatorship of the proletariat," of "the masses," "the people," really a new kind of democracy whose only enemies were White Russians and rich kulaks and, of course, Trotskyites. In all this, beginning with family background, I can see something approaching inevitability, not in fine detail of course, but in the main trajectory.

On the day of the student-strike, I was on a "soapbox" in front of my school; for protection, there was a burly young fur-worker from

Manhattan. (Flushing High was unfriendly territory and I a slender young fellow far from fully back to health.) But Agnes was there too and spoke, and not merely to give me support. I joined the Young Communist League and organized a small branch of the National Students League, Communist counterpart to the Socialists' Students League for Industrial Democracy, which we N.S.L.ers held in disdain. My hours outside school were taken up, besides local meetings, with collecting money for the American League Against War and Fascism, leafleting a factory gate, attending a class in Russian at the Workers School, going to mass meetings at Madison Square Garden (usually with one or both parents) and joining fifteen or twenty thousand people in singing the Internationale and chanting slogans. Was it the times or was my conviction persuasive? On petitions to free Angelo Herndon, Negro Communist organizer in the South, I got the signatures not only of nearly all the black service employees at the Russell Sage Foundation but also plenty of signatures on the streets of Flushing. Like my mother years before, I found the world of Jewish radicalism exciting; a Jewish Communist family, with whom friendly relations continued for some years after, was a kind of second home.

About my doings, and especially my dogmatic opinions, my father remarked in a moment of exasperation, "Not yet dry behind the ears." Agnes was ambivalent—both proud and concerned. She wanted me to be a "boy," as in many ways I was; yet she wanted a son who shared her feelings about the evils of the society.

A Women's Magazine

Agnes's papers include virtually nothing from the middle thirties, as if, perhaps no "if" about it, she meant to forget. Although we did many things together—attending plays, films, public meetings— and discussed books and current events, we did not talk much about our own activities. That must have been due in part to my need to establish a certain independence; more important reasons will appear shortly.

Agnes wanted to be "in the struggle." Always a spontaneously united-front person, she was impatient with sectarian causes. But after the Seventh World Congress of the Communist International, in the summer of 1935, Communist parties everywhere began their shift to Popular Front, including political alliances with socialist parties, no longer denounced as "social fascist," and with liberal and even not-so-liberal "bourgeois" parties. That pleased Agnes. Concurrently, she was getting from Mary Van Kleeck, whose chief political activity was with the Friends of the Soviet Union, a highly laudatory picture of the Soviet system.

As Van Kleeck presented it in her *Creative America,* published in early 1936, Soviet society was an example of "a planned economy under workers' control," whose Five-Year Plans had brought harmony between industry and agriculture. The Soviet version of "scientific management," she maintained, including the "Stakhanov" version of the Taylor System so hated by American labor people, was the spontaneous initiative of Russian workers, just as it was purported to be.[5] That official descriptions of the Soviet system fit so closely with her own social vision, her ideal of rationality, no doubt made it easier for Van Kleeck to believe those claims. For skeptics like Ed, Stakhanovite "socialist competition" was simply old-fashioned speed-up. For her part, however, Agnes tried to learn everything she could about Soviet Russia—read, listened, went to Russian films—for she would have liked to believe that one-seventh of the land surface of the globe was a workers' paradise. The capitalist press, certainly, could not be expected to tell the truth.[6]

An effort to recruit the Wiecks into "the party" was indeed made. My father told of this in a letter to me ten years later in the course of reminiscing upon his several encounters with Louis Budenz, who had recently left the editorship of the *Daily Worker* to join the Catholic Church.[7] During Progressive Miner days, Louis, then a follower of A. J. Muste, had come to Illinois to try to organize the unemployed and had stayed with us a night or two.

In the fall of 1935, shortly after he abandoned Muste to join the party, Budenz was required (my father wrote) to give a series of talks to party members. "By a chain of circumstances," Ed and Agnes Wieck were present at one of these talks. "It was the one and only time I ever witnessed such a public confession of 'error.' It gave me a queer feeling to see someone talk that way about himself, especially to an audience of several hundred. He got into the Catholic Church with infinitely less self-humiliation."[8]

Soon after, Budenz invited my parents to dinner at his apartment. Besides denouncing himself, he should try to convert old acquaintances. I'm not sure who was the principal target. Both of my parents could have been very useful — Agnes as a public figure in "front" organizations and Ed as an analyst and garnerer of information. (Should I make it clear that I am *not* hinting at "recruiting for espionage"?) The other guests: Jack and Elizabeth Johnstone, not exactly second-echelon party-people. The time: very soon after Lewis had raised high the banner of industrial unionism, had broken with the A.F.L. leadership, and had formed the Committee for Industrial Organization. "That was the first and only time," my father wrote,

> that I ever had a Commie "recruiting speech" really turned on to me. Jack was there to reinforce Louis. At the time I did not know about that technique of "recruiting speeches" which are carefully designed in their general approach by the party, and open for minor adaptations to fit the subject addressed. One of the chief arguments was to get us to see that John L. Lewis was now "different"; that he could now be safely embraced. Jack was the chief orator on that point; indeed, [that was] the chief reason he was brought to the dinner, besides the fact that he had a long history as a labor organizer before the party was ever organized. Anyway all their efforts came to naught.[9]

A few months later (March 1936) a new thirty-two-page magazine, *The Woman Today,* began publication; it was the work of women, published for an audience of women, nearly all its articles written by women. High on the list of members of its advisory board appeared the name Agnes Burns Wieck. (I believe she had some part in the planning.) Like *Soviet Russia Today* and *China Today, The Woman Today* was one of the "united front" periodicals of the time. Communist policy now called for concentration on building the C.I.O. and a complementary Farmer-Labor Party on a national scale. I see no reason not to describe the magazine, similar in format and artwork, as successor to *The Working Woman,* published from April 1932 to June 1935. The latter, whose office on the ninth floor of the *Daily Worker* building I visited once with my mother, had mirrored the earlier, so-called Third Period policies of the Communist Party. For both magazines, the Soviet Union was lodestar.

So far the picture is clear enough. But my knowledge of Agnes's year and a half with *The Woman Today* is severely limited. In the spring of 1936 her course and mine began to diverge sharply. The Communists' turn to Popular Front, which delighted Agnes, affected me quite oppositely. I had enlisted under the old banners and was still a revolutionary; anything else was compromise, which I detested. I was free now to discover that the Soviet Union was not as I had imagined it, in either its past or its present. I can understand why my mother would not have wanted to talk with me about her work with the magazine, for I was practiced already in that withering sarcasm, a developed art, of which Karl Marx set a splendid example, that many young Communists seemed to acquire and not easily to lose. I gave her my views on the first "Moscow Trials," summer 1936; pointed out that all the Communists I knew voted (that fall) for Roosevelt, whose job it was to save capitalism; expressed my enthusiasm about the social revolution of anarcho-syndicalist inspiration that was taking place behind the "Loyalist" lines in Spain and my outrage about the counterrevolutionary role of the Russian government and the Spanish Communist Party. It was not Agnes's habit to dismiss my arguments on grounds of age and inexperience and she did listen; but if the word "compromise" was missing from my dictionary, in hers it appeared in boldfaced type.

Agnes's initial contribution to *The Woman Today* appeared in the third issue, May 1936, where she was introduced with the title "Editor of *The Woman Today*'s Auxiliary Department." There would be much news to report.

Steelworkers' auxiliaries were "flourishing" in the Chicago area, where Elizabeth Johnstone had organized an autoworkers' auxiliary. An Auxiliary Council in St. Louis (ten years old) was organizing a chain-store boycott in support of a warehousemen's strike and several P.M.A. auxiliaries, including Belleville's, were doing their part. The auxiliary of the Maritime Federation of the Pacific, in the Bay Area, appears to have been strong. A rather different sort of news: In the auxiliary, long established as a social organization, and lily-white, of the International Association of Machinists, a fight was under way, led by the New York Transit employees' auxiliary, to abolish its white-only rule. An Auxiliary Council, to bring together the auxiliaries in the New York City area, was being initiated by the New York Women's Trade Union League. Flint, Michigan, decisive battleground of the General Motors sit-down strike the past winter, had its Women's Emergency Brigade of four hundred women on twenty-four-hour call. Another such brigade, in Detroit, green berets their insignia, was able on short notice to mobilize two thousand women for picketing of a cigar factory in support of women strikers. And there was much more.[10]

Compared with the Progressive Miners' auxiliary of 1933, numbers in the newer and more militant auxiliaries appear to have been small. At Flint, site of four huge General Motors plants, there was massive participation of women in support of the sit-down strikers during the long siege but the auxiliary, the Emergency Brigade included, counted only eight hundred members; in other cases too the auxiliaries probably functioned as militant nuclei whose size did not at all reflect the role of women in the organizing strikes of the time. With the subsequent history of auxiliaries I am not familiar; that women's organizations based on the job-community of their husbands proved to be viable except in emergencies, or as social or benevolent organizations, I very much doubt. Agnes's hope, of course, and not hers alone, was that the auxiliaries would become means for self-education and for action on a broad range of problems.

With the December issue, the ninth, Agnes formally joined the twelve-member editorial board. Soon after, she developed plans, which were approved, for a free correspondence course, based in the magazine, open to all women. Under the heading "We Start a School," Agnes reported that the idea had "clicked." She was excited: "At the typewriter this spring, pounding the idea into form, my eye was caught by the scene outside my window. In nearby Van Cortlandt Park, winter browns were changing. Beyond the New York horizon my mind's eye caught the larger scene, the American labor movement surging with new life. In the forefront of the marching ranks of labor, I saw the determined glowing faces of young girls and mothers. *THE WOMAN TODAY* had done much to inspire and inform such women. *It must do more.*"[11]

The course would focus on the practical: "In drafting such a course, I delved into a rich experience, gained from years of organizing women in industry and wives of workers. I have answered hundreds of letters with 'what to do' questions. I know there is excellent talent among untrained women who, with more self-confidence, can develop into able writers and speakers."[12] Women associated with the magazine, or willing to help out, teachers for example, would go over the homework. The very first lesson called for a short autobiography; some of these, Agnes hoped, might be worked into articles for the magazine. But by then the magazine was announcing terrible financial problems; the June and August issues were skipped and the September issue, the last, was drastically reduced in size. One of the autobiographies did get into print in the penultimate issue: "My Life in a Steel Town," by Anna M. Dzapo of Brookville, Ohio, just the kind of piece that Agnes was hoping for.[13]

Early in Agnes's association with *The Woman Today* there had been a disturbing incident. Katie DeRorre was very active in the Illinois Workers Alliance, an organization dedicated to organizing and working in behalf of the unemployed, including many members of the Progressive Miners' union who were stranded when the strikes were lost. For that reason, and also to refute accusations that she, like Agnes Burns Wieck, was a traitor to the Progressive cause, Katie had continued to be active in the P.M.A. auxiliary. On her way home from a convention of the national Workers Alliance in Washington, D.C., Katie stopped in New York, where Agnes had arranged a *Woman Today* luncheon. Mother Bloor—Ella Reeve Bloor, a founding member of the Communist Party—"honored Katie with a ringing speech," Agnes reported. Besides women from the magazine, Tom Tippett was there, and Roger Baldwin, and also Marion Maxwell, one of the Progressive auxiliary's left-wingers, now living in New York, who for the occasion "sang songs of labor and women" in her "sweet Scottish voice."[14] But very soon after, one of the *Woman Today* editors, Margaret Cowl, reported in the *Daily Worker* that Katie, at a conference of the I.W.A., had advocated unity of the Progressives and the U.M.W., that is, return to Lewis's union. This was not only untrue but seriously damaging to Katie's efforts to get the unemployed from both unions to work together for common interests. Agnes retained, with the notation "the *Daily Worker* ignored this," a copy of Katie's letter of protest.[15] It took considerable reassurance from Agnes to persuade Katie, who did eventually write for the magazine, to risk a possibly disastrous rewriting. Perhaps coincidentally, Cowl left the editorial board with the issue at which Agnes joined it.

In the fall of 1936, before Agnes joined the board, *The Woman Today* was confronted with a feminist issue. In the September number there appeared an article, "Soviet Russia's New Family Welfare Law." The new Soviet constitution (formally adopted in December) was being acclaimed for its proclamation of sex equality. But the new law, Hannah Stone wrote, not only was unsatisfactory with respect to its provisions for divorce and alimony: it decreed the "practically complete prohibition" of abortion, the only exception being abortion to save the prospective mother from death or serious injury. The law, she said, was especially objectionable because no evidence existed of serious efforts to develop effective contraception or to provide adequate birth-control information. "The chief aim of the newer laws is to bring about an increased population growth in Russia." Stone's article was accompanied by an editorial note indicating, depending on how it is read, that the board was troubled, or that there was trouble on the board, or both. Without tremendous improvement of economic life, the note said, contraception "would not eliminate the evils of abortion," which left the implication that at worst the Soviet Union was not wrong in prohibiting an otherwise ineradicable evil.[16]

In the December issue, a month late—the first such occurrence—Margaret Sanger, not formally connected with the magazine but sympathetic to the Soviet Union, addressed the question. More effective contraception, she agreed, might not eliminate abortion but it would appear to be the way to reduce its incidence, if that was actually the government's aim. But the government, evidently, no longer had need for working women—it wanted mothers. She stated flatly: "As a feminist, I protest against any woman having children if and when she does not want them."[17] In the next issue two letters were featured. One reader couldn't see how there could possibly be anything wrong, in a socialist society, with having a child. But the other, Cheri Appel, a medical doctor who had worked in clinics in the Soviet Union, told of being disconcerted by the poor quality of contraception and lack of interest in providing birth-control information. Most galling surely, for those at whom it was aimed, was Appel's reference to the "my country right or wrong" posture of defenders of the Soviet Union. It was an especially stinging remark, given the unlikelihood of there being a member of the board who was comfortable with the law. So ended the debate, without further editorial comment.[18]

I can't identify with certainty Agnes's role in this conflict. With "my country right or wrong" she had no sympathy. I believe myself on solid ground in asserting, further, that her position was identical with or very close to that of Sanger, whose campaign for birth control was motivated by horror at abortion. Contraception, fail-safe contraception, which she pursued vigorously, was Sanger's goal. My mother, I know, hated abortion as she hated divorce. Like Sanger, whom she greatly admired, she was, in the best sense of a horribly abused term, "pro-life." I can't believe, however, and got no hints to the contrary, that she saw abortion, any more than divorce, as a crime—except, in the case of abortion, when performed by a butcher. Did she also see the new Soviet law, as critics of the regime did, in parallel to the "cannon fodder" population policies of the fascist states? Maybe not at that time, when she was still trying to see the good in the Soviet Union.

In the spring of 1937, a few months after that debate terminated, Elizabeth Gurley Flynn, who had recently joined the Communist Party and was high in its councils, no longer the "Wobbly girl" of an earlier decade, became a thirteenth member of the editorial board. Whether she came to save the magazine, or to wind it down, she would be executing a party decision. Such magazines depended heavily, of course, upon financial "angels." It would be a not unreasonable hypothesis that the magazine's financial crisis following hard upon the abortion controversy was connected with it causally. Two more issues, at two-month intervals, and the magazine was gone.

That fall, Agnes suffered a new breakdown in health. "Low blood-pressure, slow heart," low metabolism, perhaps already a thyroid condition, were the problems. "I have had to slow up and my doctor has ordered me to stay out of all activities." The prescription, if not for its medical cause, would probably have been welcome. My sense is that she felt that her name, as a militant auxiliary leader, had been what was wanted of her.

I wish, a sorry wish, that my mother had written her "united front" experience. With at least some of the women on the magazine she had enjoyed her association. In my memory certain names have resonance of that character, including Margaret Lamont, wife of Corliss Lamont of House of Morgan millions. She had come to know some of the prominent Communist women of the period and a number of the women writers, including Josephine Herbst and Mary Heaton Vorse, who were at the periphery, and she was in close touch with many of the more active women in the New York labor movement. But apart from all other reasons not to write, there was the conclusive one: she would not provide any information that could be used by any of the "Red hunt" Congressional committees, from the Dies Committee of the thirties to the post-McCarthy committees of the sixties. In our family, people who did so, Louis Budenz for example, were despised, especially those who did so to safeguard a career or for other personal advantage.

A Quieter Life

In the summer of 1936, several months into Agnes's work with *The Woman Today*, we moved to the Bronx, to an apartment in the Amalgamated Clothing Workers' housing cooperative, across the street from Van Cortlandt Park, at the northern edge of the city. Among its residents, almost entirely Jewish working-class, were a goodly number of Socialists and Communists and a few anarchists. There were buildings of four and five stories, 650 apartments, an auditorium, a library, a tea-room, a tailor shop, a shoe shop, a cooperative store; pleasant grounds; and not far away, the older Sholem Aleichem houses, an anarchist initiative, no longer (consequence of the depression) co-op. Amelia, visiting, loved the views from our windows, with the park on one side, and on the other a large courtyard with flower gardens, and she loved especially the plenteous supply of hot water. Ed and Agnes didn't feel that they could afford to buy an apartment, modestly priced though they were; they would have had to borrow, and "going into debt" when not forced to was something of which Ed disapproved sternly, a rule that made sense to Agnes also; besides, Ed's job, though not insecure, was not secure either. We were able to rent only because there were in those hard times occasional vacancies. Although we remained in the same neighborhood for seven years, just the first two and the last were in the co-op apartments.

Beginning in 1935 with a New England tour that included a necessary pilgrimage to Thoreau's pond, my father's vacations were times for Model A travels. In the summer of 1937 it was Illinois and Detroit, where Amelia and her family were now living. On my mother's side only my Aunt Mag and Uncle Dan were left in Illinois; Gordon had gone to Detroit several years earlier.

Two years earlier, Amelia had nailed up the house in Johnston City and brought her younger daughters to Michigan, where the men of the family were beginning to find jobs in the auto industry. In the twenties, during long strikes or spells of slack work, the Cobbs had tested Gary and Detroit; their roots at home were too deep. But after the Progressive strike failed there was nothing left for them. The youngest boy had gone to a "C.C. camp" for forestry work in the Civilian Conservation Corps, one of the New Deal's methods of dealing with unemployment. The others had leased land at the old Lester strip pit; they could dig the coal all right, but who could afford to buy it? For years to come, the whole family, married sons and daughters included, just as "tribal" as the Burnses, lived within what I recall as walking distance in River Rouge, an industrial suburb of Detroit. When the drive to unionize the auto industry got under way, son-in-law "Babe" and two of Amelia's boys were among the numerous ex-coal miners who contributed to the rise of the United Automobile Workers of America. Babe (Albert Nace) was elected shop steward at a Murray Body plant, a position which (I believe) he held until retirement. For Amelia, though, "down home" was still "home." Unless she just couldn't, every Memorial Day meant a trip to Johnston City. Eventually there would be a Cobb family tombstone down there.

The move had saved Amelia's life. In Michigan hardly a couple of weeks, she was taken to a hospital, in critical condition. Her gall bladder was five times normal size and gangrenous. Good medical treatment of a quality not to be found in southern Illinois pulled her through. Agnes, convalescent from an operation and forbidden to travel, wrote to her: "I always seem to be up and down, but you are always down and up, for no sooner do I hear that you are down, than I find that you are up and plugging away as usual."[19] She didn't have much choice. Even before they left Johnston City Amelia's husband, considerably older than she, could no longer do hard work; in a few years he had a terrible cough and in a few years more Lee was dead. Was Agnes just playing with words? No, she envied Amelia's resilience. But maybe it wasn't "resilience"; maybe it was that Amelia didn't expect much out of life, expected to die poor but with confidence that she would be able to take along with her just as

much as the next fellow. She felt no shame about being on relief—
and Michigan was better for that. Her sons, with families of their
own, helped as they could. Not until war production ("defense")
began in 1940, and Amelia was able to put together a boarding
house with eventually a dozen or more roomers, did she have a
reliable, hard-earned minimal income.

All the while—a while that most probably began when Agnes left
for Chicago in 1915—more or less weekly, letters flowed between
Melia and Ag. With occasional complaints from Melie when Ag had
time for no more than a "John Hogg," complaints not entirely
justified, given that my mother could squeeze a short letter, a
hundred and fifty words, say, on one card.

In Illinois on that 1937 trip, besides visiting family and Progressive Miner friends, Agnes and Ed traveled to southern Illinois's
Menard penitentiary where "the DuQuoin boys," four of them
lifers, the fifth with forty years, were confined. Regardless of the
deed, these men, as much as Tom Mooney, were class-war prisoners
and victims. Agnes was able to visit Barney Bossetto, about whom
Katie was particularly concerned. Agnes began corresponding with
Barney and from the Catholic chaplain in whose office he worked,
she learned that her letters were a big lift to his spirits; she grew
very fond of this articulate, painfully sensitive young man, obliged
to live in a perpetual, bleak present.

A year later, quite unexpectedly, two veterans of the Progressive
Miners' left wing were elected to office, Dave Reed as president and
Jack Battuello as a board member. (Reed had been a leader in the
1919 Wildcat and both he and Battuello, an anarcho-syndicalist,
had been active in an I.W.W. organizing drive in Illinois in the late
twenties.) Coal operators, exploiting the rivalry between the unions,
were undermining working conditions, including safety. For their
efforts to achieve cooperation between the unions in dealings with
the companies and the state, Reed and Battuello were within a year
deposed and suspended from membership.[20] After Lewis took the
United Mine Workers into the C.I.O., the A.F.L. had taken in the
Progressive union, renamed, Progressive Mine Workers of America. A.F.L. president William Green no doubt suspected, rightly, an
intention on the part of the left-wingers to bring the Progressive
union into the U.M.W., and thereby into the C.I.O.; but he would
not, in any case, tolerate cooperation with a C.I.O. union. The

P.M.W.A. reverted to what it had become but not before the left-wingers got underway a campaign, in which the U.M.W. joined, to pardon the DuQuoin Boys, which resulted in their release at Christmas 1940. From New York, Agnes and Ed did their part by recruiting labor and liberal supporters. When Agnes and Ed visited Illinois the following summer, Barney was working in a small cooperatively owned mine that Katie's husband and friends had opened several years earlier. He had pulled very tough time— before and after photographs show a man aged by many more than eight years. Except that Agnes regularly sent a money order to a Belleville friend, for payment of her dues in the Women's Auxiliary and Ed's in the union, really I believe as a symbol of allegiance to the labor movement, the Progressive Miners of America was now something of the past.

In those years before the war, Agnes began to accept a quiet home life, punctuated by trips to Manhattan for the theater or for shopping or visiting. *Hamlet, The Skin of Our Teeth, The Little Foxes, Pins and Needles, Arsenic and Old Lace, Tobacco Road, Waiting for lefty, Triple-A Plowed Under*—the stage was always a miracle. She could not go anywhere without striking up a conversation, and for that our neighborhood afforded abundant opportunity. To a friend, amazed at the ease with which she initiated conversations with strangers, she explained that she had grown up in "the free and easy ways of people of the wide open spaces."[21] These conversations were also, she added, her "Gallup poll," her way of keeping in touch with what people were thinking and feeling.

Home after a day at the office, Ed relaxed with an old-fashioned, about the (authentic) making of which he held very decided views; he believed it well to learn, when young, how and how not to drink, and I participated sometimes in his ceremony. (He also instructed me in preparations for a night of hard whiskey-drinking, if need be. Agnes, not keen on that kind of education, confined herself to praise of moderation.) Agnes's cooking was simple, "American," nutritious by accepted standards, though her desserts were more than a little heavy on sugar and cream, and butter too lavish. The availability of a Jewish delicatessen was a delight.

After supper Agnes and Ed would keep each other company in the living room. He would light his pipe and they would read, often aloud. There was always the *New York Times* and an evening paper, the *World-Telegram* usually, for Heywood Broun's column and for sports. There was the LaFollettes' *Progressive, The New Republic,* Ameringer's *American Guardian,* maybe *Harper's* or the *Atlantic,* and *The New Yorker* pretty faithfully. WQXR would be bringing in classical music. The radio was always tuned in for the Metropolitan Opera's Saturday broadcasts and for Toscanini's orchestra. But not everything was so weighty: these folks enjoyed W.C. Fields and Charlie McCarthy and Fred Allen. When Ed turned in for his eight hours he would by self-command banish affairs of the day and news of the world and pass instantly into "the arms of Morpheus." Agnes was a nighthawk. In order to sleep she seemed to have to tire herself, "nervous energy" had to be dissipated. Ed, always attentive to physical fitness, put on no weight; he stayed at 175 pounds and kept muscles hard and stomach flat by night and morning calisthenics. Agnes tried, but her body just didn't work like that.

Until wartime rationing made the car too expensive to maintain, there would likely be, on a Sunday in nice weather, a family drive up the lovely serpentine Westchester parkways.

New York was a place people liked to visit; friends and relatives showed up now and then, quite a few for the World's Fair. Agnes, tour-guide, became well acquainted with Radio City Music Hall and the boat cruise around Manhattan. For a while, also, there were Illinois friends in the city or nearby. With Bill Maxwell, a super in a Bronx apartment house, Ed liked to "dig coal" and drink beer; his wife, Marion, she of the sweet Scottish voice, a devout Catholic, a scrapper, was the life of a party. Then there were the Bessons— when hope for the strike in the Taylorville field was gone, Ruth and Leon had moved on. Leon and his son by a previous marriage, both of them big and strong and good workers, got jobs in tunnel construction in North Carolina and they were doing the same work upstate. On our visits to them in Newburg the time would be filled with stories of the battles in Illinois, the shootings, the bomb that blew up the house next door, and tales of the horrors of tunnel work, the cost in lives of the Holland Tunnel. Ruth I remember as handsome and bright and a maker of good cheer. Later on it was more tunnels, in the Northwest. During the war they worked in the shipyards and dreamed about getting a little farm somewhere some day.

During some or all of these years the Allards and the Normans and Tippetts were in the city. Loren Norman had been Gerry's assistant on the *Progressive Miner.* Alongside each other, he and Gerry were, in stature, Mutt and Jeff. Tippett liked to joke that he had discovered Loren in southern Illinois and taught him to wear shoes; I had the impression that Loren enjoyed playing a hayseed-in-the-big-city role. There was nothing hayseed about Bette Norman, a very bright person. For a while Loren had a job at the copydesk of one of the New York dailies. Later, he and Bette went to Wisconsin, where Loren edited *Racine Labor* for (I think) decades. Gerry, who had been editing the *Socialist Call,* first in Chicago and then in New York, got in trouble because he wanted to advocate, contrary to party policy, military assistance to Finland following the Russian invasion. My impression is that Gerry was, by now, very weary of the political life. Finally he decided to join his family in its shoemaking business. Agnes felt that though he did well in business financially, he wasn't happy. Living once more in the Midwest, he did in time resume contact with left-wing Progressive friends, the circle around Katie DeRorre and Jack Battuello. I remember especially, from better times, his infectious laughter — his whole face laughed, the kind of face one calls mischievous.

The Tippetts lived near 86th Street in Manhattan. Mary was a very warm person, with whom I enjoyed talking. Handsome, articulate, businesslike, urbane in the better sense of the word, that's how I remember Tom. A Guggenheim fellowship enabled him to finish his *Horse Shoe Bottoms,* which Harper's brought out in 1935.[22] The novel, intended to be the first of a trilogy, celebrates his mother and father and the early struggles for union. I still find many parts of it extremely moving and it is, like his *Mill Shadows,* strong in its portrayal of women. (Ed "recognized" the miners in the novel.) Tom's father, a coal miner from Wales, one of the local leaders in the Peoria field of northern Illinois, had died at forty-four, his health destroyed by the mines, when Tom was five years old. Just about Agnes's age, Tom had gone into the mines early and got out as soon as he could. The best friend he ever had, he said, was killed while working a few feet away from him and Tom was himself trapped by an explosion on the day before he was to be married. (No wonder, then, that the description in *Horse Shoe Bottoms* of a miner's escape, following an explosion, is both technically accurate and humanly real.) A self-educated person, he prized education, especially the kind that the labor movement had given him. Writing and teaching were what he wanted to do. During the Second World War he found himself in a bureaucratic job he hated and ended up in the higher echelons of the Office of Price Administration. After the war he set up an educational department for the International Association of Machinists and served as its director until retirement age, only to un-retire and take charge of the Seattle Machinists' educational program.

The story told earlier of Mother Jones and the tobacco-sack of bullets from Ludlow is Tom's. On a speaking tour she had come to the town where the Tippetts lived, and stayed at their house as usual. As she was about to start her speech, she ordered him to go home and get the bag out of her knapsack—"I can't speak without it." He had no idea what it contained—could it be precious stones? Finally she reached her peroration, telling of how, by lantern-light, she inspected the bodies of dead miners. Then with a gesture she tore open the little bag and there rattled to the floor bullets taken from the miners' bodies.[23]

An ambition of Ed's was to write the history of American coal-miner unions. In 1940 Russell Sage published his *American Miners Association,* now recognized as a definitive work.[24] Among other places, his research took him back to Belleville's public library, whose splendid newspaper collection was of very considerable assistance. With Daniel Weaver, one of the moving spirits of the association, he felt strong kinship. Two years later appeared *Preventing Fatal Explosions in Coal Mines,* in which he analyzed the causes of a series of major mine disasters in 1940.[25] That book helped the United Mine Workers' campaign for federal mine-safety regulation, to supplement and override often-venal state supervision; even more significant was Ed's argument for making safety a standard subject of collective bargaining and for strengthening the role of mine-safety committees. The book was crisp, objective, totally knowledgeable, and damning.

Toward the labor movement Agnes had mixed feelings, preponderantly positive. Millions of workers now enjoyed the benefits of union membership. On the other hand, the close ties that were developing between the unions and the government were becoming a vulnerable dependency. When the United Mine Workers' union revived in 1933, all power remained with one man. With few exceptions, members of the International Executive Board and district officers were all "provisional" officers appointed by Lewis and so it would remain. There were pockets of dissidence but the old traditions of democracy had been shattered and Lewis would be long dead before the machine his lieutenants inherited would be seriously challenged by rank-and-file rebellion and finally over-thrown by the Miners for Democracy movement.[26] The Commu-nists, who contributed importantly to the rise of the C.I.O., had entrenched themselves in positions of control in a number of major unions and did not react mildly to challenge from any direction. Many more women were organized now but old patterns tended to persist. The International Ladies Garment Workers Union, more than four-fifths of its three hundred thousand members women, maintained its "old-established rule" by which exactly one spot on its twenty-three-member executive board was held by a woman.[27] The A.F.L. was known to still be sheltering racketeering unions. Loyalty to the labor movement, as Ed and Agnes understood it, meant, as it did to many others I knew, that one did not talk about such matters outside the labor union family—no ammunition was to be provided to the enemies of unionism, who were still strong.

John Lewis—well, even if the C.I.O. was the work of an irresist-ible force welling up from the ranks, Ed and Agnes felt that his leadership could not easily be faulted. A shrewd judge of men and motives, fully aware of the significance of the concentration of political power in Washington, he was now a celebrity, loved by these, hated by those. Had the Wiecks misjudged him? No, they were amused by hagiographers who copied down his self-glorifying and frequently apocryphal anecdotes. They saw every move, past and present, as a move for power. His political ambitions frus-trated, himself spurned by F.D.R., into whose plans he no longer fit, he was going to make a place in history as labor champion and give his enemies grief. Agnes and Ed were willing to give the devil his due.

An Anarchist in the House

Agnes's relationship with me was undergoing further change. She had entertained an idyllic view of mother-son companionship but I was in a hurry to be grown-up, wanted independence, accepted the advantages of dependence. It was part of Agnes's character to be helpfully manipulative, "helpful" being in the forefront of her mind. She had a son who was not managing well the social-sexual hurdles of male youth and whose "nervousness" was obvious and who did not want to talk about his personal life and problems. Agnes's Victorianism, tolerant and respectful of others, blocked her speaking of her own life and growing-up in a fashion that might have prepared the way for confidences. The atmosphere of the home was asexual to the point that I did not perceive my parents as sexual beings. Nor was I invited to participate in any fashion in the family's financial planning and decisions. For a single-child nuclear family, all this was a not unusual constellation, for which, in this case, everything was in place before we came to the city. The fact that Agnes's life now lacked a vital center outside the home must have made this partial scission extremely painful.

But about "the world" we did talk. When I left the Communists I was looking for an alternative that would lead to a genuinely socialist society. My furious preoccupation with "saving the world" would surely have been mad, had I been living in a reasonably sane world. But this was a monstrously unjust world, hell-bent on a war more frightful than the last, about which I had heard and read more than enough.

My temperament, explainable both by my parents' lives and the way I was raised, was anti-authoritarian. While I was struggling with my "politics" during the summer of 1936, the time of the beginning of the civil war in Spain, I was beginning to learn more about the Spanish anarcho-syndicalists, descended from the anti-authoritarian, anti-Marxist wing of the First International; a labor movement kindred in spirit, apparently, to the Wobblies, and possessing a long heroic tradition and having strong popular support. (I wanted to go to Spain—Agnes feared that I would—but I knew that youths of less-than-rugged physical constitution and no technical skills were not needed.) Not many months later, in the Amalgamated Co-op's library, I discovered the memoirs of Kropotkin and Berkman and Goldman; biographies and histories were more meaningful than theories. And Emma and Sasha, who had been in Russia during the early years of Bolshevik dictatorship, told a history whose authenticity I recognized immediately. Here was a spirit with which I could identify. The state was not a potential means to freedom, through the conquest of power, but rather the evil common to capitalism and what the Stalinists called "communism." I hadn't really freed myself from Marxist ways of thinking—was rather more a dissident Bolshevik than an anarchist. But I became convinced enough that in the spring of 1937 I was "the anarchist" among Socialists and Communists on the executive committee of the American Students Union, a united-front fusion of the previous organizations, at DeWitt Clinton High School, and a speaker for a third year at an anti-war anti-fascist observance, a school assembly.

Agnes sympathized with the spirit of my search, but it violated a fundamental tenet of her thinking. Anarchism was a wonderful ideal, but did I imagine that such ideas would be comprehensible to more than a tiny minority of working people, to my cousins for example? Did I think they really wanted anything more than steady work and good wages and union protection? And there was more. Italian anarchists she had known in Illinois had impressed her, they were fighters, and of course she honored Sacco and Vanzetti and the Haymarket martyrs. But anarchists were unrealistic, impatient, didn't understand the working class, believed that unions existed only to keep the workers in line, and were much too prone to think in terms of direct action (meaning dynamite). We must have had conversations about Goldman, but I don't remember them specifically. But I know that although Agnes was on the same side on many issues and admired Emma's participation in the free-speech fights, her courageous advocacy of birth control, and her stand on the war that had led to prison and deportation, Emma's way of living her life was just not one with which she could identify. Nor, I think, did she understand what Emma meant by "free love."

If she ever heard Goldman speak, I'm sure that Agnes would have mentioned it. My father did hear her, at the United Mine Workers' international convention at Columbus, Ohio, in 1911. The union officials rejected a proposal that she be invited to address the convention but the delegates overrode the officers. When the county officials barred the doors, a problem that Emma encountered frequently, the delegates, in great majority, paraded across town to a hall that had been hired to cover the eventuality.[28] Ed liked to tell that story—he was proud of his fellow coal miners. Anyway, Ed was, in his heart, a kind of anarchist.

I was convinced that compromise paved the road to hell. But I too was accustomed to thinking in terms of mass movements; how else to change this rotten world? In New York, it turned out, there were only a few English-language anarchist groups. I stayed on the sideline. I was going to college in the fall and I should concentrate on that; a choice very welcome to both my parents.

For Agnes it was of capital importance that her son get the best possible education. When we came to New York, she had inquired immediately about the Walden School, known as "progressive"; it was not within our means. For college, Columbia seemed a sensible choice. I had an interest in journalism and Columbia had the prestige school. Since I would be living at home and had my parents' frugal habits, the college would be affordable, just. Agnes still had her proletarian respect for elite universities and distinguished professors; not only the rich should have the best. Were jobs not so scarce, next to nonexistent, Ed would have pressed, more than tentatively, for apprenticeship at a trade, after which I could decide what to do—I was not yet sixteen. At Columbia the brief rebelliousness of a couple of years before had died down. There was a chapter of the American Students Union, but I found it to be dominated by Communists, as was the national organization. For *Challenge*, one of the New York anarchist papers, I wrote a little piece, "Death on the Campus."

In the college dropouts of a much later decade I can see myself, except that Agnes and the college made dropping out difficult. Worst was the feeling that nothing mattered. I could not visualize a "career" or even a future for myself. There would be a war in Europe and the United States would get into it. (The invasion of Poland came at the beginning of my junior year.) I did find opportunities to do research on topics of interest, such as comparative study of revolutions, a history of the anthracite miners, a paper on European syndicalism, a study of the breakdown of the medieval guilds, and, postgraduate, intended as a master's thesis in economics, a lengthy detailed examination of the process of centralization of power in the United Mine Workers' union, from its origins to date.[29] (In October of 1942 I accompanied my father to the International convention of the U.M.W.A. in Cincinnati, observed from the press seats John L. Lewis in oratorical action, noted the perfected techniques of control, and met Lewis but avoided shaking hands.) I was trying to find laws of social change and of the evolution of organizations which began with democratic and often highly idealistic philosophies and degenerated into dictatorships. My advisor, Leo Wolman, formerly an economist for the Amalgamated Clothing Workers, who had ideological reasons diametrically opposite mine for disliking John Lewis and what he stood for, tried to interest Macmillan in my manuscript; Agnes and Ed felt that I had found a direction for myself. But by then the U.S. was at war and I, twenty in the month of Pearl Harbor, was going to be wanted by the army. Long ago, I had made up my mind that I would not go.

"Big and Strong Like This"

In writing about my conversion to communism, I said that I see in it something like inevitability. The same could be said at this juncture. Our views on social justice had for me the force of a religion, without god or priest or church, but with heroes and martyrs and renegades. The "inevitability," however, was now more within me: part of my family education was that I think for myself and act by my own principles.

The only kind of war in which I could imagine myself fighting was a revolution by "the people" with the aim or hope of bringing a new society into being; the ruling classes would yield only to force. In Spain there had seemed to be just such a revolution, but the Stalinists had gained the upper hand and that war had degenerated into pure-and-simple-war in which only the Stalinists or Franco would be winners and the people the losers. The capitalist classes had all welcomed fascism and had no quarrel with Hitler until Nazi Germany became a threat to their own power. Virtually the whole of Africa and virtually the whole of the southern rim of Asia, many hundreds of millions of people, were ruled and exploited by European colonial powers. I was aware of what had been happening in Germany since 1933: the concentration camps, the Storm Troopers, the oppression and humiliation of the Jewish people, the pogroms. But I also knew the history of Russia under Stalin. As for Pearl Harbor, I was certainly not going to fight to defend America's Pacific empire.

I had many reasons and they were, I found out, much the same as those expressed by Emma Goldman in 1939 and 1940, before her death in the spring of the latter year.[30] Exiled from America, voluntarily exiled from Russia—an exile that undoubtedly saved her life—she had lived in Western Europe through all the years of the rise of fascism. The depression that she, and even more Alexander Berkman, for whose suicide it was at least one motive, experienced in those years is manifest in their letters. Then came "Spain," and a brief moment of hope. Emma knew that she was fighting pessimism. To take sides in an imperialist war, on the side of "the lesser evil," would have been to abandon the faith for which she had lived, the only faith she thought worthy of loyalty. In several shades it was the faith of young anarchists in New York City with whom I was in touch. As I look back, I see myself as moving steadily, without renouncing that faith, toward a somewhat different place: if murderous violence is the only way humankind knows to live, I could not, as the price of belonging to this human community, participate in its massacres and counter-massacres.

Within the family there was no fundamental disagreement. My father was more and more inclined to regard the human race as a hopelessly irrational species. Individuals could be sensible enough but when gathered in a crowd, as a lynch mob or as a nation, they were capable of anything. The victors in the last war, by the Treaty of Versailles and their determination to destroy Germany as a commercial rival, had helped prepare the way for Hitler. But it had always been that way, one war leading to another, one empire succeeding another, since (at least) the wars of extermination recorded in the Old Testament. It wasn't that he didn't care. He no longer expected people to learn from history, which had ever been a succession of wars for empire.

The truth about Agnes, on the other hand, is that she was simply a pacifist. Not that she had a program like Gandhi's, even though she admired his leadership of resistance to British rule in India, or an articulated philosophy of love in a Gandhian or Christian sense. She thought in terms of struggle, and she could not understand voluntary suffering; she would have been able to kill a Nazi to save a Jew or any other victim and she could have steeled herself to accept the violence necessary to overthrow a tyranny or to protect liberty. But war between nations was mass murder and modern war was war of annihilation, directed against women and children and the helpless as much as against enemy soldiers. She could not say yes to that, but only grieve for the dead and the mothers. I have made no mention of Hitler's "final solution" for the reason that the transformation of the concentration camp into the death factory did not become public knowledge until after the war. But tens of millions had died in this war, there were endless horrors, and the Jews were not saved. Those who ordered the incineration of Dresden and Tokyo, the obliteration of Hiroshima and Nagasaki, were also guilty of murder of the helpless. Agnes's emotion about the war, before, during, and after, was emotion at this totality.

Immediately after Pearl Harbor I made a choice I regretted. I felt I should refuse to register for the draft, state my position, and go to jail. I knew that doing so would have no significance except as (in my view) the right thing to do. There were many arguments in the family, centering on the futility of it. Agnes understood why Debs made a speech, during the other war, that was calculated to send him to the penitentiary, but what meaning would my going to jail have? The sentence could be up to five years. Why shouldn't I register and apply for conscientious objector status? It came down to this: she would suffer more, do tougher time, than I and it would be an enormous physical strain on her. To the morning of the appointed day, I remained undecided. I registered but it didn't feel right. It was not likely that I would be recognized as a C.O.; the law called for objection to war by reason of "religious training and belief."[31] Time passed while the case was processed. A friend of our family from Belleville came to visit in his captain's uniform. Sure that I must be activated by concern for my skin, he swore that he could get me into Officers Candidate School and a safe desk job. Whether or not things worked that way, I was not going to serve in the army in any fashion. Agnes bought a trunk and winter clothing in case I should be classified as a C.O. and assigned to a Civilian Public Service camp. Early in 1943 I impulsively made a trip south, without informing my parents. I do not fully understand my motives. Consciously, I was considering expatriation and I was going to look into possibilities for getting to Mexico, a foolishly impractical idea. Unconsciously, I think I wanted to be arrested. Rather fortunately, I was picked up in New Orleans and spent several weeks in the federal jail on a charge, technically incorrect, of not notifying my draft board of "change of address"; I got a free ride back to New York, where I was released on my own recognizance. The effect, whether I intended it or not, was to break the deadlock between my mother and myself. Of that New Orleans jail I had many stories to tell; of car thieves (Dyer Act), pimps (Mann Act), "draft dodgers," and of an ex-governor of Louisiana awaiting trial, a fate not unknown among Louisiana governors, who did not lack for hangers-on even in jail.

In July 1943 I began serving a three-year sentence for refusal of induction. For these next years, Agnes's life was going to be centered on the Danbury, Connecticut, Federal Correctional Institution, a relatively new medium-custody prison designed for short-timers. Of the prison population of six hundred or so, Jehovah's Witnesses, who kept to themselves, were the largest single group. The C.O.s were of many varieties but most were pacifists who belonged to the wrong church or none; a few were "absolutists" who refused to cooperate with the draft in any fashion.

Danbury had a nice, modern-looking front. No high walls. A rectangle of cellblocks and other buildings enclosed a large central yard. It was a good solid prison, not tough, as prisons go, but big enough and strong enough, in which all customary routines were observed religiously. In the press, it was sometimes represented as a "country club," which was true for, and only for, white-collar crooks. I was still in quarantine when the grapevine brought word that a group of eighteen war objectors had stopped work, in protest against racial segregation in the mess hall, then universal in the federal prison system. (A statement by one of the strikers: "I believe it is my right as a human being to treat other human beings with equality if I so desire." But prisoners had no "rights," only revocable "privileges.") I knew that joining the strike would jeopardize any possible parole, or "good time" for early release, but I had already decided that I should think "three years" and the issue of the strike was one on which I had to take a stand. Released from quarantine I refused to report for work; because the cellblock in which the strikers were confined was full, I spent the first five weeks in an isolation cell (in Danbury, "the bing," elsewhere, "the hole" or "solitary"), close by another late joiner, the one person of color to participate in the strike action, a deeply religious pacifist. Agnes, who had been glad to hear that I was no longer in the cages of the federal jail in New York City and had been assigned to Danbury, within a reasonable visiting distance, was not prepared for my suddenly being in a jail within a jail. But she knew that in the same circumstances she could not have acted otherwise.

For three and a half months, the Bureau of Prisons took a hard line; race segregation was and would be the policy. Confinement to cells except for a very brief exercise period, reduced diet, harassment, and intimations that we would be "shipped out to Lewisburg" were all part of a clear intention to break the strike. Prison is the father of ingenuity. For ourselves we "published," with revolving editorship, "The Clink," initiated by Lowell Naeve, an artist, who had discovered that carefully washed-off pages of *Life* made usable paper. "The Clink" was circulated from cell to cell under the doors by means of what a guard recorded in his log as an "ingenious device," which he failed to capture. In fact, it was a long string attached to a metal ring from a radiator pipe. But most days were long and morale went up and down.

The turning point was our beginning to get publicity, good stories, in November, not only in *PM*, the New York leftist daily, but more importantly in the Negro press. Ed's job, which took him to the American Federation of Labor convention in Boston in October, furnished an opportunity. He wrote me that he had a long talk with A. Philip Randolph, president of the Sleeping Car Porters.[32] He was scant with detail—letters passed through censorship—except to mention that Randolph issued a weekly newsletter to the Negro press.

He did tell about Randolph's speech to the convention, in which Randolph reviewed the race records of the A.F.L. unions. The federation bigwigs, at the rear of the stage, behind the podium, "all appeared to be sitting on hot seats," getting up from their chairs, walking around, talking to one another, pretending indifference, while Randolph "skinned" them one by one. But so thoroughly prepared was Randolph's indictment that the delegates on the convention floor, in great majority hostile, hung on Randolph's every word, waiting to find out whose turn would be next.[33]

A copy of my father's letter surely traveled from the censor to the warden and thence to James Bennett, director of the Bureau of Prisons. (During the strike censorship was lenient, probably in hope of gleaning information.) From the strike-log, two days before Thanksgiving: "David Wieck's folks came today. Bennett says no go absolutely. Wieck's folks brought [from] and taken back to train, which seems to refute the idea that the Bureau is not interested. Committee went down to see Wiecks. Dave went first. Mr. and Mrs. Wieck talked with warden 2½ hours."[34] Agnes wrote: "I do feel, and so does your father, that there has been a clearing of the atmosphere and that we laid the basis, intangible though it was, of which something good can come."[35] My dad, in fact, had bet me an old-fashioned, collectible at some later date, that the outcome would be favorable.

Shortly after Christmas, at the end of four and a half months of strike, the warden brought us a compromise, which we accepted. Clearly it was a way to save face: a month later, no longer appearing to yield to pressure from inmates, mess-hall segregation was abolished entirely, without incident. The federal government wanted to keep racial matters cool during the war, yielding of course only to pressure, and the bureau was professing to set new standards of prison modernity. This particular new standard, however, did not to my knowledge apply beyond Danbury.

When the strike ended, five of us informed the administration that we were not going to "cooperate with our imprisonment." I didn't recognize the right of the government to imprison those who objected to war, whatever their reasons or absence of reasons. I could deal with confinement; what I believed no one should have to endure was the regimentation, mild though Danbury's was. If it came to it, I had found out, one could be free in a cell; not the most preferable form of freedom, but freedom. Except for a few unpleasant individuals, I found it easy enough to deal with the "hacks" (elsewhere, "screws") despite their uniforms and ours, just as persons, so long as I didn't take their orders and answer to the name "2674" and follow the rigid prison routines.

In the last weeks of the strike, doors had been left open afternoons; on Christmas Day, our comrades gone, we were locked into cells. After five meals went untouched the warden, who wanted no more trouble, granted us in effect a "free zone"—five cells adjacent to a dayroom that overlooked the yard, and open cell doors—along with an adequate yard-period and standard prison diet. On the assumption, fortunately not quite accurate, that we were sealed off from the rest of the prison, our cells didn't suffer the routine "shakedowns" that, short of rectal searches, are probably the most repellent, and psychologically destructive, detail of prison life.

Agnes had been under terrible nervous, physical strain during the Jim Crow strike, the strain of achieving a goal. At a family visit that Christmas Day there were sharp words on both sides. (The controversy had begun several weeks before when I had written that I was seriously considering non-cooperation.) Agnes did not want her son to become a "monkish hermit"; he should be out in "population," helping other prisoners. I have tried to imagine her in an analogous situation. Probably like Jim Peck, who had a cell next to mine during the race-strike and eventually joined our noncooperation, she would have been an "agitator," constantly in and out of the bing for not-minding-your-own-business, a terrible offense in any prison.

We agreed to disagree. Ten days after Christmas, a postscript to a letter from my father: "You know after we left the last time we were there I said to myself the Wiecks just had an old-fashioned knock-down and drag-out fight just like at home. Well, I hope we can keep from having any more like that."[36] A week later, my mother: "With the long strain over, and with the 'peace' you said you have settled down to, I have been having more peace of mind myself, though still hoping you will eventually be with the rest of the fellows. I trust you will have shed the grim look with which you met us. Last time was the only occasion when your mother didn't meet you with a smile, regardless of how I felt. I have no thought of meeting you with hammer and tongs this time, but neither do I want to be greeted by a stoic!"[37] A month later, after a "swell visit," she wrote that she accepted my right to decide as I had. No more "feuding."[38] And very soon, "I finally conquered the feeling that overwhelmed me for months about your being there. I found myself indulging in happy memories."[39] Her health, which had taken a bad turn, improved sharply. In a letter summarizing the Danbury story to date, my dad wrote to Powers Hapgood that he didn't "blame them for not being 'good boys.' I wouldn't be one either."[40]

Extremely helpful to Agnes, right from the beginning, had been her finding a new "community," the Families and Friends of Imprisoned C.O.s, its center Esther and Julius Eichel; a small group, by far more radical because of the Eichels' presence than any of the major pacifist organizations. Julius made his views known through a little mimeographed paper, *The Absolutist*. In the First World War Julius had spent more than two years in military prison, under truly rugged conditions. An anti-war Socialist, Jewish but non-religious, his stand against conscription was so strong that he refused "farm furlough," then the one "out" for those judged "sincere." A non-registrant in World War II, jailed briefly but because over military age not prosecuted, Julius gave unconditional support to war objectors who refused to cooperate with their imprisonment, as did Dr. Evan Thomas (brother of Norman), who had also been an objector in the last war. The group was much concerned about two C.O.s on hunger strike for freedom who had been transferred to the dreaded federal prison hospital at Springfield, Missouri, a couple of months before I went to Danbury. Agnes was neither by principle or temperament an absolutist and the idea of hunger strike she did not like at all, in any cause, even in the woman's suffrage campaign. But she respected Julius highly and the Families and Friends enabled her to give direct support to wives and girl friends and relatives of imprisoned objectors, and thereby to the men themselves.

For me the next year and a half passed quickly, in the main. A number of C.O.s went on strike after being denied one-third parole and were shipped to Lewisburg, an emotional event for us in Upper Hartford, for many, like Ralph DiGia, who has labored mightily these past forty years for the War Resisters League, were comrades from the Jim Crow strike. In our group I became particularly friendly with Lowell Naeve, an Iowa farm boy who had left Sioux City to study art; a non-registrant doing a second Danbury sentence. Before the war in Europe started, he had gone to Mexico City, intending to sit it out. But when the military draft was inaugurated, he returned in order to take an open stand of refusal. In his first sentence he spent most of his time in "isolation" or "segregation" because "in doing prison work we were only building and maintaining a prison to keep ourselves in." "The Original Hermit," Agnes called him, an epithet she eventually withdrew. Permitted now to have paints and materials, he kept busy. He and I did pretty easy time, as prison time goes. A sea of time, Jim Peck called it; for Jim, who had been a seaman and had made the Australia run on a freighter, we were on a ship that never hit port. With Jim and George Kingsley, a union lithographer from Rochester, I found that I had a lot in common.

On Christmas morning 1944, when breakfast was brought, George and another of our men walked past a dumbfounded guard into the prison yard to stroll and to visit. Christmas is a bad time in jail and they just had to do something to relieve the tension of same walls, same people, indiscriminable days. They were apprehended quickly and put in the bing; no yard period, no fresh air, no sunlight. Lowell and I felt we had to help them. We refused to return after yard period, explaining why, and I had my first experience of vigorous nonviolent resistance and of going limp. We were dragged and carried a long route back to our cells and locked in. A couple of days passed. I stopped eating. Shortly the pre-Christmas status quo was restored. There was better feeling now in the whole group, among men who were getting on each other's nerves. I was finding myself comfortable with nonviolent methods, in which I was receiving an education. Solidarity was a principle with which Agnes had no trouble identifying.

Letters to Danbury

All this time there were lots of letters from Agnes, from notes scribbled on the subway to two- and three-page single-space-typewritten. Almost always they were cheerful.

Sometimes my big white cat was allowed to tell about the goings-on in the house from his point of view, in which "she" was The Cook and "he" The Big Fellow. Sometimes there was family news. Uncle Gordon had wished that the judge who granted his wife a divorce was dead and in hell. "Now he is dead and I'm sure he's in hell."[41] Sometimes humor. She knew I enjoyed my Aunt Mayme's remarkable spelling. Mayme, about me: "Every body is glade to here he is looking goode again." A reproach to Agnes: "Well, what is rong with yous did you loose your pen and paper when you mooved."[42] Well, "glade" and "here" are Chaucerian spellings; "every body" and "mooved" appear in the past of our language; and "yous" recorded Mayme's pronunciation, which differentiated plural from singular. "Rong" is a little odd, however, given that her father's name was Wright.

While I was still in quarantine, Ed and Agnes had made a vacation trip, by rail, to Illinois, the last they would make together. Their visit to Mag and Dan was good for a couple of letters but before quoting them it will be pleasant to go back a few months, to the spring of 1943 and what could be called a comedy of error.

In the March 7, 1943, issue of the *Washington Post,* of Washington, D.C., there appeared an article by Agnes E. Meyer, wife of its publisher, under the heading "War Plant Jobs Tame 'Bloody Herrin' Illinois." Foreseeably, that article had incensed mightily the editor of the *Marion Evening Post,* of Marion, Illinois, Elva R. Jones. Meyer's was an ordinary piece of peregrine journalism that reported alleged civilizing effects, upon a dreadfully primitive community, of a recently installed ordnance plant. "The special cotton underwear, which munitions workers must use, and the bath prescribed for men working in explosive dust, were also a novelty in Herrin, and something to boast about to the folks at home," etc.[43] Truth was not absent from Meyer's article—truth as the management of Sherwin-Williams's Crab Orchard plant perceived it.

Erelong the Marion editor got the lowdown on this awful Agnes E. Meyer: "Agnes Turns Out to Be Former Teacher from Williamson Co." "None other than the former Miss Agnes Burns, later wife of a Washington, D.C. editor." More wonderful still: "She is the same dynamic 'Gracie Allen' whose school room the editor swept out as the son of a janitor of Johnston City schools more than thirty years ago." (Would this Elva Jones be the son of the janitor whose smile, in the photograph of the staff of Johnston City's East Side School, caught my eye? I think so.) Did poor Agnes ever get hell from Jones for "sending her childhood county down the river." "Well, Agnes, all we can say is that we think you sold your old home town too cheap!"[44]

From Detroit, Gordon, to whom someone down home had sent a clipping, expressed the hope that Agnes would sue that goddamned paper "till Hell freezes over."[45] Elva Jones must have received more than a few protests; soon, the editor scooped himself by announcing his own error, "It Was Not Our Former Teacher."[46] Agnes Burns Wieck now rose to the defense of her county as well as of her name, and in a letter that the Marion paper published, she lectured Mrs. Meyer severely. Among other corrections she pointed out that Illinois miners were not unfamiliar with baths; thanks to the union, the mine washhouse was a decades-old institution. If many homes still lacked plumbing, that didn't prevent people from bathing: "City folks often ask, how do you get clean in a laundry tub? Perhaps Mrs. Meyer would consider herself ridiculous, huddling in a wash tub behind the kitchen door, but with patience she would soon be as familiar with the effectiveness of such sanitation as she is with drawing room fitness. Experience is a great teacher."[47]

Agnes was not in a better mood for the condescending placation extended by the managing editor of the *Washington Post*, to whom she had written—another Jones, mark you, to go along with two Agneses and two *Posts*. The Marion editor's mistake, said this Jones, was "not uncomplimentary, for Agnes E. Meyer is a very distinguished lady and a very able journalist."[48] In her letter to the Marion *Post* Agnes made note with pride that unlike that other Agnes, living with her husband "in luxury that befits their wealth," Edward and Agnes Wieck "now live in New York City, but still eat in the kitchen."[49] Indeed, except for a Vermont hard-rock-maple platform-rocker, with matching table, their furniture was just about what Edmund Wilson had seen.

The Williamson County that Agnes visited was now nearly indistinguishable from many another poor and culturally backward county. The Herrin Riot, the Ku Klux, Prohibition gang warfare: after twenty years, memories of these were fading and nobody wanted a reminder. It wasn't the ordnance plant that "tamed" Williamson. Between past and present was the enormous fact of the Great Depression, from which few of any class were spared. Emigration to war-industry centers, and the military draft, had now brought unemployment down. After the war, the county would succeed in attracting a bit of industry to take the place of its defunct coal industry; eventually it would acquire a federal prison. In Norman Mailer's *Executioner's Song* Marion, the location of a maximum-security replacement for Alcatraz, is a significant stop in Gary Gilmore's life. In 1986 an observer for Amnesty International reported that there was "hardly a rule in the Standard Minimum Rules, established by the United Nations, that was not infringed in some way or other."[50]

When Agnes visited, she found Mag's family and Dan's better off than they ever had been. Mag had a front porch at last, painted, even, if lacking steps. (A year later, electricity came down the hard road; there were lights in the house and on the porches, and the barn and henhouse were next in line. There was already a light in the Chic Sales; it will cost David twenty-five cents to get in, Mag, who like all the family except for Agnes had a sly sense of humor, told Agnes.[51]) Dan had finally been granted a "decent" medical pension from World War I and wouldn't have to try to work any more. His son Pat, "Mickey" in those days, would be able to get through high school now.

On her return to the city, Agnes wrote me, rather to my astonishment, as follows: "Absence makes the heart grow fonder, you know, and it really is true of your mother in regard to old Egypt, for I would really love to be back there on the soil, rather than amid all this brick and mortar of the city. The city has its advantages but I guess I'll never stop longing for the wide open spaces." She was particularly pleased with "the general improvement of educational facilities." "Did you know that our friend [Roscoe] Pulliam, President of the Normal University [at Carbondale] is endeavoring to make it a liberal arts college? We always felt he would achieve something big in Egypt."[52] Pulliam, alas, didn't live to see it; he died at forty-seven, the following March. The nostalgia, however, is hardly to be taken at full face-value. While there, she wrote about an encounter with a six-foot chicken snake—she was mortally fearful of snakes, and being non-venomous was no excuse—and of the ferocious heat and the threat of a tornado. Perhaps she just would have liked to be able to turn back the clock.

Agnes reported certain other observations. She had talked with a nephew, living in Detroit, whose marriage had collapsed, and she was trying to resolve her feelings about the effects of the war on families and on the lives of women:

> This trend of the new emancipation of women was reflected in big advertisements I observed around St. Louis—offering war plant jobs where husband and wife could both work the same shift. I tried to explain to poor bewildered and heart-broken C—— how the pendulum was swinging to the opposite extreme now, how the upheaval of war is bringing this "women's freedom." On the one hand the war breaks up homes, on the other it brings an avalanche of marriages. And everybody uprooted. Men going off to war, war wives filling the buses in all directions, to live for a little while near the camps. Thousands of mothers, like N——, going out for the "big money" and the new life. . . . I think back to the struggles for woman suffrage, the parades, the demonstrations, the hunger strikes, and the victory! . . . When some future historian deals with the rise of women in the twentieth century, the victory of woman suffrage will appear as hardly a ripple.

The rise of the machine and the resulting crisis of the war—those two great economic facts tell the story.[53]

In another letter she recalled her enthusiasm for nurseries, which she had never thought of replacing family as the center of the lives of small children.[54]

Periodically there was news of a close friend of mine, a pacifist from a Jewish anarchist family, of whom my parents were extremely fond. (Agnes would have liked it if I had been more like him, in the way of gentleness and considerateness and utter lack of arrogance.) My friend felt very much at home with my parents, as did all my friends, both fellows and girls. Spinoza and Tolstoy were his inspirations. Although non-religious, indeed anti-religious, he had been classified as a C.O. and assigned to a Civilian Public Service camp. The government camp at Mancos, Colorado, at which he wound up, after finding unbearable the pious atmosphere of a camp run by one of the "peace churches," turned out to be even worse. He and another man went on strike in protest against this alternative form of conscription, forced labor of questionable social value, and were in due time arrested. "Walking out," choosing prison, was a decision that men in a number of camps were beginning to make. Out on bail and back in the city, my friend decided, after a long struggle with himself, to accept service in the Army medical corps and ended up in Burma. What Agnes saw was that my friend, with whom she had long conversations, would have been miserable in jail, feeling himself to be of no use to anyone.

My father's letters dealt mainly with his work. His assignment, which took him to conventions and conferences, was to keep track of wartime labor-controls and their probable postwar significance. But there were occasional asides. In a series of letters over a couple of months he told about a book, *De re metallica*, published in 1556, of which he had found an English summary; the first treatise on mine engineering, a very impressive one, it gave special attention to safety and health. The author, G. Agricola (Georg Bauer), was born in Saxony not far from my grandmother's home town of Grimma. Reading about sixteenth-century Saxony, he recalled the dozens of Saxon miners, from Zwickau, whom he had known in Staunton in his youth, "all bow-legged, and very short-legged, with stout and long bodies, which I always attributed to not generations of miners but centuries of mining families that must have dug metallic ore [silver, principally] at the time of Agricola, in the Erzgebirge."[55]

The White House Revisited

Finally, the war ended. Over most of the globe the killing had stopped but the road to peace did not exist on any maps.

Soon, from Danbury, Agnes was hearing good news. There were many war objectors with a lot of time to do, some with recent five-year sentences. The Bureau of Prisons decided to bring a number of non-cooperators from other prisons to Danbury and authorized a new warden to give all of us full equality with the rest of the prisoners, except for confinement to cellblock during work hours. Agnes was not happy about it, but there was no fight over my decision not to accept any parole conditions and to finish out my sentence.

The trouble was that the Bureau of Prisons had no power to grant a postwar amnesty. Lowell and I wanted nothing more than to get on with our work (he too had chosen to finish his term). I was allowed to have my United Mine Workers manuscript, which I was revising, and I was helping Lowell write a book, *A Field of Broken Stones*, about his experiences as a war objector.[56] He was still painting. But we were not looking at five-year sentences.

Among the new men: —Wally Nelson, still a very good friend, a wonderfully thoroughgoing pacifist, a "person of color" immovable in his insistence on respect for all persons, all his life a non-payer of taxes for war. Wally was surprised to find that I, from a non-Christian background, was so close to his ideas; I was equally surprised. We had many long talks. —Joe Guinn, one of the founders of the original Committee of Racial Equality (CORE) in Chicago in 1942. Wally and Joe had initially accepted assignment to a C.P.S. camp; having decided to cooperate with conscription no longer, they had "walked out" together. At the Milan, Michigan, federal prison they had refused to cooperate with the prison system and had been shipped to our Danbury concentration point. —A black nationalist from Harlem, from whom I learned a lot during a late-into-the-night talk in which I mainly listened. Later, when I read Ralph Ellison's *Invisible Man*, I felt I knew what Ellison was talking about. —Bob, a "walkout" from a V.A. mental hospital to which he was assigned for "alternative service"; he could not have anything further to do with an institution where inmates were treated with such deliberate cruelty. —Two young Nisei pacifists, whom I didn't really get to know. —Brooks, a pacifist lawyer who had made a beautiful statement in court of the grounds for his opposition to war and conscription. —Lou Linden, an expelled member of the Socialist Labor Party, whose policy seemed to be to expel as many members as it recruited; with Lou I enjoyed many political discussions. —Clif Bennett, early in a five-year sentence after leading the F.B.I. a merry chase, who, like me, had while still free written articles for the New York anarchist paper *Why?*[57] —Leni Mehr, an objector to the "imperialist war," active in labor and radical movements, who remembered being much impressed by Agnes Burns Wieck's Annual Report to the Women's Auxiliary, of which he thought he still had a copy somewhere.

On the whole we were a pretty militant group. Some, like Brooks, disagreed on pacifist principle with the activist orientation of the majority. There weren't any votes or general meetings, the spirit was anarchist, and things began to move so rapidly that the grounds of disagreement never became fully clear to me.

As it turned out, I missed another Christmas dinner. A letter home, dated December 25, 1945:

> I hope the thought of us up here did not interfere with your merriment, because we have really had one hell of a good time here today. I think you know me well enough not to think that I am saying that just to make you feel good, because I have made it a point to tell the truth (like that little cold you got to worrying about) so you won't imagine worse.
>
> As I wrote you [that we would], we began the 72-hour non-eat today. There are now 16 of us and it is practically a unanimous demonstration. Well, at noon time, as the men came out of the mess-hall with Xmas dinner in their bellies and Xmas packages from the company [Jim Peck's term for the prison administration] in their hands, they were greeted by a big sign "FREEDOM NOW" on the Xmas tree in front of the mess-hall. Across the yard, strung up to the top of the baseball backstop, could be read the words, "THE BEST GIFT FOR CHRISTMAS IS FREEDOM." All around the yard, stuck in the snow along the walk at intervals, were 50 signs of the "keep off the grass variety." Half of them read "FREE ALL S.S. [Selective Service] MEN"; and the alternate signs read, "FREE THE POLITICAL PRISONERS." Before dinner, a leaflet "POLITICAL PRISONERS," giving the dope on amnesty all

over the world except America, was posted on the bulletin board of each cell-block and dormitory. It was a very nice-looking leaflet, and attracted a lot of attention.[58]

The category of political prisoners included not only C.O.s but also pure-and-simple "draft dodgers" and civilians, mostly homosexual, imprisoned for "wearing a uniform."

The climax came a month and a half later, on Lincoln's Birthday: demonstrations without and within. Members of the Families and Friends, and a few ex-Danbury men and a sizable contingent from the *Why?* group, picketed the jail. Agnes was ill and couldn't make it but Ed was there. One of the delegations that met with the warden included, from the *Why?* group that published the New York anarchist paper of the same name, Paul Goodman and a young woman, Diva Agostinelli, whom I had known only slightly, and who became my companion before the year was out. In his introduction to Lowell's book, Goodman remembered the warden's admission, "Society would not be hurt if every one of them were set free at once." But "I can't, I have orders." Diva pointed out to the warden that the court in Nuremberg was not accepting that plea.[59] Not that the warden's acts were equivalent to those of Hitler's subordinates, but that the principle of responsibility either applied everywhere or nowhere. Within the prison there was a one-day strike, the more popular because of work-on-the-holiday. Except for Jehovah's Witnesses ("J.W.s"), hardly anyone showed up for work. Parading and banners and slogans; chanting "We Want Out"; and singing the chorus of "Solidarity Forever." It was completely peaceful, a holiday spirit with nothing resembling a riot. The answer was foreseeable: Upper Hartford closed in once more.

Agnes was now furiously busy. A letter of February 21 tells of her having been on a picket-and-leaflet line, on a bitterly damp, cold night, in front of Town Hall in New York City where the U.S. Attorney General was speaking. She noticed that people were not throwing these amnesty leaflets away. A "John Hogg" two weeks later: "The Amnesty campaign now in high gear and I am giving it all my time. So don't be any longer concerned about my doing tough time for you. Have gotten over that by this work of hard licks for the boys with years to do. Amnesty work now organized on a solid basis. When you write that you have been able to get back to your work program after being catapulted back to constant confinement there is nothing I can't do out here."[60] A Committee for Amnesty for All Objectors to War and Conscription had been formed: A. J. Muste, chairman. Among the sponsors were Victor Reuther of the U.A.W. and Clint Golden, vice president of the Steel Workers.

A picketing was set for May 11 at the White House, just before the U.S. Selective Service Act was due to run out. Through the Amnesty Committee we sent out a call from Danbury for simultaneous demonstrations at other prisons. Two weeks before the date, the expected finally occurred: transfers of seven men to various destinations, which we resisted physically but nonviolently with locked arms and bodies and barricades of beds, tables, chairs, and benches; two more went the next day; and myself, the day after that, to the West Street federal jail in New York. On the eleventh, while a hundred and fifty people picketed outside, a delegation went into the White House to present an appeal for amnesty for all war objectors. Four of the five, including Agnes, had family members who were or had been in prison; the fifth was Dave Dellinger, one of the Union Theological Seminary non-registrants in 1940, whom I had met in Newark when I was between sentences. (During our Jim Crow strike, Dellinger was one of a group of C.O.s at Lewisburg whose hunger strike in protest against mail censorship resulted in an easing of restrictions.) This time there was no audience for Agnes with a U.S. president. In Harry Truman's stead she met an associate of a presidential assistant for minority issues, in the same room, but redecorated, Agnes noticed, in which the Women's Trade Union League delegation had met Joseph Tumulty, secretary to the president, prior to audience with Woodrow Wilson.

Agnes spoke for the non-cooperators. She had no more reservations about our position. "Mrs. Wieck," said the delegation's report,

> dealt with non-cooperation with the prison system by objectors who regard themselves as political prisoners, whether their objection is religious or political. She spoke of protests against racism and other injustices; refusal to perform forced labor; refusal to accept conditional

release; amnesty committees and activities inside prison; and the present wave of hunger-strikes protesting continued imprisonment. Principled protests cannot be stopped by physical or psychological punishment, but such men pay in health for their convictions. With many sentences not expiring until 1950 or 1951, amnesty agitations will be intensified inside and outside prison.[61]

She and Dave truly represented our group and our comrades in other prisons. We did not want preferential treatment as "sincere" conscientious objectors. To Albon Man, secretary of the Amnesty Committee, Agnes wrote: "When Nash asked about 'all Selective Service violators?' Dave was excellent. Nash polled the committee on this and we were unanimous."[62] "Dellinger," according to the delegation's report, "said that after a year in Lewisburg, he had ceased to draw the line between himself and the so-called draft-dodgers; that he was sure his fellow COs felt the same way."[63] Dave's position was no doubt too strong for most of the people involved in the amnesty campaign, and for the more conventional C.O.s, but he and Agnes were saying just what we wanted said. Later, in a letter to Edmund Wilson, she put it this way: "The fellows in prison knew that the difference between men regarded as sincere by the government and those considered draft-dodgers, was often one of family background, money and education. One group could speak in conventional pacifist or religious language; the other sounded phony."[64]

At West Street I learned that several friends still at Danbury had begun hungerstrikes. At the Springfield prison hospital, Bent Andresen had been refusing food for six months; there was going to be more hunger strikes. When the amnesty campaign began, I was already "short" and my participation in the Danbury protests had been motivated by friendships and solidarity; for myself, all I wanted to do was to finish my time, preferably in peace and quiet. The time I had left, you could do "standing on your head." But I had to give support.

I didn't know that my parents had begun a campaign to get me out; justifiably, they would have expected me to oppose an individual appeal on my behalf. Ten days before the White House visit, shortly after I was moved to West Street, Agnes had written to Charles Ross, Truman's press secretary, an old *St. Louis Post-Dispatch* hand whom she and my father had known. Agnes could sure make a case, I excerpt:

For a protest that abolished racism in a U.S. prison, my son and fellow conscientious objectors were kept in solitary confinement, on restricted diet, four and a half months. For his stand against forced labor, my son was kept in segregation for two years. For observance of "Amnesty Day," held on Lincoln's birthday this year, my son and his fellow objectors have been without outdoor air and sunshine ever since. Non-cooperative war objectors need no prison rehabilitation. Moreover, their refusal to work springs from fidelity to conscience and deep-embedded principle. Our son was brought up in the tradition of free labor and was not trained to fit a prison mold. When the St. Louis reporter [at the time of the Yereb case] wrote that our boy was named for Henry David Thoreau, Concord philosopher and individualist, he compared the "radical Wiecks" to the "radicals of Thoreau's day. Radical in that they thought their own thoughts and expressed them." My son has two and a half more months to serve his full sentence of three years. His health is in jeopardy. They tell him now he can come out of prison if he will sign on the dotted line. Like Thoreau, he will come out only when he comes out free.[65]

Two weeks passed without answer. (I was still unaware of any of this.) Meanwhile, I had stopped eating, with no duration decided; I didn't know how else to give support to the other men and I left it to the jailers to surmise my intentions. In the *Post-Dispatch* there appeared a brief news item headed "Prisoner from Belleville one of 13 on Hunger Strike." We were, the Associated Press story said, on strike to protest the death, in Dublin, of an I.R.A. hunger-striker![66] Somebody on the Amnesty Committee had apparently worded badly an expression of sympathy. Through a friend on the *Post-Dispatch,* who called Charlie Ross in Washington, Agnes and Ed learned that her two-week-old letter had never reached the Secretary's desk ("a bushel of mail a day"). Two days later, May 17, 1946, I was home, two months ahead of schedule, thin and hungry after ten days' fasting, but healthy.

There Will Always Be a Congregation

For a while there were good times. Before my release and for a time afterward, the Wiecks' apartment at 33 Indian Road, in the northwesternmost building in Manhattan, within sight of the higharched Henrik Hudson Bridge, was a welcoming place for fellows from Danbury. Agnes had found a bargain, the only drawback being the northwest winds of winter. Ed liked to take "the boys" for nature-lesson walks up the hill into semiwild Inwood Park, directly across the street, and tell them about the Indians who once lived there.

One of the "ex-cons," Lou Linden, remembered Agnes as "a warm, voluble, outgoing person," someone whom he came to feel he had known all his life. "No stiffness, no formalities, just the friendliness of an understanding, compassionate woman." Jim Peck and George Kingsley often came together. During the national strike against General Motors, the two of them did volunteer picket duty in New Jersey, and Jim did publicity work as well, in off hours from part-time jobs in the city. "I would look forward to the Sunday get-togethers at their place," Jim wrote me later. "Each of them was such a great individual (and so different) in their own right."[1]

Jim, born into a well-to-do New York family, envied me my parents. His father died when Jim was still a boy; his mother, who according to Jim, focused totally on the social ladder she was climbing, he disliked intensely. He inherited money but wouldn't spend it on himself. He had loathed Lawrenceville School and Harvard (he quit after a year) and had chosen to go to sea and to share the "underdog" life. My parents saved him and another of our

Danbury companions, Jim told me, "from a total depression"; Jim from suicide, my mother said. He had a keen mind and a sharp eye for the phony; was an enthusiast of modern art, to which he tried unsuccessfully to introduce my parents, and of modern literature, good jazz, and French cuisine. A glimpse of something beautiful or real would light up his face instantly. But he never stopped pulling tough time. For Jim, who scorned intellectual talk and had no patience with those who "peeled the onion of doubt," action was all. Year after year, he put his body on the line, sometimes literally his life. He was almost killed in Birmingham on the Freedom Ride, and did time in Hawaii as a member of the crew of the Golden Rule, which attempted to sail into the bomb-test zone. But he never talked the pacifist language of love. The truth, I think, is that Jim, who loved the French phrase "écrasez le patronat!" was not at heart a pacifist, only in his mind, which said that violent methods only create a new class of upperdogs.

Some of the prison activists were trying to convert pacifism from conscientious objection into an active nonviolence based on a program for social change. But for some, freedom was no freedom, life after prison was not endurable. Was it the war? prison? Hiroshima? the German death-factories? The world into which I emerged seemed dead, insensitive; this war had killed something in America, as the absence of guilt about Hiroshima made clear. Everything seemed pointless. I was two months out of jail when the first Bikini A-bomb tests were carried out—I think we were ten, including Jim of course, a group that picketed the Pentagon. We were ignored, busted for carrying our placards through the streets of Washington.[2] Massive indifference. But I was fortunate in friendships, friends in the *Why?* group but above all Diva, with whom to share a life; a person of utter integrity who never hurts others, never rejects others, yet never fails to take a stand and who has lived, not for lack of opportunities otherwise, by the wisdom that success in "career," as the world is, is failure as person. Slowly I began to realize that many of my ideas were not ideas at all but slogan-phrases or bad abstractions.

Agnes very much liked Diva Agostinelli, daughter of an anarchist family, coal miners, from the Pennsylvania anthracite. Deceptively soft-spoken in a voice with musical qualities, Diva made her presence felt and did not hesitate to speak up strongly and with passion when the occasion merited it. Ed appreciated that. It brought quiet chuckles from him, especially if the differing was with me; he didn't much care for women who let themselves be overwhelmed or who faded into the background.

It wasn't long before "the boys" went their several ways, though there were a few, Jim especially, with whom Agnes remained in touch. Diva and I had a railroad flat on West 49th Street in Hell's Kitchen and were working part-time, Diva as a librarian, and both of us were active in the *Why?* group and the anti-conscription movement (including draft-card burning). I was writing regularly for the paper, the name of which changed after a while to *Resistance.* Lowell and I were busy completing and revising *A Field of Broken Stones*; he was doing the drawings, the style of which the text complements nicely. My contribution was, while pruning and rearranging, to preserve Lowell's natural style: simple sentences, rarely emotional, "reportorial and nearly colorless," a style of nonviolence a friend characterized it, while the drama and Lowell's emotion found powerful expression in his drawings. The copy from which we worked had made "bush parole" in a hollowed-out portion of a large papier-mâché picture-frame that Lowell made from a New York Times-and-oatmeal base; the copies we tried to take out openly must still remain in Department of Justice archives.

The labor movement was always on my parents' mind, of course. In May 1946, the war nine months over, President Truman invoked the wartime Labor Disputes Act to "seize" the bituminous coal mines and terminate a national strike; about the events that followed, Ed worked up an interpretative chronology, published as a Russell Sage booklet, *The Miners' Case and the Public Interest.*[3] (During the war, his work had centered on the increasing role of government in industrial relations.) The secretary of the interior negotiated with Lewis an agreement that inaugurated unprecedented welfare and retirement and medical-hospital plans—the latter would in time add "black lung" to the public's vocabulary— and a mandatory federal mine-safety code, with recognition of miners' safety committees. (Whether Lewis quoted Ed's *Preventing Fatal Explosions* I don't know but it wouldn't be surprising if he did, given that the union had distributed the book to all its locals.) The companies balked at the safety provisions, the mines remained "seized," the government refused to reopen the agreement for wage adjustment against inflation, and Lewis called another strike. On the utterly specious pretext that the miners had become federal employees, the government secured an injunction which was upheld by the Supreme Court. (A line runs from here to the Taft-Hartley Law; power concentrated in union presidents was to be superseded by power concentrated in the welfare/warfare state, except that racketeering "unions" have rarely suffered indignities. The New Deal and the war had prepared the way.) The moves were all Lewis's, of course—the union "policy committee" was a mere rubber stamp—but Lewis was fighting in the miners' interests, and with their full support, and for Ed and Agnes there was no question about which side they were on.

Less than three weeks (March 25, 1947) after the Supreme Court's ruling, 111 miners died in an explosion at Centralia, Illinois, a half-dozen miles from Agnes' birthplace. It was just the kind of disaster that Ed's book had analyzed in fine detail.

Ed and Agnes knew that for the great majority of their members the unions were merely agencies which, in return for payment of dues, rendered certain services, efficiently, inefficiently, or not at all. Except here and there on the local level, the kind of democracy for which the old Progressive Miners' left wing had fought was nowhere to be found. Back in 1938, when the Auto Workers' union was still young but competition for leadership positions was already keen, Ed quoted in a letter to a Detroit friend a remark by another friend, "I hope the U.A.W. survives and that whoever runs the show will be afraid of the rank and file." "This," Ed had added, "expresses my thought and hope."[4] Things hadn't worked out that way but my parents' loyalty to the labor movement was so strong that they did not welcome criticism of it from any source.

The world of which Agnes became conscious, in the years just before the First World War, appeared (to people of her sentiments) to be an intelligible world, a world moving toward justice, liberty, equality, an end to exploitation and poverty. She undoubtedly thought of that evolution chiefly in terms of the American Revolution, the abolition of chattel slavery, the rise of the labor movement, and the increasing pressures for recognition of the rights of women. She was not a revolutionary—she hoped to participate in an evolution. As for many people in many countries, the war of 1914 blasted those hopes. (Ed, who had read about the cycles of empires over thousands of years, was for Agnes a sobering teacher.) Even so, the world of the twenties and thirties was still for Agnes an intelligible world: a world of class struggle and (often) of warfare between exploiters and exploited. Although the rise of big government, and for that time, big bureaucracy, via the New Deal, disturbed her, as did the unions' increasing dependency on that government, the struggle to establish the unions in the mass production industries was heartening, thrilling. About big government and bureaucracy she was in the same camp as her one-time mentor, Margaret Dreier Robins. The latter, however, seems virtually to have turned against the materialistic working-class and labor movement, both acceptant of the prevailing values. (Ed, who adhered to the belief that what government giveth government can also take away, a point on which he agreed with the conservative Samuel Gompers, made the same criticisms but not unsympathetically.)

But about the world that emerged from the Second World War, Agnes wrote to Edmund Wilson, she and Ed were no longer sure about anything.[5] A great exaggeration of course, and she was probably thinking especially about the atomic bomb and a World War III. But I take the remark more broadly as including the Cold War, the "American Century," the world empire, the encirclement of Russia, American armies in Europe, navies all over the world, the ferreting out of "subversives," are you loyal "American" or subversive "Red," a nation permanently militarized. With the hydrogen bomb, the very continuance of life on earth was in question. How could one think about this new world, which seemed to allow no ground for hope to make its stand? But of course she gave her moral support, and her voice so far as it would reach, to those who spoke out or took a stand.

I could write analyses and criticisms of the status quo, with which Agnes agreed by and large. But what were the answers? If popular revolution of a libertarian character may once have been a justifiable hope, and if its time might sometime come, it was impossible if people were neither prepared for nor desirous of the life of mutual aid that the "free society" represented and if people preferred the irresponsibility of being taken care of by the bureaucratic institutions of the welfare/warfare state. In our group we talked about, and I tried to formulate, a "modern day anarchism" focused on efforts to create relationships of mutual aid within the statist society, to create new traditions, to try to discover the psychological basis of acquiescence to authority and power—which seemed to have its source in childhood, in the destruction of ability to be free and responsible persons. So there tended to be more talk about A. S. Neill's school in England than about the labor movement which, I had to conclude, was no more than a practical necessity, irrelevant to the problem of fundamental social change. Needed above all was refusal to cooperate with, and to resist, the war-making and exploitative institutions. We were, according to Paul Mattick, a libertarian Marxist friendly to our group, putting ourselves "outside of history," which meant becoming irrelevant. But "history" was the history of nation-states, of empires, and to that history it seemed necessary to be irrelevant.

Agnes understood the logic of my thinking and agreed with much of what I wrote, with the conspicuous exception that she, like my father, was unwilling to give credence to psychoanalytic psychology, Freud's and to a certain extent Wilhelm Reich's, which I thought important in understanding our "civilization." (I found valuable challenges in the writings of Paul Goodman, a frequent contributor to *Why?* and *Resistance*.) In fact, though she didn't realize it, Agnes was on Freud's side on a crucial issue: the necessity for repression as a condition of civilization. (I am not using the term "repression" in Freud's technical sense.) She did not trust our animal nature, our bodies; self-denial was fundamental to her way of living, fundamental to unselfishness and to helping others. So, without our talking the language, she was defending the "super-ego" and I was making claims for the "id"; both of us, I believe, with autobiography in mind.

Agnes had invested, quite naturally, too much hope in my future. Maybe it wasn't my nature to be an organizer or agitator but she had imagined me as (perhaps) a Gerry Allard or a Loren Norman, if not an Oscar Ameringer. Or as a scholar-researcher like my father, the track I had seemed to be on; I didn't seem to have any *good* reasons for not completing work on my old U.M.W. manuscript. (In fact, I thought it would be read and appreciated by just the wrong people, such as my old advisor.) The articles I was writing, instead, for a very small audience, expressed a perspective that might have been understandable to young people twenty years later. To Agnes, the name "Thoreau" meant "rebel," but she enlisted Thoreau into a labor movement that had never quite existed.

In Agnes's life there were still pleasures, however. Early in 1947 she and Ed heard from an old friend whose career they had always followed. After retirement from Chicago, where he was retained several years past the normal date of retirement in order to express the university's contempt for a state senate committee that recommended dismissal of this "subversive," Robert Morss Lovett served during the war as government secretary of the U.S. colonial Virgin Islands. In 1943 the Congress, unappreciative of his having lent his name liberally to organizations, some fifty-six of them, that it deemed subversive, cut off his salary. Particular umbrage was taken at his paraphrase, "All governments are rotten," of Lord Acton's apothegm. With correct logic, the congressmen inferred that what was being said about all governments was being said about them. The Supreme Court eventually ruled that the Congress had committed a bill of attainder, but the Congress was not hasty about paying its debt.[6] Lovett was now writing his autobiography and wanted to be sure that he had his facts straight about the Progressive Miners and the Social Justice hearings. When *All Our Years* came out, Agnes and Ed were very pleased to make this further acquaintance with their esteemed friend, even if it was the least "personal" that an autobiography can possibly be. He had waited too long, perhaps.

But 1948 was not otherwise a happy year for my parents. Mary Van Kleeck retired. At the same time, the Russell Sage trustees, having decided to restrict the foundation to its social work and social welfare mission, narrowly defined, abolished its Industrial Studies Department. Ed was sixty-four that fall and entitled to a leisurely retirement, even if there was much that he was leaving unfinished. But he was still, after nearly fifteen years, a temporary employee with no retirement benefits; because Russell Sage was a nonprofit institution, he was not covered by Social Security. The foundation provided him with a $1,500 annual allowance, something less than half his salary, which had been raised hardly at all from the deep-deflation salary at which he had been hired; their savings were very modest and their rent was equal to more than half their income. Ed had expected to work at least one more year; the

difference financially was less significant than the shock psychologically. He felt more like an unemployed person than a retiree.

Agnes had always managed the household economy carefully.
Literally a string-saver, she had never discarded anything before
convincing herself, a severe judge, that it had outlived its conceiv-
able usefulness. Nor did she have any embarrassment about retriev-
ing the odds and ends of furnishings that their middle-class neighbors left in the incinerator-closet for disposal, not just for economy
but because she and my father had strong feelings about waste. I
was taught that things represented human labor, not only the labor
to earn the price but, looked at from the other direction, the labor
in the factory, on the farm, in the processing plant, to say nothing of
transportation, that the item embodied. You didn't throw a coat
away if you or somebody could still use it, or refuse what you could
use. Most of my wardrobe, while I was in college, had come from a
friend of my Uncle Gordon's, valet for a man (about my size) who
could afford a valet. There was one anomaly: my father would
defend stubbornly the law requiring the smashing of empty whis-
key bottles, on the old trade-union ground of protecting bottle-
makers' jobs.

From "careful," Agnes's economy became minutely scrupulous:
I find old envelopes on the back of which she recorded every
expenditure from rent to postage and set these against income.
(Diva and I, who were now living in quasi-Bohemian marginality
on the Lower East Side, were in no position to help, and Agnes did
not want to become a burden on us.) I don't see how they could have
been breaking even; on that pinchpenny budget, helped by rent-
control, it was just possible. Still, Agnes managed to pay their one
outstanding debt. Lovett, now eighty, had a year's appointment at
Fisk University and Agnes must have wanted to express her and
Ed's gratitude and perhaps give Lovett a lift in his old age. Gordon
had returned a twenty-year-old loan—he probably had hit a number—and the money seems to have burned a hole in her purse. Off
to Lovett went a money order for fifty dollars, the amount of the
loan he had made to the Wiecks in 1932—if it was a loan.

An obituary in *The New York Times*, February 5, 1949, brought
Agnes grief and stirred memories. Powers Hapgood died, hardly
fifty. A quarter-century had passed since that too polite (and very
idealistic) Harvard-graduate coal miner appeared in the kitchen

doorway of the Wiecks' flat in Belleville; although she often had news of him, many years had passed since she had last seen him. But the image remained bright in her mind, strengthened by another bond. During the last stages of the fight to save Sacco and Vanzetti, Powers had worked with, fallen in love with, and wed Mary Donovan, whom Agnes remembered fondly from her Boston years. When word of the marriage had reached Belleville there was head-shaking among Powers' friends—young man, older woman. But the marriage had survived.

Immediately after she read the news, Agnes wrote a long letter to common friends. A vivid memory: "Before Barta was born [named of course after the anarchist martyr] when they were fleeing from Lewis' killers in the anthracite, Powers to seek a job in the Colorado coal mines, they stopped off in Belleville. It was early winter. They were driving an old Plymouth, with their bedding and dishes and clothes stuffed in the back seat. Nothing about them had any Hapgood look. Mary, as in the Boston days, was still scorning cosmetics. I felt Mary would always be Mary, and would use no wiles to hold Powers. They both flamed with idealism."[7] Another vivid memory: we are living in the country, hard, hard, times. "As their car went down our driveway hill Barta was screaming at the top of her voice and reaching back for the rabbits she had been fondling."[8] (White rabbits I was trying to raise—and couldn't stand the thought of eating.) Then an excruciatingly painful memory: "I haven't seen Mary since 1932 and I haven't seen Powers since 1934, when he visited us in New York, on his way to see Lewis—before CIO was ever talked of. I pleaded with him so hard not to do it—all the terror and bloodshed of Illinois was so fresh in my mind—I guess Powers never felt like coming back, though he and Ed always visited at [labor] conventions. I wish he had come back."[9] From then on, Powers had had a union career, first with Lewis, then (after the break) with the C.I.O. That Mary's life at home on the farm in Indiana was not an easy one Agnes knew; but she would not judge. Her last words about Powers: "A pretty wonderful person."[10]

Finally, in 1950, *A Field of Broken Stones* got into print (innumerable publishers had turned it down). A group of C.O.s, among them Dave Dellinger and Ralph DiGia, had founded a community centered on a print shop (the Libertarian Press) in Glen Gardner, New Jersey. A. J. Muste hustled pacifist money to finance publication. Agnes sent a copy to Edmund Wilson, who was reviewing for *The New Yorker*; told a bit about the career of the "Boy, eleven" of the Illinois household; and closed with, "If the book does draw an Edmund Wilson review, that would certainly save it from making box parole."[11] In the issue of May 13, 1950, under the heading "American Political Prisoners," Wilson reviewed *Stones* together with an anthology of writings by imprisoned objectors, *Prison Etiquette*, also "printed privately."[12] Agnes liked the book and enjoyed being helpful, even though she wondered why her own son hadn't written something of his own, or perhaps published some of his prison letters.

But the year 1950 closed on a painful note. Hank Mayer, a long-time friend, one of the "vagrants" arrested in Belleville with A. J. Muste in 1934, now business agent for the Hod Carriers on a New York City aqueduct project at the headwaters of the Delaware River, managed to get Ed a nightwatchman's job so that he could qualify for the Social Security retirement minimum. Ed and Agnes stayed with Hank and Ada in Shavertown, a village whose site is now at the bottom of the Pepacton Reservoir. (Also in the household were the Mayers' youngsters, Scott Nearing Mayer and Eugene Debs Mayer.) But Ed was not well. "When my husband had to take the midnight shift on mountain construction," Agnes later wrote to the director of the Russell Sage Foundation, "often exposed to snow and sleet, he was still bothered by dizziness that had first beset him in 1948." "We stuck it out away from home, until his tension brought us back."[13] There was little their doctor could do for Ed, and they had to return to the mountains; it would be another year and a half before he had enough time in.

Once more, King Coal struck a blow that hit close to home. According to a *New York Times*, December 25, 1951 article: the New Orient mine, at West Frankfort, Illinois, had blown up. Sixty hours after the explosion, the last of 119 bodies were brought out; there was one lone survivor. Many were the houses in Franklin and Williamson counties in which Christmas trees came down.

Earlier that year Gerry Allard had made a survey of mine safety in Illinois for the *St. Louis Post-Dispatch*. He had distributed copies of Ed's *Fatal Explosions* where he thought they would do the most good: he had been alarmed at what he saw. Gerry was familiar with New Orient—he had worked there in pre-Progressive days. He was distraught. In answer to a letter from Gerry — "Agnes and I regard you as the one authentic voice left out there" — Ed wrote on January 6, 1952:

> Gerry, I believe you have heard me say how astonished I have been all these years that Franklin County had escaped such a major mine tragedy. From my own experience as a miner, and my familiarity with the southern Illinois coal field, as well as the things I learned gathering material for my book on explosions, I knew this fate was hanging over Franklin County. In fact, the most experienced and ablest mine safety expert in the United States [Daniel Harrington, then Chief of the Health and Safety Branch of the U.S. Bureau of Mines] joined in my fears, at that time, that "one of these days the top will be blown off Franklin County." In other days, as you well know, it could have taken a thousand lives. Mechanized mining has lessened the number of men exposed but still great numbers pay the toll.[14]

The company blamed the miners; the Illinois Department of Mines, which had rejected a key recommendation by federal inspectors, agreed; Governor Adlai Stevenson backed the Illinois Department.

During the summer of 1952, while Ed was still working in the Catskills, he and Agnes rented a small cottage in Grahamsville and they returned to that area during the three summers following. Ed could enjoy digging a little garden, something he'd had no opportunity for in many years. But now Ed and Agnes weren't spending their summers upstate just for the pleasant surroundings. Ed was in more and more serious trouble; eventually the doctors would diagnose "cerebral arteriosclerosis." In the city in the winter Agnes became a virtual prisoner; as Ed's memory became worse and he began to experience periods of extreme confusion, she became afraid to leave him alone in the apartment. Agnes's life was coming to a standstill.

She gave Ed every possible encouragement. She got him to do little paintings, mostly of trees. He had always loved trees, especially the tough long-lived ones that survived amputations by disease and weather, became twisted and gnarled but persevered stubbornly; his trees have that character (he had always said he planned to live to a hundred). In the summer he filled the cottage with wild flowers, and there were good days when he would catch sight of an unusual bird and verify his identification by consulting his bird-book. But Agnes was under enormous strain. And Ed's illness was progressive.

Finally in April 1957—my father had by then few completely lucid intervals—I drove the car that took him to Rockland State Hospital. I was naive enough to think, or hope, that he would get genuine hospital care, as Agnes's trusted doctor assured her he would, and I was aware of how utterly exhausted she was, not so much from physical burden as from her need to be constantly alert that he would not stroll out for a walk and lose his way. On the very eve of that trip she had congestive heart failure, a condition from which she would from then on suffer recurrently. (Perhaps congenitally, almost certainly from an early age, she had a weakness of the heart muscles.) At the hospital they took away my father's false teeth, took away his glasses, and doped him heavily like they doped all prisoners. I have sometimes wondered whether the drugs shortened his life—Rockland's doctors were doing a lot of uncontrolled medical experimenting on patients—but it was true that his life was over.

During the two and a half years that Ed was in the hospital, Agnes took the bus from George Washington Bridge every visiting day that Jim and I were not free. On this bus were relatives and friends of other inmates. She heard their stories of how their dear ones, youngsters and oldsters, were treated, in many cases far worse than Ed, for he was only occasionally "difficult" from confusion about what was wanted of him or where he was and why. (I remember so vividly his confusion at admission. I could see at once, by the way he was "welcomed," what kind of institution this was.) Most of the visitors were women. Before long, Agnes drew out more and more of their stories, not all of which could have been exaggerated.

The people on the bus were timid about questioning psychiatrists and afraid of reprisals. There existed an officially recognized Rockland Hospital Guild, of families and friends, with an office in the city, but it had concerned itself only with benevolence acceptable to the institution. Still the persuasive organizer, Agnes got a number of them, mostly women, to master courage to join her in presenting their grievances, the grievances of their relatives and friends, collectively. They could not change the basic conditions, they could always be lied to, and of course the complaints of inmates were regarded as symptoms of illness. The revolt against psychiatry and institutionalization was still in the future; people who were psychiatrically suspect for having institutionalized relatives and friends had nowhere to look for allies. But Agnes felt that she had accomplished, in considerable degree, something important: that these women had changed themselves, that they saw themselves as sharing common or similar problems. For a time, so long at least as Agnes was about, they would feel a certain solidarity.

On October 24, 1959, nine days past his seventy-fifth birthday, Ed died. Agnes insisted on an autopsy; the report read "stroke."

At the funeral, attended by New York pacifist friends and friends from the Hospital Guild and Diva's family and Hank and Ada, A. J. Muste delivered the eulogy. Beyond a doubt, Muste was just the right person. An ordained minister, he had abandoned the church to work with the labor movement—first as an organizer, then with Brookwood—a career that took him to the Trotskyists in the thirties. Disillusioned with political revolution, he had returned to Christianity and pacifism. (I recall, in the late thirties, the weightily pious atmosphere in the Muste home the evening I had dinner there.) As executive director of the Fellowship of Reconciliation, he was seriously at odds with, and antagonized, the social-activist pacifists in the jails and in the C.P.S. camps; but after the end of the war Muste moved quickly into the camp of Gandhian nonviolent direct action, and not merely as advocate.[15] I was not alone in seeing A. J. as manipulative and "political," but what mattered more was his energy and zeal and total commitment, his energy amazing in a man only a few months younger than my father. Edmund Wilson, in a postscript to *American Earthquake*, confessed a "foolish nostalgia" for "the Mustes, the Wiecks, the Frank Keeneys, along with how many others with whom I then [in the early years of the depression] came into contact but whom I have not revived in this volume," and added that he found in the Muste of the present-day a symbol that "the American tradition of political courage stubbornly and toughly lives."[16] Just right, A. J., for this moment.

"Ed Wieck was an informal person," Agnes quoted A. J., in a letter to Ed's brother John, "let us be informal on this occasion."[17] So he talked his eulogy, quietly, seated in a circle of thirty or forty. He reviewed Ed's life nicely and he knew how to use a clue provided by Agnes: Ed's fondness for the Book of Ecclesiastes and the poems attributed to Omar the Tentmaker. "Muste chose to talk a bit of Ecclesiastes and its meaning to a person like Ed Wieck. 'Vanity, vanity, all is vanities,' but Ed Wieck 'did not choose to draw from this that life was not worth the struggle for one's convictions." I wish I could quote the beautiful phrases describing Ed's integrity. Never laudatory but deeply moving. He closed with a quotation from one of the books of the prophets which he said did not get incorporated into the Biblical Canon. His interpretation was that for a man to whom the rivers and oceans and winds spoke the oneness of life, whose life was lived on behalf of mankind, there could be no lure of money or power or glory, but that for such a man there would always be a congregation.[18]

> Everyone remembered Muste's tribute as a thing of beauty. The Hospital people, new to such an informal service, said it was an unforgettable experience, that for once they had attended a funeral service and really heard what the person was like in life. The Jewish friends from the Guild remarked that at their funerals only the rich and important got much attention and that too often the praise of the dead is not merited. An Irish Catholic friend remarked that at Catholic funerals you hardly know what is said, the prayers go so fast. Protestants, too, remarked that nowadays the funerals are so impersonal you hardly know who died. But Ed's story they will all remember.[19]

Ed'a body was cremated, as Agnes wished for herself. So far as anything could reconcile her to loss of her companion of nearly forty years, Muste's eulogy had accomplished that. There only remained for her to make sure that Ed's papers, all his unpublished research, would be placed where labor historians could make use of it.

A Hard Death

Ten years had passed since Ed began to fail, during which Agnes's energies had been devoted almost exclusively to a single cause, although even then she found reserves of energy with which to help and inspirit others. Perhaps I don't have that quite right: it must be that her helping others generated energy. She may have been right that even toward the end, when Ed would sit mute, apparently seeing and hearing nothing, he still heard and enjoyed her readings from his favorite poets, that she had kept something in him alive. What was there now that she could do? I don't believe she wanted to outlive Ed but she did, by seven years. Those life-trails of which Ed wrote to Agnes during their courtship had become one trail, and Agnes must have imagined and hoped that she and Ed would disappear into the darkness, into the "everywhere," together.

My life, meanwhile, had been undergoing change. *Resistance* had stopped publication, by my choice, at the end of 1954. The original group, brought together by the war, had scattered; newcomers were few; there seemed to be no point in persevering. I had no expectation that something new was soon to begin in Montgomery, Alabama, and that the sixties would be "the sixties." I was now writing for *Liberation*, a new pacifist monthly, among whose editors were Muste and Dellinger and Goodman; a couple of my articles, based on a trip to Little Rock in connection with the school integration "crisis," pleased Agnes very much. In the fall of 1956 I had begun taking courses in philosophy at Columbia; in 1960, my work finished, I took a teaching job upstate, none being available locally.[20]

For two years after Ed's death, Agnes stayed on in the apartment on Indian Road; she seemed to want it that way. I felt that living alone with thoughts of my father was not good for her, especially in her poor state of health. (Jim found it difficult to get her out of the apartment and felt she was finding reasons for not going downtown and seeing people.) Diva and I rented a larger house and urged her to come live with us. In the fall of 1961, after sorting out Ed's papers, she came to Latham, across the river from Troy, to join us. At a going-away party, her Rockland friends presented her with a watch in expression of their appreciation and love. Maybe some people should be left alone with their memories. The climate up north was much colder; Diva and I had demanding jobs, she as librarian for a high school, myself teaching a full load of courses at Rensselaer Polytechnic Institute; and we lived fairly secluded lives. For Agnes there was one distinct compensation, the airport a few minutes away. She immediately transferred her love of trains to love of air travel and visited friends from here to Texas, including a visit to Freda Ameringer, whom she hadn't seen for many years.

The first winter Agnes spent mostly in Michigan, with Amelia. In the early fifties, Amelia, by then around sixty-five, had given up her boardinghouse and gone to live with her youngest daughter, Lillian Faye, and Lillian's husband, of both of whom she was very fond. She immediately regretted it, though life with daughter and son-in-law was pleasant and easy. She was "homesick," especially after a cataract operation restored her sight, homesick for the men who had been another family for her to look after, one long-time boarder in particular, who regarded her as mother. But she had settled down very comfortably. Mag's daughter Geneva, who thought the world of Agnes, as did her husband, also lived near Detroit. There, too, Agnes was a well-loved aunt.

Amelia's philosophy of life was quite different from Agnes's. Melie lived and let every day take care of itself. Maybe there wouldn't be a morrow; she had had enough "bither and bother" all her life. She took things easy whenever she could. She suffered terribly when her oldest remaining son, not yet fifty, died. I don't know exactly Amelia's views on religion; churches didn't scare her but she didn't find much need to go. She had her opinions about each of her children and grandchildren, as well as about their choices of husbands and wives, but she managed pretty well with "what will be, will be" and was pleased enough with her grand-children. If she couldn't possibly convert Agnes to her philosophy, she could calm her anxieties by poking fun at them.

But the sisters had gone as far as they could together; a year later Melie's health took a downturn and before many months went by she was dead at seventy-five. Agnes was shaken. Mag had died the year before. Of the children of Pat and Florence Burns only Dan and Gordon, besides Agnes, were still alive. The people of her past were disappearing. Mayme was dead, Ed's brothers were dead, Katie DeRorre was dead. The year Agnes moved north, Gery Allard, in his mid-fifties, died of a heart attack. Agnes's weak heart could not prevent the accumulation of fluids; already in 1961, at sixty-nine, she had what she counted as her fifth heart attack. Her vision was failing, she had trouble gripping a pen; she had frightful attacks of shingles, close to the ultimate in pain, visited upon a person with low tolerance of pain, and her half-sleep at night was broken by crying and moaning.

For years her friends had importuned her to write about her life and experiences, or at least record them on tape. She always said, who would be interested? Which, in that period, was probably true. A letter from Mary Van Kleeck seems to have stirred her to try. "Always I have wished, and still wish, that you would write your memoirs, describing as you can so well much that is still vital—the life of a coal miner's family, the miners in Illinois, your work in rallying the women, the Progressive movement and, also, the Women's Trade Union League, and then Ed's activities and later writings. . . . Why don't you begin? Just write a page at a time, as you think of it and it will grow. You write so well!"[21] Too late.

Amidst steady decline there was one brief period of what seemed like recovery which her doctor, she said, diagnosed as return to health; due, perhaps, as she thought, to wise medical treatment, or perhaps to a flaring up of spirit. In the summer of 1965 she went to South Carolina to visit Hank and Ada—Hank was organizing furniture workers—and thence to Illinois where she hadn't been for more than twenty years. From Belleville she wrote a seven-page single-spaced letter, excellently typewritten, her fingers for once cooperative again, packed with interesting news and commentary. There was a bright spot: a visit to Katie's family, and with Barney Bossetto, now in his sixties, with snow-white hair and two grandchildren. "He is nice to talk with, a sense of humor, and has a very nice wife." She went to see the monument at Katie's grave: "It was Gerry's idea, having it designed to show the miner and his wife and child."[22] But this was a small island of the faithful; elsewhere, she did not feel at home—quite the reverse. The civil rights movement had reached the stage where demands were being made not only upon the South but upon the North; old friends were now indignant (to put it moderately) about the "niggers," who wanted to "go too fast," and the trouble they were making; some were ready to defend their property with guns.[23] It was nothing out of the ordinary except that these were people from whom Agnes did not expect such talk. Perhaps she could no longer overlook certain things she had been unwilling to face in the past.

In her feelings about the civil rights movement and the northern ghettoes and the war in Vietnam, she was in the same world as Diva and myself. In the letter quoted above she wrote: "I wonder if Jim [Peck] feels as foolish as I do about the lesser of two evils in the 1964 election. Johnson is doing everything predicted for Goldwater. I never believed TV commercials could get to me; TV campaigning did."[24] She would have liked to be able to get out there and march.

To a young man who consulted her in connection with his research, she wrote, "I find this a most exciting generation." And she meant it. She had never turned her back on the young, never had the resentment, or condescension, that so many older people display. She didn't think of the old days as "good old days" and she was open to the new, and hopeful. Of course, she could have no sympathy with the cult of drugs or the language of "motherfucker" or with the hippie culture. The music, literally and figuratively, was not hers. The young, too, could be wrong.

Whether Agnes's voyage was a defeat, or whether she had exhausted herself in making it, when she returned to Troy she was back where she had been, physically and mentally, before that last thrust of energy. From morning to night, a night she could not sleep through, and from Sunday to Saturday, suffering occupied the forefront of her consciousness. She was dying a hard death. But she had one more journey to make and she managed to make it the following summer—to Detroit once more, this time principally to visit the Labor History Archives, now part of the Walter Reuther Library of Labor and Urban Affairs, at Wayne State University, and to inspect the Edward A. Wieck collection. But her energy was quickly spent.

Finally her torment, and her struggle to live, ended, October 22, 1966, in a hospital in Troy, two days before the anniversary of Ed's death, a little more than two months before what would have been her seventy-fifth birthday, alone, at a pre-dawn hour, as Ed had died alone; by a stroke (a scribbled note suggests) either anticipated or willed. I am inclined to think that the near-coincidence of dates is significant.

Epilogue

On our way home from the conference at Jacksonville, Diva and I spent our first night with my cousin Pat, son of Daniel Burns, and Pat's wife, Lois, and we got glimpses of their kids, college-age and older and starting to marry. Pat reminded me very strongly of my grandfather. Lois, whom we had never met, made us feel right at home. We had last seen Pat, then still "Jimmie," at my uncle Dan's when Diva and I made an excursion from a multi-stage bus trip to San Francisco; that was 1947. We remembered how Dan had taken his time, quite a long time—in Williamson County time did not proceed at a rapid pace—before saying to Diva what he had to get said. "I never thought Aggie's boy would marry an Eyetalian girl." To which, Diva, who looks people right in the eye, had responded in a manner every way appropriate. (We weren't married, either— and my Aunt Mayme had warned Diva that the Wiecks were not to be trusted if there wasn't a license—but I think we let that fine point go by.) Dan, whose experiences in France in the First World War had left him with a violent hatred of war (he was highly pleased that Aggie's boy was a conscientious objector), could barely stand it when his son was drafted for Korea. That was very hard on Agnes too, who corresponded with Jimmie, for whom Aunt Agnes was a very important person.

Pat and Lois live on the outskirts of a small town in east-central Illinois. Shelbyville is one of those places where the denizens of the Underworld, should they surface, would have no doubt about the infinite flatness of the Earth. It was a night of silence, the darkness interfered with only by the searchlights of the local airport and an occasional passing car. Pat and I stood for a long while in the front yard, enduring an intermittent light rain and talking (mostly)

237

about family and the town and Pat's frustrations in his work as counselor and teacher at the local high school. Each of us hoped that the other had some news of our Burns family cousins. Neither of us, it turned out, had kept in touch. With the death of the three sisters within a few years of each other, the connections had snapped; the tribal spirit, the life of which I as favored nephew might have tried to preserve, was gone.

What I got from that evening, above all, was that my mother would have been delighted with this family.

Some months went by before I understood what I had been doing at the Jacksonville conference. When my mother died there had been no funeral. It is not a ceremony that either Diva or I feel right about; our notion of the appropriate is that friends gather to rejoice in having known the friend no longer present. But my mother's friends were far from Troy, and scattered, so it was Diva and myself with our thoughts.

At Jacksonville I was uncertain of my audience, was apprehensive as I usually am. But I began immediately to feel that these people, few of whom had any memory of Agnes Burns Wieck, wanted the connection I could make to a person from a past they wished to appropriate. When A. J. Muste had spoken of a "congregation," I took him to be referring both to an ideal and an actual congregation. I now describe my feeling at Jacksonville, at this scholarly conference, as my sensing the presence of a kind of "congregation." For all my care not to idealize the portrait, I was delivering a eulogy in my own style but a eulogy nevertheless, validated as such by its reception.

We need real communities, not merely communities of the moment. As the case is, we must be glad of the communities of the moment, whose yield is a certain strengthening of spirit. But our need is great and more desperate as our species devises ever more ways of making social existence problematic. Agnes Burns Wieck had dreams in her youth of a heaven on earth, a practical, everyday heaven at least. She was one of numberless precursors, from the famous to the anonymous, of a life we do not yet know how to reach. Her more realistic enterprise was to seize every opportunity to create friendships, and encourage mutual aid among people, to nudge and urge others to act on their own behalf, and to persuade women to assert their presence in the human community. My friend Giovanni Baldelli in his *Social Anarchism* speaks of the ethical capital of a society, by far the more significant kind of capital: our disposition to be cooperative and peaceful human beings, its antithesis being power and privilege and hubris.[1] In her way, Agnes made a contribution to that ethical capital.

That was the spirit of the final remarks with which I closed my talk at Jacksonville:

> I have come here, not to praise Agnes Burns Wieck, but to describe her and to describe the work she did and tried to do. Taking a certain view of her life, one might say that she was a failure. That does not trouble me — for the same is true of nearly all the people I admire, all the idealists down through the ages. Agnes lived by her principles, lived by her convictions, did not seek to lead people to a Promised Land but tried to persuade them to become seekers in their own behalf and in the common behalf. Such a teaching is almost bound to be ignored or misunderstood, but it is the only teaching that I find to be worth teaching.

Notes

Index

Notes

Foreword

1. Anthony F. C. Wallace, *St. Clair: A Nineteenth-Century Coal Town's Experience with a Disaster-Prone Industry* (New York: Knopf, 1987); Herbert G. Gutman, *Work, Culture, and Society in Industrializing America: Essays in American Working-Class and Social History* (New York: Knopf, 1978), chap. 3.

2. *The Autobiography of Mother Jones*, introduction and bibliography by Fred Thompson, 3d ed. (Chicago: Charles H. Kerr & Co. for the Illinois Labor History Society, 1976).

3. For a fuller perspective on these broader developments in the history of the labor movement and reform, see Nick Salvatore, *Eugene V. Debs: Citizen and Socialist* (Urbana, Ill.: 1982); Nancy Schrom Dye, *As Equals and as Sisters: Feminism, the Labor Movement, and the Women's Trade Union League of New York* (Columbia, Mo.: University of Missouri Press, 1980); *If You Don't Weaken: The Autobiography of Oscar Ameringer* (New York: H.P. Holt, 1940); Melvyn Dubofsky and Warren Van Tine, *John L. Lewis: A Biography* (New York: Quadrangle, 1977).

Prologue

1. Iver F. Yeager, ed., *Sesquicentennial Papers, Illinois College* (Carbondale: Southern Illinois University Press, 1982). Also, *Encyclopaedia Brittanica*, 11th ed., s.v. "Jacksonville, Ill."

2. Edward A. Wieck (hereafter abbreviated EAW), *Preventing Fatal Explosions in Coal Mines: A Study of Recent Major Disasters in the United States as Accompaniments of Technological Change* (New York: Russell Sage Foundation, 1942), 116n.

3. Hon. Andrew Roy, *A History of the Coal Miners of the United States from the Development of the Mines to the Close of the Anthracite Strike of 1902*,

including a Brief Sketch of Early British Miners (Columbus: J. L. Trauger Printing Co. [1903]), 202–7.

1   Do You Know What "Radical" Means?

1. *Proceedings, 33rd Constitutional Convention of the United Mine Workers of America, Indianapolis, Ind., Jan. 23–31, 1934,* I, 315.

2. Although Lewis did not become acting president until 1919, he had been in command since 1917. See Chap. 4.

3. EAW, "Rise of the Progressive Miner's Union" 80. MS, 103 pp., Edward A. Wieck Papers, Archives of Labor and Urban Affairs, Wayne State University (collection hereafter cited as EAW Papers).

4. Agnes Burns Wieck (hereafter abbreviated ABW), *First Annual Report of the Illinois Women's Auxiliary, Progressive Miners of America* (Springfield, Illinois, 1933).

5. Editorial, "Coal Diggers' Wives," *New Republic* 73 (28 December 1932): 176.

6. ABW, *First Annual Report,* 8.

7. Ibid., 11.

8. Jean E. Rosinos, "Marching Women of Illinois," *Labor Age* 21 (November 1932): 6.

9. ABW to Robert Morss Lovett, 21 November 1932. Copy, Agnes Burns Wieck Papers, Archives of Labor and Urban Affairs, Wayne State University (collection hereafter cited as ABW Papers).

2   Babies, Strikes, Shutdowns, Blacklists

1. ABW, "Diary of a Miner's Wife" (1922–1923), 170. MS, ABW Papers.

2. ABW to David T. Wieck (hereafter abbreviated DTW), 13 December 1944, 1.

3. ABW, "Diary," 170.

4. Ibid., 171.

5. Ibid., 173.

6. Ibid.

7. Ibid., 172–73.

8. Ibid., 173.

9. Ibid., 174.

10. ABW, Notes, 11 July 1966, ABW Papers.

11. ABW, "Diary," 173–74.

12. ABW, "The New Freedom," *Illinois Miner,* 20 April 1926, 6.

13. ABW, "Diary," 152.

14. Ibid.

15. ABW, Notes, 11 July 1966.

16. Margaret Tolbert to ABW, 1932, ABW Papers.

17. ABW, Notes, 11 July 1966.

18. Ibid.

19. *Proceedings, Biennial Convention, District 12, United Mine Workers of America, Springfield, Illinois, March–April, 1916,* 329.

20. ABW, "The New Freedom."

21. ABW, "Diary," 174.

22. Mrs. Lotta Work [ABW], "Better Communities," *Illinois Miner,* 20 June 1925, 6.

23. ABW, "Our Children's Schools and the Splendid Program of the Pioneer Youth Movement," *Illinois Miner,* 3 October 1925, 6.

24. *Proceedings, District 12, 1916,* 318–19.

25. ABW, "Debs," *Illinois Miner,* 18 July 1925, 6.

26. Ibid.

27. *Proceedings, District 12, 1916,* 325–26.

28. Patrick J. Burns to DTW, 1 December 1984, 4.

29. Ibid., 2.

30. ABW to DTW, 29 December 1943, 2.

31. Margaret Tolbert to ABW, n.d., probably ca. 1930, ABW Papers.

32. On the other hand, union policy was clear: a member was a member, regardless of race. Unlike many other A.F.L. unions which, especially in the South, had separate local unions for blacks and whites and, in many trades, systematically excluded blacks, the miners' union had a fine record. Not so the mining communities.

33. ABW to DTW, 29 December 1943, 2.

34. Margaret Tolbert to ABW, n.d., probably ca. 1930, ABW Papers.

35. For Carterville, see Paul M. Angle, *Bloody Williamson: A Chapter in American Lawlessless* (New York: Alfred A. Knopf, 1952), chap. 5.

36. ABW, "A Miner's Wife Writes a Letter to Lady Mosley Relating Leiter Story," *Illinois Miner,* 10 October 1925, 6. Agnes was moved to write the story by learning that Lady Mosley, the former Lady Cynthia Curzon, granddaughter of Joseph Leiter and wife to Oswald Mosley, was standing for Parliament as a candidate of the Labour Party.

37. Ibid.

38. Ibid.

39. Ibid.

40. For the Leiter mine, see also Angle, *Bloody Williamson,* chap. 7.

41. Roy, *A History of the Coal Miners,* 452–53.

42. ABW, "Big and Little Houses and the Story of Jane Addams and Hull House," *Illinois Miner,* 29 August 1925, 6.

43. Ibid.

44. ABW, "Diary," 152.

45. Anne Sims, University Archives, Southern Illinois University at Carbondale, to the author, 8 August 1984.

46. ABW, Notes, 10 July 1966.

47. Rosinos, "Marching Women of Illinois, 6.

48. ABW, Notes, 10 July 1966.

49. ABW to Ella Southers, president of the O'Fallon chapter, Women's Auxiliary, Progressive Miners of America, 2 March 1933, ABW Papers.

50. Ibid.

51. ABW, "Trains," *Illinois Miner,* 5 May 1928, 6. "From the time I started to school and had to cross the Wabash track, where the boys would lay pins on the rails to have them made into scissors by the fast mail, trains have never ceased to thrill me." But trains were also bound up with her mother who had had "to drag herself and children from pillar to post in the constant move from one mining town to another" (ibid.).

52. For the West Virginia strikes, see David Alan Corbin, *Life, Work, and Rebellion in the Coal Fields: The Southern West Virginia Miners, 1880–1922* (Urbana: University of Illinois Press, 1981), chap. 4, esp. 88–90.

53. Rosinos, "Marching Women," 6–7.

54. *Proceedings, District 12,* 1916, 323.

55. Agnes Burns to Margaret Dreier Robins, 17 November 1916. National Women's Trade Union League Papers, The Arthur and Elizabeth Schlesinger Library on the History of Women in America (hereafter cited as National Women's Trade Union League Papers).

3   *It's Awfully Hard for a Woman to Sit Still*

1. Efforts to trace the *Chronicle,* by Professor Ralph Stone and myself, have been fruitless; libraries know only of a nineteenth-century *Harrisburg Chronicle,* no connection. The miners' paper, which received financial assistance from the union, seems to have been a perennial problem for the latter. Initial publication in 1914 seems probable; at some point (perhaps 1919) it was renamed the *Illinois Miner.* The later *Illinois Miner* (1922–33) took over the name and nothing else.

2. ABW, "Debs," 6.

3. Ibid.

4. Ibid.

5. Ibid.

6. Eugene V. Debs to Oscar Ameringer, 18 July 1925. Original, ABW Papers.

7. The telegram of invitation, dated 27 May 1915, from Agnes Nestor, Chicago, to Miss Agnes Burns, "care the Chronicle, Harrisburg, Ill.,"

reads: "Can you serve as a delegate to the National Women's Trade Union League convention in New York June seventh to twelfth — Illinois State Committee will elect you and pay all expenses — We are all going from Chicago — Wire Reply — Will write more particularly — Make every effort to go." ABW Papers. In the photograph of delegates to the convention in Elizabeth Anne Payne's *Reform, Labor, and Feminism: Margaret Dreier Robins and the Women's Trade Union League* (Urbana: University of Illinois Press, 1988), Agnes Burns is in the front row, extreme right, next to Nestor.

8. Perhaps because its principal branches, Chicago, New York, and Boston, each had its distinctive history, and because the league changed character after Robins's retirement in 1922, there is no general history of the National Women's Trade Union League of America. Elizabeth Anne Payne's *Reform, Labor, and Feminism* is valuable both as biography and as exploration of Robins's philosophy of womanhood and society. Two autobiographies by friends of Agnes have provided helpful background: Mary Anderson with Mary Winslow, *Woman at Work* (Minneapolis: University of Minnesota Press, 1951) and Agnes Nestor, *Woman's Labor Leader* (Rockford, Illinois: Bellevue Books, 1954).

9. Nestor, *Woman's Labor Leader*, 166–68.

10. Information on Agnes's life in Chicago is chiefly from notes (dated 1964) on fly leaves of her copy of Robert Frost's *Mountain Interval* and a copy of a letter, ABW to Anthony B. Barrette, 22 March 1966, ABW Papers.

11. *Proceedings, District 12, 1916*, 317–33.

12. Some of these orators were said in my family to lack "terminal facilities." One such was Alexander Howat (see chap. 4) who could be unfinished after two hours of rambling.

13. *Proceedings, District 12, 1916*, 317.

14. Ibid., 318–19.

15. Ibid., 319–21. Agnes preserved her University of Chicago matriculation card, "unclassified," No. 62906, dated 13 January 1916. Her address was given as 3702 Lake Avenue, Chicago.

16. *Proceedings, District 12, 1916*, 322–30.

17. Ibid., 322.

18. Ibid., 324, 328.

19. Ibid., 324–25.

20. Ibid., 325.

21. Ibid.

22. Ibid., 325–28.

23. Ibid., 328.

24. Ibid.

25. Ibid., 330–31.

26. Ibid., 331–32.

27. ABW to John H. Walker, 19 August 1916, John Hunter Walker Collection, Illinois Historical Survey University of Illinois (collection hereafter cited as Walker Collection). For the rise of the cooperative movement among Illinois miners, and its postwar decline, see John H. M. Laslett, "Swan Song or New Social Movement? Socialism and Illinois District 12, United Mine Workers of America, 1919–1926," in *Socialism in the Heartland: The Midwestern Experience, 1900–25*, ed. Donald Critchlaw (Notre Dame: Notre Dame University Press, 1988), esp. 193–97. See also Ralph A. Stone, "Illinois Miners and the Birth of the Cooperative League U.S.A.," in *Selected Papers in Illinois History, 1981, from the Second Annual Illinois History Symposium of the Illinois State Historical Society*, ed. Bruce D. Cody (Springfield: Illinois State Historical Society, 1982), 70–85.

28. ABW to John H. Walker, 9 June 1916, 4, Walker Collection.

29. Ibid., 2.

30. Ibid., 4–5.

31. Ibid., 6.

32. ABW to John H. Walker, 4 August 1916, Walker Collection.

33. Ibid.

34. ABW to John H. Walker, 19 August 1916, 2–3, Walker Collection.

35. Ibid.

36. In the Walker correspondence there appear references to a strike of the "spar" miners of Rosiclare, Illinois, a small and isolated town on the Ohio River twenty-odd miles southeast of Harrisburg; Agnes was anxious for information about it. (Fluorspar, a fluoride of calcium, earlier used in glassmaking, had become important in the open hearth process of steel production; principal owner was John R. McLean, publisher of the *Washington Post*. The U.M.W. lacked jurisdiction over the industry but supported the strike actively.) A biographical note in the *Illinois Miner* ("Agnes Wieck Talks to Miners," 25 April 1925, 1) refers to Agnes's having had a role in the "earliest and most picturesque" efforts to unionize those mines. In her autobiography, Mary Anderson, then an organizer for the Women's Trade Union League's Chicago branch, tells of having gone to Rosiclare, accompanied by Agnes Burns (a "close friend") and a lawyer for the league; they were to report "the facts" to Margaret Robins. The facts were that strikers were being evicted from their miserable homes and that company guards directed by the sheriff were terrorizing the town and were in the habit of kidnapping the mayor. A sympathetic mine engineer allowed the visitors to hold a public meeting in his garden. Mary and Agnes were able to speak—surrounded by "about fifty mine guards with guns pointed at us" (*Woman at Work*, 57); the visitors had seen enough and did not choose to stay a second night. Free to import strikebreakers, the company had no

problems. I have no way of resolving the discrepancy between Anderson's account and Agnes's use of the term "picturesque," which fits with my fragmentary memory of the story as I heard it when I was young.

37. ABW to Margaret Dreier Robins, 6 October 1916, National Women's Trade Union League Papers.

38. Payne, *Reform, Labor, and Feminism,* 143.

39. For health of league workers, and "breakdowns," see ibid., 131–32.

40. ABW, "Shirt Makers Win," *Life and Labor* 7 (April 1917): 53. ABW, "Going to Jail," *Illinois Miner,* 6 February 1926, 6. ABW, "Moyamensing," *Illinois Miner,* 13 February 1926, 6.

41. ABW, "Shirt Makers Win."

42. Ibid.

43. ABW, "Moyamensing."

44. Ibid.

45. Ibid.

46. *Organization Report, Sept. 1917, Women's Trade Union League of Philadelphia,* 9. Carbon copy, ABW Papers, on which "Agnes Burns" is the signature, in her handwriting. Between Agnes's *Life and Labor* and *Illinois Miner* articles there are discrepancies, which I have sorted out as best I can. In the former, eight "girls" and a man were arrested; in the latter the man is not mentioned, perhaps because he would have been separated from the women in jail. On the other hand, the *Life and Labor* report, which may have been edited, makes no mention of the presence of an organizer, nor does Agnes's name appear except as author of the report—which suggests a league policy of no limelight for its workers, a policy that would accord with the spirit of the league. For the facts of arrest and court appearances I have relied chiefly on the *Life and Labor* story. The theme of the *Miner* articles is the experience of being arrested and jailed. Agnes was inspired to write the story, she told in "Going to Jail," by the curiosity of a coal miner's young daughter who wanted to know what picketing and being in jail were like.

47. *Organization Report,* 3. The report, some six thousand words in length, deals mainly with the upholsterers' strike.

48. Ibid., 2.

49. Ibid.

50. Ibid., 7.

51. Ibid., 7–8.

52. ABW, "Yetta and Clara," *Illinois Miner,* 20 March 1926, 6.

53. "Agnes on a Vacation," *Weekly News Letter,* Illinois State Federation of Labor, ed. Victor Olander, 8 September 1917, 2.

54. *Proceedings, 23rd Annual Convention of the United Mine Workers of America, Springfield, Ill., Feb. 20–March 1, 1912,* 71, 452, 451, 459.

55. EAW to John H. Walker, 21 May, 26 May, and 12 June; Walker to Wieck, 6 June, 20 June 1917, Walker Collection.

56. About Harriet Reid's career, Professor Ralph Stone provided valuable information. A letter of Reid's to the Wiecks, 2 October 1935, ABW Papers, is virtually a self-portrait.

57. ABW, "Diary," 148.

58. EAW to ABW, 7 March 1918, 11–12, ABW Papers.

59. EAW to ABW, 8 April 1918, 1, ABW Papers.

60. EAW to ABW, 7 March 1918, 1, ABW Papers.

61. EAW to ABW, 29 January 1921, 3, ABW Papers.

62. EAW to ABW, 8 April 1918, 1, ABW Papers.

63. ABW, "This Actually Happened," *Illinois Miner,* 6 July 1929, 6.

64. ABW, "Telephone Operators Hold First Convention," *Life and Labor* 9 (November 1919): 285.

65. ABW, "Our High Schools," *Illinois Miner,* 24 March 1928, 6.

66. "Mrs. Wieck National Labor Leader Elected State Auxiliary President," *Progressive Miner,* 11 November 1932, 3.

67. The warning was contained in a letter to Agnes from Stella Miles Franklin (then in London); January 1917, by Agnes's notation, ABW Papers. Henry was the first editor of the league's *Life and Labor,* Franklin her assistant; both were "allies" and Australian by origin.

68. "Letters from a Miner's Wife," *New Republic* 21 (24 December 1919): 117–19, ABW Papers. At the top of the first page on her clipping of the article Agnes wrote: "actual letters from Amelia Cobb to her sister Agnes Burns, then in Boston with the Tel. Operators union." I can't identify "Tom"—his voice is not distinctive. When she scribbled her note Agnes may have forgotten about the Tom letters at the end. But I can't say for sure that she did not provide them.

69. Agnes loved to quote the never-named "literary lady," e.g., ABW to Anthony B. Barrette, 22 March 1966, 1, ABW Papers.

70. ABW, "Letters from a Miner's Wife," 118.

71. Ibid., 119.

72. Besides the widespread dissatisfaction with the union officials' failure to press for termination of the wartime wage agreement, there was a distinct political dimension to the Wildcat. Tom Mooney's sentence, for the 1916 Preparedness Day bombing in San Francisco, had been commuted to "life" but labor people believed, with excellent reason, that he and Warren K. Billings, also under life sentence, had been framed. A.F.L. leaders sabotaged the "Tom Mooney Day" strike of July 4, 1919, which was a failure nationally. But the refusal of coal companies in the Belleville subdistrict to return fines collected from strikers under the hated "automatic penalty clause" for "illegal" strikes (strikes in violation of contract) sparked a wider

rebellion. For the Wildcat, see Laslett's "Swan Song or New Social Movement?" in Critchlaw, *Socialism in the Heartland*, 181–84. Laslett argues, in my judgment entirely correctly, that the 1920s were not the death of radicalism in Illinois but a new turning, a more profound radicalizing, in which the 1919 Wildcat was a crucial moment.

73. During that summer the Telephone Operators' Union engaged in an organizing campaign in southern Illinois; among other places, local unions were formed in Johnston City and Marion (information provided by Professor Stephen Norwood). That same summer Agnes did "Labor Party work for the Altoona shopmen and District #2 Mine Workers" ("Diary," 103).

4 *My Soul Aflame with Indignation*

1. EAW to ABW, 7 March 1918, 5, ABW Papers. My sketch of Ed's family background and life prior to marriage is based mainly on his autobiographical letter and on his "History of Staunton" or "Staunton Story," as he variously called it, a 4500-word typewritten manuscript, undated, probably early 1920s; in the author's possession.

2. EAW, "Staunton Story," 6.

3. Ibid., 9.

4. Ibid., 7.

5. Ibid., 8.

6. Ibid.

7. Ibid., 9.

8. EAW to ABW, 26 December 1920, 7–8, ABW Papers.

9. EAW to ABW, 31 January 1921, 1, ABW Papers.

10. About Belleville history I have been assisted by two publications of the Belleville Public Library: *The Belleville Public Library, 1838–1936: An Historical Sketch*, compiled by Bella Steuernagel, 1936, and *A Walking Guide to Historic Belleville*, n.d.

11. *Encyclopaedia Britannica*, 11th ed., s.v., "Belleville, Ill."

12. ABW to Mary Donovan Hapgood and Powers Hapgood [1929], Powers Hapgood Papers, The Lilly Library, Indiana University (collection hereafter cited as Hapgood Papers).

13. ABW, "Diary," 136.

14. Ibid., 165.

15. "Deportation," *St. Louis Post-Dispatch*, Sunday Magazine, 17 September 1922, 6–7, ABW Papers. No by-line; Agnes identified the reporter on her clipping of the article.

16. Agnes Burns Wieck, "A Deportation and the Aftermath," *New Republic* 26 (2 August 1922): 278.

17. Ibid., 279.

18. Ibid., 278.

19. Rudolf I. Coffee, Rabbi, Temple Sinai, Oakland, California, to ABW, 18 August, 1922, ABW Papers.

20. ABW, "Deportation," 6.

21. Ibid.

22. See Corbin, *Life, Work, and Rebellion*, 195–224.

23. The account of the rise of John L. Lewis given here is based mainly on the author's "United Mine Workers of America: A Study in Centralization," 1942, 24–45. Typescript, 539 pp., Archives of Labor and Urban Affairs, Wayne State University. About Lewis's career my father was of considerable assitance.

24. ABW to DTW, 20 March 1945, 1.

25. EAW to ABW, n.d., early October 1921, ABW Papers. The beginning of the letter is missing.

26. See Heber Blankenhorn, *The Strike for Union: A Study of the Non-Union Question in Coal and the Problems of a Democratic Movement* (New York: H. W. Wilson, 1924).

27. For the Herrin Massacre, see Angle, *Bloody Williamson*, chaps. 1–4.

28. EAW to DTW, 25 September 1945, 2.

29. EAW, "Bloody Williamson County," *Nation* 116 (3 January 1923): 11.

30. Ibid.

31. ABW, "Diary," 102.

32. Ibid., 122.

33. Ibid., 127–28.

34. Ibid., 107A.

35. Ibid., 122–23.

36. Ibid., 123, 147.

37. Ibid., 147.

38. Ibid.

39. For Lovett, see his autobiography, *All Our Years* (New York: Viking Press, 1948).

40. ABW to Robert Morss Lovett, 19 August 1923. Copy, ABW Papers.

41. ABW, "Diary," 110–11. Fortunately, Herstein gave another lecture in the area ten days later and Agnes was able to go and to enjoy a visit (ibid., 128–29).

42. ABW to Lovett, 18 September 1923. Copy, ABW Papers.

43. ABW, "Mrs. Mason Marches," *Nation* 119 (24 September 1924): 309. Reprinted in *Illinois Miner*, 11 October 1924, 6.

44. Ibid.

45. Ibid.

46. Ibid., 309–10.

47. ABW to Robert Morss Lovett, 30 September 1923. Copy, ABW Papers.

48. ABW, "Mrs. Mason Marches," 310.

49. ABW, "Ku Kluxing in Miners' Country," *New Republic* 38 (26 March 1924): 122. Reprinted in *Illinois Miner,* 5 April 1924, 1 (cont'd. on 4). Angle, in *Bloody Williamson,* acknowledges use of EAW's "Bloody Williamson County" and ABW's "Ku Kluxing" and (137–38, without attribution) quotes from her conclusion.

50. ABW, "Ku Kluxing."

51. Ibid.

52. Ibid., 122–123.

53. Ibid.

54. Ibid.

55. Ibid.

56. Ibid., 124.

57. ABW to Freda Kirchwey, 10 February 1925. Copy, ABW Papers.

58. ABW, "Condemned uv God," 2. Typescript, probably 1925, ABW Papers.

59. Ibid., 2–3.

60. Ibid., 6–7.

61. Ibid., 7.

62. Ibid., 8.

63. Ibid., 9.

64. ABW to DTW, 21 January 1944, 1.

65. EAW, "A Coal Miner's Journal," *Atlantic Monthly,* July 1924, 5–16. The full diary, "Six Months on the Pit Committee," 193 pp., runs from 22 October 1923 to 9 May 1924. Typescript, EAW Papers. The mine was the Taylor mine, operated by a company that was by no means scrupulous in adherence to the terms of the contract and constantly threatening to shut it down.

66. Carter Goodrich, *The Miner's Freedom: A Study of the Working Life in a Changing Industry* (Boston: Marshall Jones Company, 1925). EAW is quoted on 64, 71, and 90–91.

67. EAW, "Mines into Factories," *New Republic* 45 (3 March 1926): 53–54.

68. ABW to Lovett, 26 July 1948. Copy, ABW Papers.

69. *Digs,* 49. Sixty-four-page booklet, n.d., published by the *Illinois Miner* but neither author nor publisher is identified.

70. Ibid., 31.

71. *Illinois Miner,* Woman's Page (p. 6): ABW, "Our Children's Schools and the Splendid Program of the Pioneer Youth Movement," 3 October

1925; ABW, "Mothers Wake Up!" 13 March 1926; Mrs. Lotta Work [ABW], "The Ignorant Chinamen," 19 September 1925; "What's Wrong in China," 8 August 1925; Mrs. Lotta Work [ABW], "What's Wrong with the Schools," 25 April 1925; ABW, "The High School Graduate," 6 June 1925; Mrs. Lotta Work [ABW], "More about Bed Bugs," 31 May 1925. Noteworthy also: ABW, "Murder in the Mines: — A Miner's Wife Speaks," *Illinois Miner,* 7 March 1925, 8; inspired by outrage at the death of fifty-one miners (one survivor) at a Sullivan, Indiana, mine on 10 February 1925.

72. Mrs. Lotta Work [ABW], "More Trials and Tribulations," *Illinois Miner,* 15 April 1925, 6.

73. Workers Education Bureau flyer, ABW Papers.

74. Banquet program, ABW Papers.

75. "Agnes Wieck Talks to Miners," *Illinois Miner,* 25 April 1925, 1.

76. ABW, "Debs," 6.

77. Ibid.

78. Ibid.

79. Ibid.

80. Agnes's one-day diary was written in a ledger book in which Ed had (earlier) begun a diary prior to his pit committeemen's diary; it fills most of five pages. Of the St. Louis day I have no memory. Agnes, who did not fix events into the geometry of time, always talked of "Debs just out of Atlanta prison" — as she indeed wrote, at some late date, in the margin of the diary. When I came to realize that I was born in the month that Debs came out of prison, I assumed that I must have been wheeled through the streets of St. Louis in a baby carriage; and so I often told the story to friends. I wasn't drafted into service — indeed I feel sure that Agnes explained to me, in my language of the time, that this man was a brave champion of poor people who was put in prison because he wouldn't stand for it that young fellows were being sent off to far places to kill other young fellows. (She knew how to do that.) Agnes, of course, had not seen Debs since his release and probably not since their meeting in Harrisburg a decade earlier.

81. EAW, "Gambling with Miners' Lives," *New Republic* 42 (15 April 1925): 205–8, and "Gambling," (a letter) *New Republic* 44 (2 September 1925): 48, in response to a critic. In the same period he reviewed a novel of the mines: "Lights and Shadows of the Yorkshire Pits," *New Republic* 44 (7 October 1925): 182.

82. EAW, "General Alexander Bradley," *American Mercury* 8 (May 1926): 69–74. Reprinted in *Belleville News-Democrat,* 20 April 1926.

83. EAW, "General Alexander Bradley," 71.

84. Ibid., 72.

85. *Amerikareise deutschen Gewerkschaftsfuhrer* (Berlin: Verlagsgesellschaft des Allgemeine Deutschen Gewerkschaftsbunde, 1926), 12.

86. *New York Times Index*, 27 April 1935. Ed noted Husemann's death on the inside cover of his copy of *Im Lande der billigsten Kohle: Eine Amerika-Studie* (Bochum: Verband der Bergarbeiter Deutschlands, 1926), below Husemann's and Berger's autographs.

87. Margaret Dreier Robins to ABW, 8 July 1922, ABW Papers.

88. ABW, "Labor Women of Great Britain in an Inspiring Conference," *Illinois Miner*, 25 July 1926, 6; based on a report of the Birmingham conference by Cheryl Eastman (source not given).

89. Ibid.

90. Ibid.

91. ABW, "The New Antis," *Illinois Miner*, 27 February 1926, 6. See also Woman's Editor [ABW], "Odds and Ends," *Illinois Miner*, 25 February 1928, 6, where she chastised Mrs. O. H. P. Belmont, president of the Woman's Party, for her refusal to vote so long as the Woman's Party did not have a candidate on the ballot, which Agnes, who believed that everybody should exercise the right to vote, regarded as irresponsible.

92. Woman's Editor [ABW], "Odds and Ends," *Illinois Miner*, 4 June 1927, 6.

93. The most interesting, if in the end frustrating, of Agnes's articles touching on feminism is her Woman's Editor "Odds and Ends" of 6 August 1927, *Illinois Miner*, 6; a nearly two-column summary of an article that had just appeared in the *New Masses*—an unsigned article, in fact by Agnes Smedley. Agnes Wieck evidently did not know the identity of the author. The article grabbed her. Smedley had grown up in coal camps in Rockefeller controlled regions of Colorado, in a poverty far worse than Agnes Burns had experienced—father, mother, children in a one-room tent, father an itinerant laborer, a brutal man who abandoned his family. The mother took in washing, this daughter had to go to work very young. Like Agnes Burns's, Smedley's mother had died at an early age, Smedley's at forty-two. (The two Agneses were indeed of nearly the same age.) But this Agnes from Colorado had rebelled totally—became a radical feminist and rejected America to join the Free India movement. (Later, in the mid-thirties, my mother and I both read Smedley's *China's Red Army Marches*.) Unfortunately Agnes Wieck didn't take up the challenge presented by Smedley's claim that her experience was not exceptional, was rather the rule; she chose instead to honor the heroism of the mother who had insisted that her daughter get an education. If Agnes Wieck were inclined to probe further, she would certainly have received no encouragement from Ameringer and his staff.

94. EAW to ABW, probably December 1925, ABW Papers.

95. Ibid.

96. ABW to Wilson Midgley, an American correspondent for the *Daily*

News of London, 10 July 1926. Copy, ABW Papers. Midgley had invited a short article from Ed.

97. ABW, "Country Might Help, But It Won't Solve," *Illinois Miner*, 26 July 1930, 6.

98. EAW, "Mother Jones Herself," *New Republic* 45 (3 March 1926): 53–54 and "Will Coal Dust Explode?" *New Republic* 48 (6 October 1926): 199–200. His review of *The Autobiography of Mother Jones* is carefully nuanced, with a reservation that may have been suggested by Agnes: "In relation to her own sex she has been most puzzling. Miners' wives marching with Mother in command—they were crusaders! Women wage-earners themselves the leaders in the march for political and industrial justice—career-seekers!" (53).

99. ABW, "Belleville Stoves," *Belleville News-Democrat*, 16 October 1926.

100. DTW, Diary, 3 April 1927; in author's possession.

101. ABW, "A New Kind of Coal Miner," *Illinois Miner*, 7 March 1925, 6. Agnes liked to tell the story of Hapgood's having come to the Wiecks' flat (probably 1922) looking for Ed—Ed might help him get a job in the Belleville field. She and Maud McCreery of the Federated Press, who was visiting, could not believe that this fellow with a Harvard accent and the habit of bobbing up and down whenever either of them rose or sat could possibly be a miner—and were suspicious of him (ABW, "Diary," 112–14).

102. *Visions: For the Boys and Girls of the Illinois Miners: Little Journeys within the Realms of Art, Science, Literature, Life, and Labor* (Springfield: Illinois Miner, 1928).

103. ABW, "West Frankfort," *Illinois Miner*, 6 April 1929, 6.

104. Adam Coaldigger [Oscar Ameringer], "Timely and Untimely Observations," *Illinois Miner*, 17 November 1928, 8.

105. ABW, "Intolerance," *Illinois Miner*, 10 November 1928, 6.

106. ABW, "Our Children's Schools and the Splendid Program of the Pioneer Youth Movement," *Illinois Miner*, 3 October 1925, 6.

107. ABW, "The New Freedom," *Illinois Miner*, 10 November 1928, 6.

108. DTW, Diary, 28 and 29 March 1927, in author's possession.

109. ABW, "The Women Get on the Job," *Illinois Miner*, 12 October 1929, 6, "The Stool Pigeon," *Illinois Miner*, 19 October 1929, 6. Amelia Cobb, "Miners' Wives Urge Membership to Kick Lewis Out," *Illinois Miner*, 26 October 1929, 1 (cont'd. on 2).

110. ABW, "Women Urged to Rally to Aid of Illinois and Help 'Clean House' in U.M.W. of A.," *Illinois Miner*, 2 November 1929, 6.

111. In his *Rise of the Progressive Miner's Union*, EAW noted that only a small percentage of the membership, and of officers and or-

ganizers, of the N.M.U. were Communists: "The miners joined it . . . to free them from the thralldom of the officialdom of the U.M.W. of A." (4).

112. Oscar Ameringer's autobiography *If You Don't Weaken* (New York: Holt, 1940) is delightful to read — Oscar was a great storyteller — but of next to no value for understanding Illinois miners' history of the twenties, nor is it reliable factually.

113. ABW to Mary Donovan Hapgood and Powers Hapgood, 19 February 1931, Hapgood Papers, "The Great War to Make Safe the Leaders' Jobs. The hell with the cost. . . . All of the crimes they piled mountain-high against Lewis, all the atrocities — that was nothing but kidding the rank and file. . . . Ed says the union is bound to go down, if this thing turns out to have been only a quarrel among the leaders."

114. DTW, Diary, 1 April and 9 May 1932.

115. Ibid.

116. "Flash!" *Illinois Miner,* 13 August 1932, 1.

117. In Studs Terkel's *The Great Divide: Second Thoughts on the American Dream* (New York: Pantheon Books, 1988): 169–70, one of the persons interviewed, originally from Franklin County, speaks of the Progressive Miners' movement and the Mulkeytown March. His immediate family had stayed with the United Mine Workers (while helping out relatives who joined the Progressive strike). Only long afterwards did he learn that the march was unarmed and that its repulse was not a glorious victory.

118. Amelia Cobb to ABW, n.d., probably August 1932, ABW Papers.

119. ABW, "Remember Virden!" *Progressive Miner,* 14 October 1932, 1. EAW, "General Alexander Bradley," reprinted in *Progressive Miner,* 14, 21, and 28 October 1932.

120. ABW to Robert Morss Lovett, 21 November 1932, 1. Copy, ABW Papers.

121. Ibid.

122. Ibid.

123. Ibid.

124. Ibid., 2.

125. Ibid., 1.

126. ABW, eulogy of Andy Geynes, typescript, ABW Papers. In "New Miners' Union in Illinois Grows," *Labor Age* 21 (November 1932): 9, Tom Tippett wrote that the funeral procession was fifteen miles long and that 25,000 persons came to the funeral.

127. ABW to Laura Manick, 14 September 1933. Copy, ABW Papers. ABW to Mrs. Laurenti, 1 November 1933. Copy, ABW Papers. A friend would translate it.

5   *This Heroic Struggle Has Come to Naught*

1. For the Progressive Mine Workers of America, see chap. 6. For an excellent summation of the background of the P.M.A. rebellion, see Tom Tippett, "The Miners Fight Their Leaders," *American Mercury* 32 (June 1934): 129–37. For events leading up to the formation of the union and for detailed reporting of its first six months, see EAW, "Rise of the Progressive Miner's Union," n.d. (completed March 1933). Typescript, 103 pp., EAW Papers. Although clearly intended to advance the Progressive cause—and sadly optimistic in its anticipation of the future of that cause—it is a rich source. Harriet Dufresne Hudson's monograph, *The Progressive Mine Workers of America: A Study in Rival Unionism* (Urbana: University of Illinois Press, 1952), although it touches on the role of "family" and of the Women's Auxiliary and credits Agnes Burns Wieck's talents as an organizer, is formalistic and evenhanded in the manner of dissertations and emphasizes statistics and legal matters—which is a pity, since she seems to have lived through some part of that history.

2. Tom Tippett, "P.M. of A. Women Issue Record of Heroic Fight," *Labor Action*, 20 December 1933, 2.

3. Ibid.

4. ABW to Tom Tippett, 15 November 1933, 1. Copy, ABW papers.

5. Charles M. Swart, "Agnes Burns Weick [sic]—Coal Field Hell Raiser," *East St. Louis Journal*, Illinois Magazine, 22 October 1933, 1.

6. Sutherland Denlinger, "Mines' New 'Mother Jones' Here Denouncing the NRA," *New York World-Telegram*, 2 February 1934, 18.

7. Swart, "Agnes Burns Weick."

8. Ibid.

9. Ibid.

10. ABW, *First Annual Report*, 12.

11. ABW to Tom Tippett, 16 December 1932, 1 (continuation missing). Copy, ABW Papers.

12. Edmund Wilson, "The Battle of Mulkeytown," *New Republic* 75 (14 June 1933): 12.

13. Edmund Wilson, "Illinois Household," *Travels in Two Democracies* (New York: Harcourt Brace, 1936): 32–38.

14. Edmund Wilson, "Illinois Household," *The American Earthquake: A Documentary of the Twenties and Thirties* (Garden City: Doubleday, 1957): 465–70. "Postscript," 470–72.

15. Wilson, *American Earthquake*, 470.

16. Ibid., 467.

17. Ibid., 470.

18. Ibid., 485.

19. Edmund Wilson, *The Thirties: From Notebooks and Diaries of the Twenties and Thirties,* ed. Leon Edel (New York: Farrar, Straus and Giroux, 1980), 290.

20. Ibid., 291.

21. Wilson, *American Earthquake,* 468.

22. ABW, "Franklin County Is Coming Back!" *Progressive Miner,* 2 December 1932, 1. See also ABW, "Southern Illinois Miners Revolt from Oppression of U.M.W.A.," *Progressive Miner,* 9 December 1932, 1 (cont'd. on 3), and ABW, "Auxiliary President Reports Progress in Southern Field," *Progressive Miner,* 16 December 1933, 1.

23. Wilson, *American Earthquake,* 469.

24. Ibid.

25. In Illinois at that time everyone had guns. Although we lived in Progressive territory it was not irrational, in view of the violence elsewhere, including bombings of homes and cold-blooded shootings, to prepare for self-defense. Besides the automatic and the usual quail-hunting shotgun, there was a four-ten shotgun with which Agnes took some target practice and the old German Mauser rifle (it had the kick of a mule and could kill a man at a mile) that Ed had owned since Staunton days.

26. ABW to Robert Morse Lovett, 21 November 1932, 3. Copy, ABW Papers. See also Edmund Wilson, "Gerry Allard," *New Republic* 75 (14 June 1933): 120–22.

27. ABW to Tom Tippett, 15 December 1933. Copy, ABW Papers.

28. ABW, *First Annual Report,* 12–13. Reported also in ABW, "Auxiliary Women Invite Progressive Members to Belleville New Year's Eve," *Progressive Miner,* 23 December 1932, 1.

29. EAW, *Rise of the Progressive Miner's Union,* 80.

30. ABW, *First Annual Report,* 15.

31. Ibid., 16.

32. Ibid.

33. EAW, *Rise of the Progressive Miner's Union,* 87.

34. ABW, "The Great March," *Progressive Miner,* 2 February 1933, 1 (cont'd. on 2). See also ABW, "10,000 Miners' Wives" (letter), *Nation* 136 (1 March 1933): 233. From the latter: "Governor Horner received us cordially—a big delegation of fifty local presidents and fourteen State officers. The day before, a Communist delegation trying to see him had been clubbed and forced out of his office when they would not accept his offer to receive a committee of five. Damage to the Governor's quarters resulted, and the next day when I arrived with 10,000 miners' wives the city was a bunch of nerves, with two companies of soldiers in readiness. . . . Our army was peaceful and well-disciplined, wanting mainly to demonstrate the solidarity of the

new miners' union, which we certainly did. We women assembled in the armory, paraded through the streets with a motorcycle police escort, and marched down Capitol Avenue to the State House grounds, where we massed about the statue of Lincoln and overflowed into the Capitol."

35. ABW to Mrs. Clarence Kinney, Moweaqua auxiliary, 20 January 1933. Copy, ABW Papers.

36. ABW, *First Annual Report*, 19.

37. EAW, *Rise of the Progressive Miner's Union*, 87. If Walker did say it, it would not be surprising for his speech always ran of its own momentum. In any case it was obviously true. The Saline County miners were about to vote to join the Progressives and except for Franklin and Williamson counties, and strategically unimportant Vermillion County, the miners had everywhere "voted with their feet."

38. ABW, *First Annual Report*, 19–20. Also ABW to Hazel Ansboury, president of the Buckner auxiliary, 21 February 1933. Copy, ABW Papers.

39. ABW, *First Annual Report*, 16.

40. Swart, "Agnes Burns Weick."

41. "Franklin Co. Strike Calls Drop from Air," *Progressive Miner*, 31 March 1933, 1.

42. *The Struggle for Civil Liberties in Illinois* (New York: American Civil Liberties Union, May 1933), 3.

43. ABW to Tom Tippett, 3 May 1933. Copy, ABW Papers.

44. Wilson, *The American Earthquake*, 470.

45. Lovett, *All Our Years*, 217.

46. Gerry Allard, "Lewis Refuses to Sign Statement Condemning Race Intolerance; Opposes Meeting and Picketing," *Progressive Miner*, 19 May 1933, 1.

47. Lovett, *All Our Years*, 217.

48. ABW, *First Annual Report*, 22.

49. Lovett, *All Our Years*, 217.

50. Allard, "Lewis Refuses to Sign."

51. ABW, *First Annual Report*, 22.

52. Amelia Cobb to ABW, 16 June 1933, ABW Papers.

53. ABW, *First Annual Report*, 22.

54. ABW to Tom Tippett, 3 May 1933. Copy, ABW Papers.

55. ABW, *First Annual Report*, 23.

56. Editorial, "Toward a National Drive," *Progressive Miner*, 2 June 1933, 4.

57. ABW, *First Annual Report*, 24.

58. "Worse" was the editors' use of the paper to promote Father Coughlin and other right-wing and anti-semitic demagogues of the time who were enjoying a very considerable popularity in the Midwest.

59. ABW to Mrs. Earl Lintz, president of the Peoria chapter of the Women's Auxiliary, 7 August 1933. Copy, ABW Papers. Also related in ABW, *First Annual Report*, 24–25.

60. ABW to Robert Morss Lovett, 21 November 1932, 1. Copy, ABW Papers.

61. Circular letter dated February 1933, ABW Papers.

62. Tom Tippett, *When Southern Labor Stirs* (New York: Jonathan Cape and Harrison Smith, 1931), *Mill Shadows, a Labor Drama in Four Acts* (Katonah, N.Y.: Brookwood Labor College, 1931).

63. "Miners Turn Actors in a Dramatization of Labor Strife," *St. Louis Post-Dispatch*, Sunday Magazine, 9 July 1933. Clipping, ABW Papers.

64. Amelia Cobb to ABW, undated, probably late August 1932. ABW Papers.

65. ABW, *First Annual Report*, 19.

66. In her *First Annual Report* and elsewhere, Agnes always used the number "twenty thousand." I think that toward ten would be about right for actual membership; it's very unlikely that anyone had an accurate count. As in all wars and crusades, numbers tended to be rounded off generously and I have tried to be careful with them. "Twenty" might still be too low, even, as estimate of the number of women who became involved in the movement.

67. Alice Henry, "Women's Auxiliaries Are Valuable Aid to Union," *Illinois Miner*, 1 December 1923, 6. Source not credited.

68. Ibid.

69. Amelia Cobb to ABW, undated, probably late August 1932, ABW Papers.

70. Curiously, both Mother Voyzey of Springfield, an auxiliary board member, and Mother McKeever of the Taylorville field, were, like Mother Jones, named "Mary."

71. "Obituaries and Eulogies of Mrs. Katie DeRorre," *Collinsville Herald*, 11 January 1960, 8. Allard's eulogy appears to have been printed in full; the soup kitchen photograph was reproduced; a message from Agnes, who was unable to attend, appears among many from numerous walks of life. Clipping, ABW Papers.

72. ABW to DTW, 29 November 1943, 2. See also, Thyra Edwards, "Sister Katie," *Progressive Miner*, 21 April 1933, 3.

73. ABW to DTW, 29 November 1943, 2.

74. Ibid., 2–3.

75. E.g., ABW to Mary Galitko, Recording Secretary, Nokomis auxiliary, 9 September 1933. Copy, ABW Papers.

76. ABW, *First Annual Report*, 2.

77. Swart, "Agnes Burns Weick."

78. "Apparent Conspiracy to Form Numerous Small Unions to Bewilder Rank and File Miner; New Confusion Group Underway in Illinois; Various Groups and Disgruntled Individuals Attempt to Deceive and Discourage Miners by Vicious Attacks on Progressives," *Progressive Miner*, 6 October 1933, 1 (unsigned). The first issue of the *Fighting Miner* was dated 2 October 1933. Allard's linking of Agnes with his paper did make trouble for her. Gerry was impetuous—from the best of motives.

79. ABW to Mary Rudolph, 9 October 1933, 1. Copy, ABW Papers.

80. Ibid., 1–2.

81. Ibid., 2–3.

82. Ibid., 2.

83. ABW, *First Annual Report*, 28.

84. Ibid., 7.

85. ABW to Tom Tippett, 15 November 1933, 2. Copy, ABW Papers.

86. "A parade of officials" is a reasonable way to characterize the scene as reported in "Auxiliary Women Elect Officers in Second Convention," *Progressive Miner*, 10 November 1933, 1 (cont'd. on 2). President Claude Pearcy made it quite clear that "closer cooperation"—with the union officials—was expected.

87. Tom Tippett, "P.M. of A. Women Issue Record of Heroic Fight," *Labor Action*, 20 December 1933, 2.

88. ABW, *First Annual Report*, 30.

89. Ibid.

90. Ibid., 11.

91. Ibid., 30.

92. Ibid. ABW, "Diary," 172.

93. Leaflet, mimeographed, "Who Sold out the Women's Auxiliary?" n.d., Belleville address given, ABW Papers.

94. Death of Patrick H. Burns, clipping, ABW Papers.

95. Sutherland Denlinger, "Mines' 'New Mother Jones' Here Denouncing the NRA," *World-Telegram*, 2 February 1934, 18. Clipping, ABW Papers. The Wiecks' view of the N.R.A. was due only in part to its favoring Lewis vis-a-vis the Progressive Miners. The Wiecks were distrustful of strong federal government—one thing would be a Bureau of Mines with power to enforce mine safety, quite another were agencies that controlled collective bargaining. As the decade of the thirties proceeded, and the term "statism" achieved currency, their distrust grew.

96. For Muste and Brookwood Labor College, see "Sketches for an Autobiography," in *The Essays of A. J. Muste*, ed. Nat Hentoff (Indianapolis: Bobbs-Merrill, 1967), 84–154, esp. 147–54.

97. Denlinger, "Mines' 'New Mother Jones.'"

98. Newsletter from Mother Jones Post, Belleville, dated 9 April 1934; mimeographed, seven legal-size pages with seal of the auxiliary, signed by Emma Wingett, President, Florence Lemler, Recording Secretary, and Matilda Glossop, Minnie Sharrock, and Mayme Belleville, Committee. Copy, ABW Papers. "Hilda" Glossop was a particularly close friend of Agnes.

99. May Day leaflet, ABW Papers.

100. Muste, *Essays of A. J. Muste*, 161. The incident is recounted also in C. H. [Hank] Mayer, *The Continuing Struggle: Autobiography of a Labor Activist* (Northampton: Pittenbruauch Press, 1989), 86–87. Unfortunately, Mayer's recollections (106–12) of the Progressive Miners' movement are marred by serious errors of fact.

James G. (Jimmy) Cross, son of a fine socialist coal-miner family of Gillespie, had attended Brookwood Labor College and was a member of the cast in the Illinois production of *Mill Shadows*. Subsequently he went on to organize bakery workers in Detroit, worked his way up, and eventually succeeded to the presidency of the Bakery and Confectionery Workers International Union of America. Muste (160): "I think that Cross is the only Brookwood graduate who achieved personal wealth and adopted the style of living which we had associated with the most deplorable type of labor leadership." In 1957 the A.F.L. expelled the entire union, essentially to be rid of Cross, who refused to resign. The smell of corruption, of which he appears to have been at the center, was just too strong for the federation to ignore. All this was terribly painful for Agnes — Cross's mother and father were good friends of hers.

6 Beyond the New York Horizon

1. Mary Van Kleeck, *Miners and Management* (New York: Russell Sage Foundation, 1934).

2. John M. Glenn, Lilian Brandt, and F. Emerson Andrews, *Russell Sage Foundation, 1907–1945* (New York: Russell Sage Foundation, 1947), vol. II, 551–52.

3. Edward A. Wieck to Oscar Ameringer, 8 February 1936. EAW Papers.

4. Swart, "Agnes Burns Weick."

5. Mary Van Kleeck, *Creative America: Its Resources for Social Security* (New York: Covici Friede, 1936), 309–11.

6. Sympathy with the Soviet Union, even among liberals and radicals who were repelled by the tactics of the Communist Party of the United States, did not seriously erode until the trial and execution of the Old Bolsheviks (1936–38) and remained strong until the Soviet "nonagression"

pact with Nazi Germany in 1939 and the assassination of Leon Trotsky in Mexico in 1940.

7. EAW to DTW, 25 October 1945.

8. Ibid.

9. Ibid.

10. ABW, "Onward Chicago," *Woman Today,* May 1936, 23; "Women Battle Chains," ibid.; "Pacific Coast Women," ibid., June 1936, 21; "Milwaukee Convention," ibid., December 1936, 25; "Housewives United in Auxiliary Council," ibid., January 1937, 21; "Solidarity in Detroit," ibid., July 1937, 25.

11. ABW, "We Start a School," *Woman Today,* May 1937, 27.

12. Ibid.

13. Anna M. Dzapo, "My Life in a Steel Town," *Woman Today,* July 1937, 24.

14. ABW, "An Inspiring Visitor," *Woman Today,* June 1936, 21.

15. Catherine DeRorre to Clarence Hathaway, 17 August 1936. Copy, ABW Papers.

16. Hannah Stone, "Soviet Russia's New Family Welfare Law," *Woman Today,* September 1938, 8.

17. Margaret Sanger, "The Soviet Union's Abortion Law," *Woman Today,* December 1936, 8.

18. "Our Readers Discuss the Soviet Family Welfare Law," *Woman Today,* January 1937, 26.

19. ABW to Amelia Cobb, 29 May 1935. Copy, ABW Papers.

20. Reed and Battuello presented their case in a small pamphlet, *The Case of Dave Reed and Jack Battuello,* n.d., apparently 1940, ABW Papers. There was no doubt in the Wiecks' mind but that they had been ousted for reasons of union politics and to please the coal companies. The Superior Coal Company, subsidiary of the Northwestern Railroad, the only major operator to accept the Progressive union, would not have forgotten Battuello's leadership, as president of the big Gillespie local, of a sit-down strike against the company in the spring of 1937.

21. ABW to DTW, 23 February 1944, 1.

22. Tom Tippett, *Horse Shoe Bottoms* (New York: Harper and Brothers, 1935).

23. The Mother Jones story comes from Harper's publicity for *Horse Shoe Bottoms,* ABW Papers.

24. EAW, *The American Miners' Association* (New York: Russell Sage Foundation, 1940).

25. EAW, *Preventing Fatal Explosions.*

26. In 1944 an old acquaintance, a Lewis "payroller" from the very beginning of Lewis's presidency, would complain to Ed, but with no

understanding of the "Why" of it, that the Appalachian field, now the heart of the coal industry and of the union, had not produced any new leadership at all, not even dissenters. (Once, a long time ago, he had been a "good rebel" and he knew the importance of dissent, Ed said, but his mind was now on pension and retirement.) "From now on," my father wrote, "Lewis can say with every truth, *I* am the State, after me the deluge." Indeed, the deluge came. Lewis remained president until he retired in 1960 at age eighty. By 1969, when he died, the corruption within the union had gotten so far out of hand as to be a public scandal; its victims, the miners. The murder in 1970 of Joseph Yablonski, along with his family — Yablonski had attempted to oppose Lewis's successor — failed to stop the Miners for Democracy movement. But only governmental intervention enabled that movement to win control of the union in a relatively honest election two years later. The conditions that inspired the rebellion had of course long antedated Lewis's retirement. Today the U.M.W. struggles for survival in an industry whose future lies in strip-mining in the Southwest. The social idealism that animated the Progressive Miners of America in its early stages and that inspired many of the rank and filers who built the C.I.O. in the 1930s is rarely to be found in the present-day labor movement but militancy survives, viz. the strike (1989) in Virginia and West Virginia against the powerful Pittston Company in which the women of the coal towns — including, now, women miners — were in the front lines. One group of forty women, arrested for strike activity, gave as their name just "Daughter of Mother Jones." (See Denise Giardina, "Solidarity in Appalachia: the Pittston Strike," *Nation*, 3 July 1989, 12–14.) Agnes Burns Wieck would have liked that!

27. Rose Pesotta, *Bread upon the Waters* (New York: Dodd, Mead, 1944), 395.

28. Emma Goldman, *Living My Life* (Garden City: Garden City Publishing Co., 1934), 475–76.

29. DTW, "The United Mine Workers of America."

30. Emma Goldman, *Vision on Fire: Emma Goldman on the Spanish Revolution*, ed. David Porter (New Paltz, N.Y.: Commonground Press, 1983), 239–46.

31. Except for an unusual draft board, the "religious" clause was construed as requiring belief in a Supreme Being; "objection to war" as requiring absolute commitment to nonviolence. While waiting to go to jail I did research on conscientious objection for an American Civil Liberties Union pamphlet, *Conscience and the War, A Report on the Treatment of Conscientious Objectors in World War II* (New York: American Civil Liberties Union, 1943). I learned that in England the law required neither religious training or belief or objection to all war. In the U.S. many Catholic C.O.s

had a hard time because of the "just war" clause in the teachings of the Church. Protestants who did not belong to one of the "Historic Peace Churches," Friends, Mennonites, and Brethren, for whose benefit the law was framed, might or might not be recognized. "Selective" objection to war and conscription, never accepted in the U.S., became an issue during the Vietnam War. The figure most commonly given for imprisoned objectors in World War II was six thousand, nearly three-quarters of them Jehovah's Witnesses who refused to fight in any war except the ultimate Armageddon, claimed ministerial status, and refused alternative service.

32. EAW to DTW, 13 October 1943, 3.

33. EAW to DTW, 11 October 1943, 1–3.

34. Strike log kept by Lowell Naeve; copy in author's possession.

35. ABW to DTW, 29 November 1943, 1.

36. EAW to DTW, 3 January 1944, 3.

37. ABW to DTW, 11 January 1944, 1.

38. ABW to DTW, 23 February 1944, 2–3.

39. ABW to DTW, 9 March 1944, 3.

40. EAW to Powers Hapgood, 6 March 1944. Copy, ABW Papers.

41. ABW to DTW, (late) October 1944, 2.

42. ABW to DTW, 22 March 1944, 1–2.

43. Agnes E. Meyer, "War Plant Jobs Tame 'Bloody Herrin' Illinois," *Washington Post*, 7 March 1943. Clipping, ABW Papers.

44. "Agnes Turns out to Be Former Teacher from Williamson Co.," *Marion Evening Post*, 22 March 1943. Clipping, ABW Papers.

45. Gordon P. Burns to ABW, 25 March 1943, ABW Papers.

46. "It Was Not Our Former Teacher," *Marion Evening Post*. Clipping, undated, ABW Papers.

47. ABW to Elva Jones, 6 April 1943, published under the heading "Agnes Burns Wieck Tells about Agnes the Crucifier . . . From County and Proud of It; Read How a Real Writer Sizes up Human, Fundamental Things; [and in boldfaced type] 'Mrs. Wieck, We Thank You.'" Letter and clipping (undated), ABW Papers.

48. Alexander F. Jones to ABW, 29 March 1943, ABW Papers. Jones ignored, rather discourteously, Agnes's request for a copy of Meyer's article.

49. ABW to Elva Jones, 6 April 1943. Copy, ABW Papers.

50. *Allegations of Mistreatment in Marion Prison, Illinois, U.S.A.* (New York: Amnesty International, May 1987), 14.

51. ABW to DTW, 18 November 1943, 1.

52. ABW to DTW, 16 September 1943, 2–3.

53. ABW to DTW, 10 September 1943, 3.

54. ABW to DTW, 28 October 1943, 2.

55. EAW to DTW, 7 March 1945.

56. Lowell Naeve (in collaboration with David Wieck), *A Field of Broken Stones* (Glen Gardner: Libertarian Press, 1950).

57. *Why? A Bulletin of Free Inquiry* was published in New York City from March 1942 to March 1947. Renamed *Resistance: An Anarchist Review*, the magazine continued until December 1954, an additional twenty-seven issues.

58. DTW to ABW and EAW, 25 December 1945, in possession of the author.

59. Paul Goodman, preface to *A Field of Broken Stones*.

60. ABW to DTW, 7 March 1946, postcard.

61. "Committee for Amnesty [for All Objectors to War and Conscription]: Report of Special Delegation Presenting Appeal at White House, 11 May 1946," 1. Mimeographed, copy in ABW Papers.

62. ABW to Albon Man, formerly of Danbury and Lewisburg prisons and secretary of the Amnesty Committee, 1–2. Copy, ABW Papers.

63. "Committee for Amnesty: Report," 2.

64. ABW to Edmund Wilson, 23 January 1950: 2. Copy, ABW Papers. In the same letter: Dellinger was "the outstanding Conscientious Objector in this war. . . . In prison he was a kind of Gene Debs, interesting himself in all manner of men. A graduate from Yale University, and from Union Theological, Dellinger had widened the outlook of the older pacifists." She also expressed her disgust at Roger Baldwin's undercutting of the Amnesty Committee's campaign for a general amnesty for draft-law violators—the same Roger Baldwin who, then an anarchist, had gone to prison in World War I as a draft refuser. But Roger had become cozy with high government officials. If she had been aware of his active collaboration in the internment of persons with Japanese ancestry, she would not have been surprised at his stand on the amnesty issue.

65. ABW to Charles Ross, 1 May 1946. Copy, ABW Papers.

66. Associated Press story, datelined 14 May 1946, *St. Louis Post-Dispatch*. Clipping, ABW Papers.

7   There Will Always Be a Congregation

1. Author's recollection of conversation with Lou Linden; letter, Jim Peck to author, 6 September 1978.

2. "Bikini Test Picket Prefers Lockup to $5 payment," *Washington News*, 1 July 1946. Clipping, ABW Papers.

3. EAW, *The Miners' Case and the Public Interest, A Documented Chronology, with Introduction by Mary Van Kleeck* (New York: Russell Foundation, 1947).

4. EAW to Joe Brown, 8 January 1938. EAW Papers.

5. ABW to Edmund Wilson, 23 January 1950, 2. Copy, ABW Papers.

6. For Lovett's troubles with the U.S. Congress, see his *All Our Years*, 297–309 and Appendix.

7. ABW to C. H. ("Hank") and Ada Mayer, 5 February 1949, 2. Copy, ABW Papers.

8. Ibid.

9. Ibid.

10. Ibid.

11. ABW to Edmund Wilson, 23 January 1950, 2. Copy, ABW Papers.

12. Edmund Wilson ended his review, "American Political Prisoners," *New Yorker*, 13 May 1950, 125–27, by quoting from *A Field of Broken Stones* the incident where Lepke, boss of Murder Inc. and on his way to the electric chair, asked Naeve about his objecting to war and, to Naeve's answer that he refused to kill, remarked, "It don't seem to make much sense that they put a man in jail for that." Christopher Isherwood, however, more than Wilson, caught the spirit of the book in a review for the *Herald-Tribune* Book Review, 23 July 1950, 3. Wilson couldn't make Naeve out— "You get the impression of a man of unusual conviction and character operating completely in reverse to the point of masochistic perversity." In 1959 Alan Swallow (Denver) published a paperback edition of "the Stones." (The year previous he had published *The Phantasies of a Prisoner, A Visual Novel*, by Naeve.) During the Vietnam War, Lowell and his wife Virginia Pacassi Naeve, also a painter who was very active in the international peace movement, emigrated to Canada to get their sons away from the draft. Lowell, who no longer believed in enlisting in jail as protest, would have nothing to do with another reprint of "the Stones." Their home in Quebec, near the border, became widely known as a first stop for border-crossers. *Prison Etiquette: The Convict's Compendium of Useful Information* (Bearsville, N.Y.: Retort Press, 1950) was hand-set and hand-printed by its editors, Holley Cantine and Dachine Rainer, who were publishing the anarchist review *Retort*. For his *Asylums*, the sociologist Erving Goffman found much useful material in *Prison Etiquette*. Jim Peck's *We Who Would Not Kill* (New York: Lyle Stuart, 1958) tells his "Danbury story" well. Lawrence S. Wittner's *Rebels against War: The American Peace Movement, 1929–1983* (Philadelphia: Temple University Press, 1984), chap. 5, "Men against the State," provides a brief history of prison activism among World War II C.O.s.

13. ABW to Donald Young, director, Russell Sage Foundation, 6 December 1959. Copy, ABW Papers.

14. EAW to Gerry Allard, 6 January 1952. See also his letter to Allard of 11 January 1952. EAW Papers.

15. See "Sketches for an Autobiography" in *The Essays of A. J. Muste.*

16. Edmund Wilson, *The American Earthquake,* 574. Frank Keeney: president of District 17 (West Virginia), U.M.W.A., from 1917 until Lewis removed him from office in 1924.

17. ABW to John H. Wieck, 9 October 1959.

18. Ibid.

19. Ibid.

20. Not long after, in an exchange in the pages of *Liberation,* Dave and I came to a parting of the ways politically over his claim to have found in Castro's Cuba an authentic democracy.

21. Mary Van Kleeck to ABW, 3 January 1964, ABW Papers.

22. ABW to DTW and Diva Agostinelli, 16 July 1965. On the program of the dedication (26 May 1961) of the Sister Katie DeRorre Memorial at Holy Cross Evangelical Cemetery, Collinsville, Illinois, Agnes Burns Wieck, who was unable to attend but of course sent a message, is listed as Honorary Chairman. Chairman, Jack Battuello; Secretary of the Committee, Barney Bossetto.

23. Ibid.

24. Ibid.

Epilogue

1. Giovanni Baldelli, *Social Anarchism* (Chicago: Aldine-Atherton, 1971).

Index

David Thoreau Wieck, professor emeritus of philosophy at Rensselaer Polytechnic Institute, has contributed articles and reviews to *Black Rose, Diogenes, Dissent, Interrogations, The Journal of Aesthetics and Art Criticism, Liberation, The Monist, Philosophy East and West, Social Anarchism,* and *Telos.* His primary interests are social and political philosophy, and social history.